ALASDAIR MACINTYRE

ALASDAIR MacINTYRE

An Intellectual Biography

ÉMILE PERREAU-SAUSSINE

Translated by Nathan J. Pinkoski

Foreword by Pierre Manent

University of Notre Dame Press
Notre Dame, Indiana

Library of Congress Control Number: 2022935757

ISBN: 978-0-268-20325-2 (Hardback)
ISBN: 978-0-268-20327-6 (WebPDF)
ISBN: 978-0-268-20324-5 (Epub)

Dilectissimae et vere amandae

Contents

A Note on the Translation

What follows is an English translation of *Alasdair MacIntyre: Une biographie intellectuelle*, and the foreword by Pierre Manent, as they were published in the original French edition. Perreau-Saussine published an edited and translated version of chapter 2, part I, under the title "The Moral Critique of Stalinism," in *Virtue and Politics: Alasdair MacIntyre's Revolutionary Aristotelianism*, edited by Paul Blackledge and Kelvin Knight (Notre Dame, IN: University of Notre Dame Press, 2011). From this published article, we can discern that Perreau-Saussine's intention was to provide a literal translation of his French work on MacIntyre into English—a task interrupted by his untimely death in 2010.

My goal has been to provide a translation that remains faithful to Perreau-Saussine's efforts to translate this book into English. Using Perreau-Saussine's published article as the template for the complete translation of the book, I aim for consistency with his published article and follow Perreau-Saussine's choices for a more literal style and language. The footnotes and quotations cite the original French or English text. Unless otherwise noted, the translations are my own. In some cases I have added additional footnotes to clarify sources, as well as notes to explain French references that may be unfamiliar to Anglo-American readers. Sometimes Perreau-Saussine alludes to private correspondence or conversations with MacIntyre; I have left those allusions as they stand.

MacIntyre's reply to some of the criticisms raised by Manent and Perreau-Saussine can be found in "Replies," *Revue international de philosophie* 67, no. 2 (2013): 203–7. Readers should bear in mind that Perreau-Saussine did not cite or discuss the following books or collected essays by Alasdair MacIntyre: they were all published after this intellectual biography was written.

- *Edith Stein: A Philosophical Prologue* (New York: Rowman and Littlefield, 2006)
- *The Tasks of Philosophy: Selected Essays*, vol. 1 (Cambridge: Cambridge University Press, 2006)
- *Ethics and Politics: Selected Essays*, vol. 2 (Cambridge: Cambridge University Press, 2006)
- *God, Philosophy, Universities* (New York: Rowman and Littlefield, 2009)
- *Ethics in the Conflicts of Modernity* (Cambridge: Cambridge University Press, 2017)

I am grateful to the James Madison Program in American Ideals and Institutions at Princeton University, as well as the Witherspoon Institute, for supporting this translation project. I am also grateful to Ronald Beiner, Dan Hitchens, Pierre Manent, Jean-Baptiste Pateron, Molly Gurdon Pinkoski, and Cécile Varry for their comments and assistance in preparing this translation.

Foreword

Liberalism, that's the enemy! Thus we could summarize the *opinion* that, in a diffuse and insistent way, inspires the works of those who offer their views on our political, social, and economic situation. At the same time, we agree to recognize that the alternatives to liberalism have lost all credibility. Never has a principle organizing human association been more criticized while triumphant, or more triumphant while discredited. What should we make of this enigma? We need not look for the answer either in the particularity of circumstances or in the universal character of human dissatisfaction. Surely it is liberalism itself that supplies the best explanation of its strange situation in opinion. But how do we conduct this enquiry into liberalism? Must we reconstitute liberalism's intellectual history? Or its political history? Or that of its social and moral effects, direct and indirect? All these approaches can be legitimate and fruitful. In the fine book that follows, Émile Perreau-Saussine has chosen another. It is, in short, an application of what Charles Péguy called "the method of eminent cases." Alasdair MacIntyre offers us the eminent case, or culminating case, of a long and complex intellectual trajectory, rich in variations and even in conversions. However, for more than fifty years, his steady core of antiliberal anger has supplied the energy and radiance for his singular and singularly revealing work. MacIntyre's intellectual biography, which Perreau-Saussine conducts with the necessary sympathy but also without letting himself be intimidated by the philosopher's often boastful tone, is not only "the story of a soul" (however endearing that may be). It is also the instrument to access a set of political, social, moral, and philosophical problems of pressing interest to us all.

One of the first results of Perreau-Saussine's enquiry is that it helps us order our past. At first glance, it seems that in the second half of the twentieth century, political and philosophical problems unceasingly renewed themselves for each generation. They differentiated according to the circumstances—in particular, the national circumstances. Who does not know that in philosophy and in politics, an abyss separates France and the United Kingdom, or the French and the "Anglo-Americans"? Well, they are not so different! Through the distinctions and connections that our young guide Perreau-Saussine draws, we are made to revisit our past. Both the polemic between Sartre and Camus and the critique of Stalinism on the one hand, and the debate between liberals and communitarians on the other, fall within one large but circumscribed argument. MacIntyre's work, surely better than any other, enables us to discern this. The existential subject, whether ceding to the prestige of History or stoically refusing to let itself be carried away, exhibits the same fragility as the liberal subject, which is responsible for managing the portfolio of its identities. Yet more essential than good action is action itself. Before "taking a stand" in society and in history, and in order to do it wisely, we need in the first place to recover the understanding of what it is to act. And good action will then appear in the first place as completed action, as that which best fulfills the nature of action. We should be grateful to MacIntyre for identifying the central lacuna in our approach to the human world—namely, our inadequate understanding of human action and our reason's abandonment of its "practical" register. First, we must understand what acting means!

With the question having been asked in these terms, the answer, at least in its outline, is self-evident. We need to look from Aristotle's perspective, simply because he is the only author, ancient or modern, to have completely clarified the realm of action on its own terms, with the corresponding notion of practical reason (what Kant calls by that name covers something else entirely). MacIntyre approaches Aristotle through the mediation of Elizabeth Anscombe in particular, who had herself rediscovered Aristotle through the mediation of Wittgenstein, and whose singular personality is well limned by Émile Perreau-Saussine. Here, however, the risk would be to allow oneself to be dazzled by such prestigious figures. On the contrary, Perreau-Saussine is very sensitive to the paradoxical particularity of the Aristotle who is here invoked: he is fundamentally apolitical! We find the strength and weakness of MacIntyre's approach in his recourse to a philosophy of man as a "social animal," disdaining real interest in man as a "political animal."

We understand how this mutilated Aristotle comes to serve the oppositional political posture from which MacIntyre has never departed. MacIntyre is always "for" the subpolitical community threatened by the political community that rises in power, and "against" the latter. Very subtly, Perreau-Saussine shows how Andrew Fletcher, the Scottish patriot and enemy of the Act of Union with England, is MacIntyre's hero and, so to speak, his model. Caught between the sovereignty of the individual and that of the nation-state, the local community—fishermen's village, craftsmen's guild, Benedictine monastery—always incorporates the *sana pars* of human practice, or is the place where this practice takes refuge. MacIntyre's contribution to the analysis of the life of practice and his phenomenology of the good as "internal" to a practice (therefore incommensurable with the criteria of "money" or "rights") are often highly incisive. But what is the ultimate validity of a conception of the human world that, in the name of practice, evacuates the human world of its political part?

Perreau-Saussine emphasizes that MacIntyre, in this respect as un-Aristotelian as possible, is interested neither in political form nor in political regime. He roundly condemns the nation-state, even though the political framework in which European man organized his life for many centuries surely merits more than some brisk expressions of contempt. There is no trace in the philosopher's work of the Aristotelian debate on political justice, holding in tension the demands of a small number and those of a great number. Incidentally, he feels only repugnance for the Aristotelian portrait of magnanimity. As Perreau-Saussine rightly says, MacIntyre broaches political questions guided by the *Nicomachean Ethics* alone and after having essentially rejected his *Politics*. He also keeps very little of the *Ethics* itself. As Perreau-Saussine indicates, this is because MacIntyre is in fact hardly interested in the particular virtues and distinctions of which Aristotle offers an unrivaled description. Rather, for MacIntyre the heart of practical life is the practice of craftsman or skilled worker, on the condition that this practice might be transformed into a habit or a tradition. Certainly, Aristotle makes a great use of "technical" comparisons in his analyses of practical life, but here, the comparison tends to obscure the matter in question. We are therefore very far from Aristotle, but very close to an author such as Michael Oakeshott. I believe Perreau-Saussine does not mention him. But while Oakeshott's social sensibility is opposed to that of MacIntyre—Oakeshott is just as "refined," even "genteel," as MacIntyre claims to be "plain"—Oakeshott analyzes "human conduct" on the model, for example, of the transmission of culinary competences. And in these two cases, the stress placed on the spontaneous or natural transmission of practices endangers the integrity and the validity of reason.

Aurel Kolnai sees a sort of perverse affectation in the way Oakeshott, so to speak, immerses human life in "idioms of conduct," above which it is impossible to raise one's head to access something like common reason or rational debate.[1] But Oakeshott does not purport to struggle against moral relativism, which constitutes one of MacIntyre's principal intentions, perhaps *the* principal intention. MacIntyre's intention is undoubtedly rationalist, and his aversion to certain deep practical irrationalities of the liberal world is often expressed in a gripping and liberating way. But how does he intend to depart from relativism or heal us, as we, though sick, are happy? By recourse to traditions, or to some single tradition of moral enquiry? MacIntyre is right to emphasize that the development of a refined practical rationality presupposes the continuity of a tradition. However, he risks mistaking the condition for practical rationality with the substance of practical rationality. MacIntyre does not ignore that it is, so to speak, a perennial experience that a tradition ossifies and loses itself. A tradition "forgets its origins" (as Edmund Husserl says) if it is not periodically shaken by ruptures with the tradition. Perhaps one such rupture, several generations later, will without scandal become part of the tradition that it had attacked. But in the end, at every moment in time, the question posed to us within each tradition is not only whether the tradition coheres but also whether it coheres with the truth of human phenomena.

This is again a point where MacIntyre essentially distances himself from Aristotle. For Aristotle, the opinions of the city and the traditions of the city are only the point of departure for enquiry. This enquiry should lead us beyond the opinions and traditions of the city, which is to say outside of the city itself. It does not seem that MacIntyre feels the slightest need or desire to accomplish this movement of rupture. He does not dream of exiting the cave, as long as the cave is unpretentious and lit by candle-light. If we have really lost all sense of practical rationality, if even the most venerable institutions—the universities and the churches—are but shad-ows of themselves (as MacIntyre himself readily recognizes), in which tra-dition can we find ourselves again, since the traditions are precisely what is lost? Are we not, so to speak, condemned to search for the truth with ele-ments detached from all traditions and accessible to the rational animal as such? Would these not be a matter of searching for truth in the human ex-perience, approached either through a "phenomenology" or through the "great books" of the philosophical tradition, which are custodians for the tradition of rupture with the tradition?

We understand that after many "variations," MacIntyre finally con-verted to Catholicism. The Catholic conception of "The Tradition" more or less combines with MacIntyre's conception of the tradition, if at least we avoid emphasizing the rigorous Catholic distinction between super-natural revelation and natural reason—natural reason being the enquiring faculty that is naturally accessible to every human being as such and that is capable of elaborating a "natural theology." Perreau-Saussine's development of the religion question makes up the book's most original and rich sec-tions. We can read in particular a luminous explanation of how the enemy of liberalism happily settled in the country that is the liberal country par excellence, the United States of America. And this explanation of an "emi-nent case" clarifies this very complicated question of the religious and moral difference between the two sides of the Atlantic, which is very important for us politically today. Let me quote several lines from it:

> Why did MacIntyre leave Europe in 1969? Why did he need to immigrate into the United States, into the most liberal of the com-mercial republics? Beyond the Atlantic, MacIntyre discovered the possibility *of not being of his time*. European homogenization entails an imperious demand for presentism. Yet, in its origins, America was intended precisely as a land where different tempo-ralities could coexist without melting together. . . . His theory of the primacy of traditions presupposes liberalism's success: it comes *after* liberalism.

. . . MacIntyre's America is the same as that which gave asylum to the Puritans of the seventeenth century: the territory not ruled by the treaty of Westphalia.[2]

So MacIntyre escaped from the powerful by taking refuge in the world's most powerful country, from money by taking refuge in the richest country, and from the nation-state by taking refuge in the last nation-state of the West. But this is because, like a Thomist of another school before him, Jacques Maritain, MacIntyre discovered in America all the possibilities and virtues of the social, active, working, and benevolent man, who is always conscious that he depends on his fellow citizens as his fellow citizens depend on him. Living in one of the innumerable social segments into which American democracy is subdivided, we can forget that money, like rights, homogenizes incommensurable things. We can forget that the individual, like the state, claims a ruinous and otherwise unintelligible sovereignty. We can forget liberalism.

Émile Perreau-Saussine's book establishes with perfect clarity the merits and the limits of Alasdair MacIntyre's return to Aristotle, and more generally perhaps of the Anglo-American Aristotelianism derived from Thomism and Wittgensteinianism. To this school, we owe penetrating analyses of practical life. But these analyses remain condemned to a certain abstraction because they refuse to consider the real concretizations of action, which always have a political mark or coefficient. This school is, in short, an "Aristotelianism of the opposition." It leaves the great city in the power of practical heresies, and to be happy, it takes refuge in the pores of liberal society—as, in the Middle Ages, according to Marx, commerce took refuge in the pores of feudal society. But this is to flee combat while claiming to still fight on. The critique of liberalism that would only define it by its errors lacks plausibility. We need to explain a bit why liberalism is still stronger than our good Aristotelian reasons. Or, Perreau-Saussine suggests, might this be because we confuse liberal politics with its most abstract philosophical formulations, or with its most ideological political formulations? Instead of lodging Aristotle in the quarter of the artisans, forbidding exit, why not remember that he is more interested in those who command than in those who obey, simply because only those who command can develop all the virtues, and in particular the supreme virtue of practical life that is prudence? The great liberal statesmen probably did not lack prudence. Today, furthermore, with the European nation-state weakening and perhaps soon disappearing, we can better recognize how much it resembles the Greek city: in its dynamism, in some of its wellsprings, and in the modality of its decline! No tradition protects us against the death of political forms and the disappearance of the practices they harbor. The only thing that does not die is the intellect's comprehension of things. Such is the teaching of Aristotle that MacIntyre would call prideful. In any case, without any trace of pride, but with much impartiality and subtlety, Émile Perreau-Saussine's contribution is to make more precise the terms of the debate between practical philosophy and liberal politics, and thereby to clarify the conditions of sensible action in the city of liberty and equality.

Introduction

The solution to the political problem pertains not so much to a dynamic of the good but to a balance of evils. It is achieved less by an improvement of human beings and more by a careful adjustment of powers. This is the thesis that presides over the working of liberal democracy. Contrary to what we too often suggest, the first movement of liberal democracy's theorists is somber and without illusions. They emphasize that human beings work to become powerful rather than to become just, that power corrupts and that absolute power corrupts absolutely. Neither moral edification nor laws are enough to render citizens good and virtuous. It is useless to look to transform tyrants into generous kings, oligarchs into aristocrats, and corrupt men into wise men. It is more efficient for ambition to counteract ambition so that one cancels out the other. Liberal democracy uses egoism and ambition, which lean in principle toward tyranny, to avoid tyranny itself. Are human beings dominated by the passion to acquire more things and more power? Do they want to possess ever more, to accumulate without limits? We will not gain by groaning about the human condition, by grumbling about it indefinitely. It is better to prove our audacity, and mount the beast to train it. Vices have an advantage over virtues: they are, so to speak, regular, stable, and foreseeable. In relying on the vices, in transforming passions into interests, we can ensure that each one pursues his interest in a way that profits everyone. We ensure order by developing this regularity in disorder itself. A little unsettled by such dexterity, we should exclaim with

Pascal: "The greatness of man even in his concupiscence, to have known how to draw from it an admirable rule!"[1]

Liberalism's adversaries have opposed this regime, sometimes in the name of *nobility* (the critique of the right), sometimes in the name of *justice* (the critique of the left).

Liberal democracy supposes that human beings are naturally unjust, and that if we allow them to, they will behave like tyrants. Socialists and communists combine this thesis with a simple sociological statement: liberal democracy comprises different social classes, bosses and employees, bourgeois and proletarians. Do we believe, socialists and communists argue, that the rich (who are powerful) love the poor (who are weak) with a pure and generous love? If every man is a potential tyrant, there is no reason for the industrialist to refrain from exploiting the workers. Why do liberals, who distrust human beings so much, not distrust the richest human beings? As human beings hardly want the good and as justice depends on a balance of forces, we should concern ourselves with the little means available to the poor. Liberal democracy provides for a balance of power, but it hardly ensures a balance within businesses or industries. As it tends to sacralize private property, it sacrifices economic equality for legal equality. In so doing, it abandons the most destitute to their own fate and to the greed of the wealthy. Liberal democracy is supposed to ensure a certain equality, but the equality that it extols remains "formal," and we need to contrast it to a "real" equality.

Antiliberals of the right upend this critique. For them, liberal democracy seems not insufficiently democratic, but rather too democratic. They compare the modern world to the ancient world and are first and foremost struck by the progress of equality. It seems to them superficial to contrast formal equality with real equality. They remark that aristocracies have disappeared, that slavery no longer exists in law, that paternal authority has withered away, and that money everywhere exerts an equalizing power. They denounce the reign of this equality, this razing to the ground that puts everyone, including the greatness of some and the mediocrity of others, on the same level. In the name of excellence and of glory, they protest against the shrinking of the soul. They call for a new aristocracy.

If human beings fight for this or that cause, then the liberal resolves— or, more precisely, defuses—the conflict by abandoning talk of it. Everyone should decide for himself. Why risk civil war by looking to decide on a common good, when pluralism, which facilitates everything, is possible? This strategy has the merit of simplicity: human beings readily agree on trivial things (a commercial contract, for example), not on important things (such as final ends). The more serious and essential a question is, the more it is liable to enrage. The liberal technique par excellence consists in "neutralizing" the public sphere, in "privatizing" its problems. For antiliberals of the right, this privatization raises two difficulties. On the one hand, it encourages mediocrity. An entirely peaceful universe, where all preciously keep their convictions to themselves, is not the paradise that liberalism promises. It is a flattened, dehumanized world, without the martyrs or the heroes who are the salt of the earth. It is a world where human beings, abandoning self-improvement, merely enrich themselves. On the other hand, for antiliberals of the right, the hypothesis of a tranquil and depoliticized world mistakenly presupposes that human beings are essentially good, that one can disregard the aggressive urges that incite conflicts and wars. In this sense, liberals do not take the reality of evil seriously. Therefore, one should turn what seems to be liberalism's principle, the primacy of evil, against liberalism itself.

Liberalism can be criticized in the name of justice or in the name of nobility. In the twentieth century, these two critiques culminate in totalitarianism. The struggle between communism and Nazism illustrates the deadly struggle between two crazed interpretations of justice and of nobility. The concern for social justice was brutally turned against justice itself: with the Soviet Union, the proletariat's advocates morphed into champions of tyranny. As for the desire to reestablish a sense of heroism and of nobility, it was turned against nobility itself: far from embodying a new aristocracy, fascists and Nazis enjoyed their greatest successes among demoted citizens dominated by resentment. The two great adversaries of liberal democracy thus demonstrated their limits. Despite themselves, they established the necessity of the liberalism they abhorred. For liberals ensure the balance of powers. They separate church from state, state from civil society, man from citizen, and politics from economics, in order that the state may be as limited, restricted, and counterbalanced as possible. It is against the backdrop of the reciprocal failure of communism and Nazism that liberalism imposes itself today, as a posttotalitarianism. Liberalism comes out of its trial reinforced, since the political shape of evil was embodied with an atrocious brutality in the regimes of Hitler and Stalin. Liberalism therefore imposes itself: thanks to modern tyrannies, the political regime that starts from the affirmation of evil finds a new legitimacy. As a famous saying goes, liberal democracy "is the worst of all regimes, except for all the others."

Is this to say that liberal democracy has no more adversaries? That it imposes itself everywhere through consensus? Far from it. The same success of liberalism brings to the fore a critique somewhat forgotten in the West today: a third critique that, without ignoring either justice or nobility, relates both to moral truth, to the objective reality of the *good*. Unlike the communist or Nazi challenges, this Aristotelian-inspired critique does not start from the primacy of evil to better turn it against the injustice of some and the vulgarity of others. It argues against the relativism or skepticism that theorists of liberal democracy share with their critics on the right and on the left.

Liberal democracy's founders emphasize, above all, the disorder of the world: human beings tend neither to truth nor to the good, but to the useful and to the pleasant. It is important to base the political order on this regular disorder. It is vain to look to teach character or to encourage the virtues. On the one hand, there is no natural tendency on which we could rely. These virtues are in fact against nature and do violence to human nature. Man is by nature asocial and apolitical. On the other hand, there is no reason to think that the good of the individual coincides with the good of the city. There is not, properly speaking, a "common good"; at most there is a "general interest." By overemphasizing the good, we come to quarrel about abstractions and incite civil wars and wars of religion. By overemphasizing the good, we are led to underestimate the perversity of which those who aspire to tyranny are capable and to forget that, in certain situations, it is perhaps necessary to violate the rules of morality to preserve political liberty. It is dangerous to rely on a natural order that does not exist. The state alone ensures the order that renders a certain peaceful coexistence possible. Since the good is reducible to the useful and the pleasant, political life should therefore not strive for the good, but for the useful and the pleasant. By contrast, for the neo-Aristotelian critiques of liberalism, the good is not reducible to the useful or the pleasant. The city should teach the natural desire to live in society, the natural desire for the good and the true. The city itself should also make good use of it. Justice and law are fully intelligible only by reference to this natural desire and the natural order that it presupposes. Man is a social and political animal; it is important to organize the city around this good nature, by ensuring the education of character and by encouraging the virtues. It is not enough to organize the state as for a nation of intelligent devils: we need to rely on the aspiration for the good.

For liberals, the state should be considered "neutral" about the idea of the good, and it is up to the individual to look for happiness and truth, for himself and through himself. It is in this sense that liberalism is a kind of individualism and positivism: morality is a private affair, and the just is separate from the good. Insofar as liberals are concerned about the good or about happiness, it is to make it an individualized question: it is up to the individual, and himself alone, to decide his morality and his religion. But can the individual discover the good and the true independent of authoritative social forms and traditions? In the eyes of neo-Aristotelians, liberalism, which looks to avoid disagreements about the nature of the good and to circumvent them by privatizing or depoliticizing the question of the good, distorts the care of the virtues and the transmission of truth by making the essentials rest on the frail shoulders of the individual. A too-exclusive concern with tyranny and anarchy impoverishes existence. The primacy of security entails forgetting the good that nourishes interior life. The state and the law cannot and should not be perfectly "neutral" in morality. Justice is unthinkable if it is completely separated from morality. Positive law is only intelligible to the extent to which it refers to natural justice. Individualism that consists in choosing for the self a reputedly private morality is an error or an illusion.

This opposition crystallizes over the question of freedom. For liberalism's founders, evil is constitutive of political life. Correlatively, freedom is in the last analysis the absence of evil; which is to say, on a political level, freedom is the absence of tyranny and the absence of coercion. It is a "negative" liberty. Freedom is understood by reference to a balance of powers and has no specific relation to either the good or the true. However, for the neo-Aristotelian school, freedom is subordinated to the good and the true. Freedom is not only a matter of security, the absence of physical or legal obstacles, or autonomy. First and foremost, it involves grasping the good.

Liberty includes a "positive" dimension. It is not enough to have freedom; we still need to become free. Subjective freedom should be related to the objective character of the good. We cannot give all of freedom's meaning to the freedom of indifference without counterbalancing it by the concern for wisdom. It is not enough to be able to do what we want and to know what we do not want; we must still give ourselves the means to know what we want, what we would like, or what we should want. The refusal of all dependence renders moral life anemic. At the most fundamental level, freedom is achieved not so much by the absence of obstacles but by a truth that enables removing these obstacles. A certain "paternalism" is at once inevitable (every society, whether it wants to or not, transmits a certain idea of the good) and desirable.

Against the philosophical skepticism that is the basis for the primacy of evil, numerous voices propose to straighten out our conceptions of justice and correct liberalism's own crookedness. Have we not lost the difference between liberty and license? This is what the contemporary critics of liberalism insist, beginning with the most determined among them, Alasdair MacIntyre, who is inspired by the Aristotelian tradition to recover an idea of the good and of moral truth.

At "MacIntyre, Alasdair," a dictionary might indicate "born 1929 in Glasgow" and should add "historian of moral philosophy." The three principal works of MacIntyre—*A Short History of Ethics* (1966), *After Virtue* (1981), and *Whose Justice? Which Rationality?* (1988)—each tell, in their own ways, the same history, which begins in Greece with Homer and comes to an end in the twentieth century with nihilism. These histories of ethics establish, on the one hand, the dependence of moral life on traditions of enquiry and, on the other hand, the progress of relativism and irrationalism under the corrupting influence of individualism. Perhaps it would be better to translate *After Virtue* as *The Misfortunes of Virtue*. If this analogy with the Marquis de Sade's novel does not suggest that philosophical digressions and narrative character are inclusive of each other, at least it suggests that the liberal category of the private is not as morally indifferent as it is said to be. In his books, MacIntyre intends to establish that the unilateral progress of freedom disintegrates rationality, feeding the moral relativism that all his work denounces.

In his eyes, the civil liberty that citizens of liberal democracy enjoy is too often exercised to the detriment of interior freedom. Individual autonomy is not self-sufficient; it ends up exhausting traditions, which it requires without being sufficiently aware of it. Autonomy, reduced to its own means, comes to undermine the foundations of the moral life and capsizes. The indefinite deepening of individualism has gradually corroded the meaning of truth that practical reasoning presupposes. The subjective character of freedom should be compensated with the objective dimension of a tradition: consent must be rebalanced with wisdom. If we grant liberalism the upper hand in all aspects of existence, human beings find themselves distraught, desolate, mutilated, and deprived of goals or ends. Against individual rights, MacIntyre counters with a conception of justice that takes into account the importance of forms of life and of moral authority. It is not enough to flee evil; it is still necessary to look for the good. Negative liberty, conceived as the absence of coercion, is not enough: it is necessary to add a "positive" dimension. MacIntyre develops a theory of freedom as participation in something greater than oneself. He subordinates the question of freedom to that of practical rationality, to demonstrate that, in the last analysis, the capacity to choose without coercion must be subordinated to the capacity to choose intelligibly or reasonably. He analyzes the limits of the absolutization of individual consent, which is to the detriment of authority and moral excellence. He appeals to virtue and character formation, which liberalism tends to neglect for "efficiency." True justice and true nobility, pursued with such relentlessness by liberalism's adversaries on the right and left, depend precisely upon virtue and character formation.

MacIntyre describes a world in which one no longer knows what one wants, a world which no longer knows toward what end it advances. He writes:

> What strikes me most basically and most finally about our society is its domination by the concept of "getting on." One gets on from one stage to the next on an endless conveyor belt. One goes to a primary school in order to pass the eleven plus in order to go to a grammar school in order to go to a university in order to get a degree in order to get a job in order to rise in one's profession in

order to get a pension. And those who have fallen out are not
people who have found a true end; they are mostly people who
have got off, or been pushed off, the conveyor belt. Last year a
student whom I knew well had a break-down as a result of taking
seriously the question, "What am I studying for?" The chain of
reasons has no ending.[2]

MacIntyre describes the triumph of instrumental reasoning, a society that has become expert in means. But it has lost the very meaning of
truth, by reference to which a worthwhile education is understood. It is an
efficient society, where utility is maximized, but for a goal that fades away
as one approaches it. As a good Aristotelian, MacIntyre deplores the absence of ends and regrets that society does not make the goods that could
nourish moral life accessible to its members. Hobbes, who is perhaps the
most eloquent spokesman for the political tradition against which MacIntyre writes, insists to the contrary that one analyzes life in terms of means
and not ends.

The Felicity of this life, consisteth not in the repose of a mind
satisfied. For there is no such *Finis Ultimus*, (utmost ayme,) nor
Summum Bonum, (greatest good,) as is spoken of in the Books of
the old Morall Philosophers. Nor can a man any more live, whose
Desires are at an end, than he, whose Senses and Imaginations are
at a stand. Felicity is a continuall progresse of the desire, from one
object to another; the attaining of the former, being still but the
way to the later. The cause whereof is, That the object of mans
desire, is not to enjoy once onely, and for one instant of time; but
to assure for ever, the way of his future desire.[3]

In the absence of a *summum bonum*, happiness is about fleeing from
evil or about the accumulation of means for the goal of self-preservation.
Aristotle ranks among the "old Morall Philosophers," from whom Hobbes
looks to distinguish himself. Hobbes does not describe life as oriented toward a determined truth or good, but as a forward march in which the
only goal is in reality a means: the "assuredness" of the route—that is to
say, the absence of danger and the absence of evils. Hobbes readily con-

cedes that in thus considering practical life, we come to lose all moral objectivity and reduce the good to the pleasant. He writes, "Whatsoever is the object of any mans Appetite or Desire; that is it, which he for his part calleth Good: And the object of his Hate, and Aversion, evill."[4] Hobbes fears first and foremost the state of nature, a war of all against all, from which he looks to have us escape in an efficient and intelligent way, with moral subjectivism as the price to pay. MacIntyre does not believe that the good needs to be reduced to the pleasant, save to impoverish human existence to an unacceptable extent. The world that Hobbes describes really is the world as it has become. But this is to be deplored, not welcomed. Whose justice and which rationality should we make our own? Not the justice and rationality of utilitarian and positivist inspiration, but the justice and rationality of Aristotelian inspiration, which draws its substance from the implementation of the good and the contemplation of the true.

Today, at least in the West, liberalism imposes itself. But an anxiety tends to spread. The soul is troubled. One comes to ask whether individual autonomy has not carried the day so well that it is collapsing in on itself. If individualism is surely in many respects a political solution, it can also constitute a psychological and spiritual problem, to the point of casting doubt on the foundations of liberalism. The present political triumph of liberalism is also the triumph of autonomy over all socially embodied authority. But does liberalism not triumph even when the meaning of this autonomy has become uncertain?

The present situation is paradoxical in that it seems that one should turn toward the traditional adversaries of liberalism to give substance to liberalism itself. The critiques of liberalism studied here come after the failure of the great antiliberal waves: socialism, fascism, Nazism, and Marxist-Leninism. *They do not cast doubt on liberal democracy as a political form or political regime*, even though they criticize the way in which most theorists give an account of liberal democracy, and they warn against the atomist, relativist, and finally nihilist dynamic of a certain liberalism.

To the extent that liberal democracy imposes itself and proves its worth, it becomes more artificial to insist on the primacy of evil and more tempting to offer an Aristotelian-inspired reinterpretation of the regime.[5] We can thus show that liberalism cultivates certain veritable goods, starting with concord and justice. We can describe liberalism as a mixed regime, which, by means of representation, reconciles democratic and aristocratic elements, harmonizing their respective parts to consent and wisdom.[6] We can elaborate an analysis of liberal democracy in terms of the natural law and the common good. From this point of view, a durable and satisfying political regime is achieved less by a balance of evils than by a dynamic of the good. The liberalism that avoids evil does not forbid the liberalism that looks for the good.

A member of the Communist Party of Great Britain in the late 1940s, an activist of the first New Left ten years later, and a Trotskyist in the first half of the 1960s, MacIntyre immigrated in 1969 to the United States, where he renounced all political engagement. As an academic, he taught theology, sociology, and philosophy at Manchester, Leeds, Oxford, Princeton, and then at the University of Essex. In Boston in the 1970s, he was successively a professor at Brandeis University, Boston University, and Wellesley College. He finally taught at Vanderbilt University (1982–88), the University of Notre Dame (1988–94), and Duke in North Carolina (1994–2000), before coming back to Notre Dame until his retirement. First influenced by the young Marx and the late Wittgenstein, he turned toward Aristotle in the early 1970s, embarrassing his old allies and bewildering his new friends. He was first a Presbyterian, and even envisioned becoming a pastor. In the mid-1950s, he embraced Anglicanism, before losing his faith several years later. He converted to Catholicism in 1983. First attracted by the theology of Karl Barth, he ended up a disciple of Thomas Aquinas. As a Marxist, Barthian, Wittgensteinian, Aristotelian, and Thomist, MacIntyre places at the heart of his reflection what liberalism keeps on the margins of politics: the soul, community, and truth. Thus from apparent chaos, something constant emerges. The critique of liberalism is at once the continuous base and the final cause of his work.

Why study this tormented thinker? I see three reasons. First, even though his intellectual journey provides a very clear understanding of the intellectual history of the second half of the twentieth century, it remains misunderstood. In France, it is not known that MacIntyre constitutes one of the great authorities for the debate in Anglo-American moral philosophy and politics. In his home in the Anglo-American world, MacIntyre's latest works are read without much concern for their genesis. Second, it is generally admitted that the range of his reflection remains difficult to grasp, even though there is agreement to see him as a storyteller of lively charm, a brilliant historian, a daring polemicist, and the author of profound views on the twentieth century's evil. Finally, if his intellectual journey is atypical to the point of being unsettling, and yet if the critique of liberalism constitutes the guiding principle of his works, then his apparent atypicalism is turned on its head. MacIntyre becomes a privileged figure in the antiliberal repertoire, one of its eminent cases. It is not so much MacIntyre that turned me toward the theme of "community." Rather, I started from the critique of liberalism and turned toward MacIntyre. His trajectory enables us to take another look at a great part of the history of the intellectual opposition to bourgeois individualism, and the internal tensions in his thought convey the tensions proper to this opposition. I did not choose his work because it offers a demarcated object of study according to the methods of the university's disciplines, but because it enables us to explore the multifaceted legacy of Aristotle, Rousseau, and Marx.[7] In reducing common life to the lowest common denominator, in reducing justice to individual rights alone, and the good to the useful or the pleasant, we kindle the need for a reaction. As a former communist concerned with justice and an Aristotelian concerned with nobility and truth, MacIntyre marvelously illustrates this aspiration.

From the 1970s, even before MacIntyre turns toward Thomas Aquinas, he is the object of a petty but significant polemic: "In the past he has been a 'Christian' without God, a 'Trotskyist' without commitment to revolution, a 'Marxist' patronized by the Central Intelligence Agency, an 'anti-elitist' adornment of the world's most mediocre and servile bourgeois intelligentsia, a 'socialist' avid for the approval of his social 'superiors.' Now he is a liberal . . . a libertarian instrument of academic authoritarianism."[8]

The text is ambiguous, for we do not know whether it suggests through its quotation marks that MacIntyre, in the last analysis, was never what he purported to be, invariably remaining a hypocritical "valet of capitalism," or whether it points to changes so crazy that it discredits him. These flip-flops, it is true, are manifest. But perhaps MacIntyre is nevertheless sufficiently single-minded, so that we should concern ourselves with the meaning of these ruptures. I would like to establish that his intellectual journey clarifies the history and the nature of anti-individualism. Moreover, I would like to treat his successive turnarounds as historiographical difficulties, while striving to show his unity of purpose. In the contemporary repertoire, MacIntyre is not a neutral figure. He is one of the rare thinkers today to have remained faithful to the antiliberalism of his youth, one of the rare critics of liberalism not to have stopped thinking after the fall of communism, and one of the rare thinkers to have been able to reorient his outlook in a new direction. Yet even though he is a complicated person, MacIntyre hardly discusses his past with us. "To write a worthwhile autobiography," he remarks, "you need either the wisdom of an Augustine or the shamelessness of a Rousseau."[9] I however intend to reconstitute his intellectual journey, as a way to outline *the biography of a problem.*

Upstream from MacIntyre's diverse political engagements, I would like to show that a philosophy is at work, and, alongside his philosophy, a theology. Through him I shall study the contemporary critique of liberalism, as it has developed after the failure of communism (in politics), after Ludwig Wittgenstein (in philosophy), and after Karl Barth (in theology). In each instance, I shall try to show MacIntyre's philosophy: that, limited to his own strength, the individual is not always able to find the good and the true to which he aspires.

In each of the three chapters, I shall take a different starting point: for politics, the history of the New Left; for philosophy, the moral critique of Stalinism (or the articulation of politics and morals); and for theology, the question of secularization. In each instance, I shall attempt to show that the starting point leads to the rediscovery of the social nature of the human being and therefore of a certain conservatism: "a new conservatism," a "philosophy of tradition," and a "theology of the tradition."

The theorists of liberalism privilege the circumvention of evil over the search for the good. On the whole, they hold to a minimalist conception of the good. They tend to subordinate the question of the good life to that of life simply, to security. They delegate the quest for the good to the individual alone: it is for him to find wisdom and happiness, for himself and through himself. In the first chapter of the book, I shall show that in the eyes of the author of *After Virtue*, lives are impoverished to the extent that one adulterates or privatizes the concern for the good. In the second chapter, following MacIntyre, I shall explain that the quest for the good life necessarily takes a collective form, for all individual reasoning participates in collective reasoning, and it is by reference to moral consensus and a tradition that the individual can judge, weigh the pros and cons, and prove his prudence and virtue. Finally, in the third chapter, I shall take up again the themes of the first two chapters from a theological angle, showing that for MacIntyre, secularization is one of the most important dimensions of the impoverishment of human existence, and that it is also by reference to "The Tradition," in the theological sense of the term, that the individual can reason morally, become virtuous, and lead a worthwhile life.

Tocqueville thus depicts the personality of Louis-Philippe, the most "liberal" of princes in France's history:

> Enlightened, subtle, supple, and tenacious, fixed exclusively on the utilitarian and filled with such profound contempt for truth and such complete disbelief in virtue that his intelligence was consequently dimmed, he not only failed to see the beauty that truth and honesty always exhibit but also failed to understand that they can frequently be useful. He had a profound understanding of men, but only of their vices. In religion he had the incredulity of the eighteenth century and in politics the skepticism of the nineteenth. An unbeliever himself . . . his ambition, limited only by prudence, was never fully satisfied nor out of control and always remained close to the earth.[10]

A liberal himself, Tocqueville a priori had some sympathy for the July Monarchy. He preferred it to the regimes that came before it and the regime that followed it. At the same time, he could not prevent himself from disdaining it. By keeping only to the perspective of what is evil, we run the risk of dangerously narrowing our range of vision.

ONE
Politics
Impoverished Lives

I. The Disappointments of Socialism and Communism

In the 1950s, most British Labourites could be content with themselves, for their struggle seemed to be coming to an end. The welfare state, for which they had fought so hard, appeared to be installed for good. The "wretched of the earth" had almost disappeared, which is to say they had won. The difference between exploited and exploiters had almost vanished. Marx had predicted the increasing pauperization of the working class. Yet thanks to economic growth and to social democracy, the postwar decades saw the great beginnings of the consumer society. Class struggle gave way to a vast middle class.[1] In 1957, Prime Minister Harold Macmillan could exclaim: "Our people have never had it so good." Macmillan belonged to the Conservative Party. But it was true that the consumer society satisfied the hopes of the Labour Party, which had been raised in the fear of the impoverishment of the proletariat and which preserved painful memories, if not of the Industrial Revolution, then at least of the Great Depression. One then spoke about the "end of ideology."

An almost centennial struggle seemed to be reaching its end. This was what most of the Labourites thought, notably the old guard, who congratulated themselves for the successes obtained. But a large part of the young postwar generation was distressed. They countered the satisfaction of Hugh Gaitskell (the British Guy Mollet) with a question: Is this really *socialism*?[2] In foreign policy, the West erected itself as the party of freedom. But for the young people marked by the complaisance of the ruling classes, this "socialism" and this "freedom" had all the appearances of a paltry lie. They felt or believed that they felt the oppressive character of the West's *Union Sacrée*[3] and the sociocultural repression then exercised in the very name of tolerance. The thesis of "the end of ideology" was seen as a mere ideological maneuver, for civic life cannot confine itself to the pursuit of comfort and of security.[4] For young intellectuals, whose idealism had not yet been either smoothed or even molded by daily toil and long-term struggle, the contentment of the Labour Party was surprising. Would *socialists* intend to be content with a scarcely reformed capitalism? Does *socialism* not first have for its object a transformation of the *social bond*? Material demands are not enough, for socialism does not consist in either obtaining or even in desiring more "things."[5] Socialism should involve first and foremost the search for another way of life. As one good observer of this epoch remarked, "The old politico-economic radicalism (preoccupied with such matters as the socialization of industry) has lost its meaning. . . . The irony, further, for those who seek 'causes' is that the workers, whose grievances were once the driving energy for social change, are more satisfied with the society than the intellectuals."[6] The above-quoted phrase from Macmillan sounded like a provocation.

The Labourites transposed James Burnham's theses about the "managerial revolution" and the transformation of the relation between the owners of the means of production and the effective direction of management. In their eyes, the two world wars had profoundly changed the nature of capitalism. They insisted that, thanks to state control of the economy, Great Britain was no longer, properly speaking, a capitalist country. Their young adversaries, who were pondering "true" socialism, vigorously criticized this analysis, for they considered that industrial nationalization hardly changed the nature of capitalism. A new elite had seized the industries. To be sure, it was a more complex elite, but in the end it was barely different from its predecessors.[7] One does not abolish wage earning by earning wages from the state. As Engels already remarked, "If the taking over by the state of the tobacco industry is socialistic, then Napoleon and Metternich must be numbered among the founders of socialism."[8] MacIntyre ranks among these young opponents of the Labour Party. The transfer of industrial ownership changes nothing about the criteria of efficiency, he then wrote.[9] "Nationalized property is only workers' property when the workers own the state."[10] In nationalized industries, he noted, the key posts come back almost always to people closely linked to private capitalism, and those people always end up profiting from lowered prices and payouts. Private property or state property hardly makes a difference, for both prevent establishing true industrial democracy and setting up an authentically collective organization of property.

Each side quarreled about the meaning of the Second World War. For most Labourites, it provided the chance to set up a welfare state. For the young generation, Prime Minister Clement Attlee was not faithful to the hopes that the conflict incited: a truly collective mobilization at the service of a radical renewal of human relations. While setting up a social security system satisfied the Labourites, the young generation made themselves the apostles of "rich relationships, endowed with meaning," and railed against the consumer society. Growing abundance, they emphasized, would not be enough to promote a democratic community. They stigmatized the separation of private and public, to which the Labour Party ended up resigning itself.

"Is this really *socialism*?" On this question, an "Old Left" separated itself from a New Left. The latter expressed itself in two journals, *The New Reasoner* and *Universities and Left Review*, born after 1956, in which MacIntyre participated. These merged in 1960 to become *The New Left Review*. At the very beginning of *After Virtue*, MacIntyre recalls, with notably manifest pleasure, that he "was privileged to be a contributor to that most remarkable journal *The New Reasoner*."[11] In the second half of the 1950s, in reaction to postwar conformism, a literary school emerged, that of Angry Young Men.[12] The first New Left embodied the political wing of this generation, and its slogan—"Out of Apathy!"—replied to the numbness of the Old Left. But the "New" Left was not as new as it sometimes wished to believe or wished others to believe. Thirty years later, turning back to their past, some of their members felt first and foremost the need to recognize honestly that they were not as original as they had then believed.[13] In fact, the New Left took up certain antistatist socialist currents from the beginning of the twentieth century. The New Left's critique of capitalist society was "informed by values which are radically different from those of Fabianism—new or old."[14] The Fabian Society, which promulgated its views around 1900, intended to bring about socialism through the intermediary of the state. Guild Socialists, the great rivals of the Fabians, proposed organizing the British working class into several great industrial federations, grouping together all the workers, employees, and technicians of each industry, as the medieval corporations and guilds did. Through G. D. H. Cole, one of the theorists of Guild Socialism, the New Left drew some of its ideas from this British anarcho-syndicalism. "The New Left has often been tempted to claim him as a patron, but perhaps it would be more accurate to say that we have caught up with him, about fifty years late," remarked one of the movement's intellectuals in the early 1960s.[15] Nourished by William Morris, Cole had constantly denounced the dangers of an omnipotent state. Sensitive to the size of the great modern nations, he dreaded gigantism and defended the autonomy of associations, calling for "communities" and emphasizing the potential for tyranny in a society deprived of its intermediary bodies. "Cole does not portray himself as a defender of old forms of community," noted one good observer, "but he thinks (with Marx, incidentally—remember the 'motley ties' of which the *Communist Manifesto* speaks) that they were preferable to no community at all."[16]

The relationship between human beings should take precedence over the relationship of human beings to things. Such was the leitmotif of these intellectuals. Originally, socialism was not so much a reaction against pauperism as a political critique of Hobbesian and Lockean psychology— think of Rousseau. Under the influence of Marx, then John Maynard Keynes, utilitarianism appeared to be reconciled with socialism, but this reconciliation could only be achieved at the cost of redefining socialism's goals: the desire to transform the social bond was subordinated to the struggle against poverty. In the nineteenth century, socialism evolved into a neo-capitalist doctrine for putting food on the table. The struggle against the impoverishment of the proletariat had to take precedence over the safeguarding or renewal of human solidarity. Thus the thought of Marx slid from a neo-Hegelian humanism to a markedly more materialist and economicist position. One hundred years later, this perspective was reversed. The New Left proposed to come back to socialism's initial goals. For the new generation, the gentrification of the proletariat raised more difficulties than it resolved. It was not true, as Marx had hoped, that by making scarcity disappear, collective enrichment reconciles society with itself. It was Rousseau who was right: the progress of instrumental reason divides and separates much more than it unites. The question of the social bond was revived. It was about rediscovering the old socialist question: "Production for what?"[17] The consumer society led back to the sources of anticapitalism. In 1958, Charles Taylor enthusiastically brought back from Paris to Oxford the news about the recently rediscovered manuscripts of the young Marx. The Hegelianism of the young Marx, his "humanism," and even his existentialism incited considerable interest. For E. P. Thompson, the rising economicism of the left was responsible for the degeneration of the socialist movement in the world. Even though he was himself a Marxist, MacIntyre criticized all determinism.[18] His reflections pertain to a popular thematic of the 1960s and '70s, that of the self-destruction of capitalist society through its "cultural contradictions."[19] Furthermore, the editors of *Universities and Left Review* expressly made sure not to separate the journal into economic, political, and cultural sections. In the philosophical realm, the journal followed in the footsteps of Antonio Gramsci and the Frankfurt School, who, from the interwar period, had criticized the economicism of *Das Kapital*, rediscovering the importance of ideology. Charles Taylor, one of the chief thinkers in the journal, wrote: "We can now see how powerless and ineffective mere delivery of the goods is to keep a society from inner division, deadlock, and possible breakdown. This experience reveals that liberal society, like any other, cannot hold together simply by the satisfaction of its members' needs and interests. It also requires a common, or at least widespread set of beliefs which link its structure and practices with what its members see as of ultimate significance."[20]

Do individualism and comfort render human beings happy or satisfied? The young MacIntyre announces the bankruptcy of these ideals—less with a notary's tranquility and more with a prosecutor's impetuousness. His best texts are also his most aggressive. Wrath gives them a particular tone. In his eyes, the Labour Party is nothing other than a second Conservative Party.

For MacIntyre, the market economy destroys the forms of sociability. Whereas Hegel considers that we can make a peaceful coexistence between "the system of needs" and the mediations or forms of life that control acquisitive passion, MacIntyre considers that capitalist economy and utilitarianism have transformed the very nature of these mediations, rendering them inoperative. Neither the family nor the unions nor the state raises awareness of the importance and the truth of duty, as Hegel had hoped. Morality requires community life, but "neither the modern nation-state nor the modern family can supply the kind of . . . association that is needed."[21] MacIntyre takes over Marx's analysis. Following Marx, MacIntyre could have written that the bourgeoisie "has pitilessly torn asunder the motley feudal ties that bound man to his natural superiors, and has left remaining no other nexus between man and man than naked self-interest, than callous *cash payment*."[22] Everything has become a commodity, and everything can be bought and sold. An endemic manipulation rules over the city.[23] Liberal "democracy" is at its core an oligarchy.

We can analyze the limits of the Hegelian synthesis and of this monetization of the world under three different angles.

1. F. H. Bradley, one of the greatest British Hegelians, insists on the link between function in the community and moral life. Because man is by nature social, happiness and self-realization depend on accomplishing the duties of his station. We would expect to see MacIntyre recognize, if not his debt toward Bradley, at least the kinship of their views. Yet this is not the case. MacIntyre is unceasingly sarcastic toward Bradley. In bringing moral life back to social roles, Bradley is right in theory but wrong in practice, for he forgets to remark that today these roles have disappeared.[24] Individualist moral philosophies invite one to distance oneself from the roles that society assigns, and they denounce all identification with these roles as a characteristic symptom of inauthenticity.[25] Even though MacIntyre reacts against this "distancing" and insists on the importance of roles and of the duties of one's station, he ends up ruling in favor of individualism's theorists. They are wrong in the absolute, but right in the present circumstances—in the liberal and capitalist regime.[26]

2. According to Hegel, administration plays an essential role in surpassing the logic of the market economy. Marx, however, emphasizes that with class struggle being what it is, the state or the bureaucracy is not so

much in the service of the universal as in the service of the bourgeoisie—
and he writes ironically about the scaffolding of mediations that Hegel sets
up. Like Marx, MacIntyre criticizes the Hegelian schema, but he relies less
on the theory of class struggle than on Max Weber's sociology. Following
Weber, MacIntyre insists that the rationality proper to administration
obeys an instrumental logic and is therefore not fundamentally different
from the system of needs.[27] Like György Lukács, Max Horkheimer, and
Theodor Adorno, MacIntyre joins the analyses of Marx and Weber together, relying on the thesis of the progress of instrumental rationality and
of bureaucracy to provide evidence for new forms of alienation.[28]

    3. Like the family, the "universal class" does not resist the overpower-
ing charms of utilitarianism. The nation-state is not, as Hegel had wished,
both the result and the foundation, a final end for the individual to find
his duty and satisfaction, or the reality of the idea of morality. The state is
not the realization and the apparition of the divine in the external world.
Reacting against Hegel, who saw in Prussian administration the realization
of Absolute Spirit, MacIntyre denounces the "fundamental contradiction
of the state." The state, he insists, could not be both an administrative machine and an agent with the right to call for death. The state cannot sometimes behave as a gigantic enterprise and sometimes as a sacred guardian de-
manding that we sacrifice our lives to it.[29] The nation-state appears to him as
an extension of particular interests, and not as a means to escape utilitarianism through the intermediary of a collective self, with which everyone would identify. It is not true that the nation-state reconciles the universal and the particular.[30] Disillusioned by social democracy, MacIntyre is
attracted by the Communist Party.

    Between 1942 and 1944, MacIntyre was a student at Epsom College,
a middle-ranking public school situated south of London. He rubbed
shoulders with the sons of some lesser notables, the sons of doctors in particular (his own parents were doctors). He seemed not to have appreciated
them very much. In fact, he must have judged the children of the English
bourgeoisie harshly; shortly afterward, while he was studying Latin and
Greek at Queen Mary College in East End, he joined the ranks of the Communist Party. In 1949, at the age of twenty, he entered the University of
Manchester, where he studied philosophy for two years. Several years later,
he was to write an article on the spirit of this university. Retrospectively, it

clarifies the nature of his choice: a choice for a provincial tradition, for a nonconformist spirit in religion, for a radical spirit in politics, and for a rupture with the establishment.[31]

In 1945, some saw the Labour Party as the catalyst for ridding the country of that England described by George Orwell: "It resembles a family, a rather stuffy Victorian family, with not many black sheep in it but with all its cupboards bursting with skeletons . . . a family in which the young are generally thwarted and most of the power is in the hands of irresponsible uncles and bedridden aunts."[32] For those who in 1945 had hoped for a more or less revolutionary Labour Party, abolishing the House of Lords and the nobility, fagging and public schools, the temperate Fabianism of Attlee could not fail to disappoint. For the young and most brazen among them, it provided a strong incentive to join the Communist Party, in spite of the mediocrity of its electoral results in Great Britain; even in its heyday, the Communist Party of Great Britain (CPGB) was hardly more than a rump party.

We must recall that immediately after the war, the USSR enjoyed the prestige of a dazzling victory against Nazism, and that one was perhaps still allowed to hope that, in the East, regimes would be established where communism and pluralism were not mutually exclusive. In 1947, communists and noncommunists could still have accepted a durable sharing of power. Moscow could have, *in theory*, tolerated autonomous Czech diplomacy. Immediately after the war, the people's democracies could have foretold a happy future. This hope, however, which MacIntyre shared for a time, was short-lived. The Prague coup, the expulsion of Tito, and the show trial of László Rajk rapidly followed.[33] At risk of losing votes, the communists seized power when the date for new elections approached. At the same moment, Stalin forbade the Czech government from participating in the Marshall Plan. In 1946–47, intellectual milieus were rather complacent toward Soviet Russia. But in 1950, the wind had changed, and many returned to their ivory towers. MacIntyre joined the CPGB only to move away from it rapidly. Devoting himself to higher education rather than militancy, he taught at Manchester first, then at Leeds. Leon Trotsky's warnings before the war and the "normalization" of "people's democracies" after the war were enough for MacIntyre. Others, even less enlightened, would wait for 1956.

In 1945, the USSR could bask in the glowing achievements of its armies. But eleven years later, the regime lost its remaining eschatological privileges. Shaken by the revelations of the Twentieth Congress of the Communist Party of the Soviet Union, a semidissident group of the British Communist Party on the organization's margins published a journal: *The Reasoner*. As early as September 1956, however, the Central Committee gave the order to stop the journal. Two months later, the invasion of Budapest by Russian tanks rattled even the most dormant consciences. Around ten thousand communists gave up their Party membership; among them was E. P. Thompson, who edited *The Reasoner*. Summer 1957 saw the appearance of the first issue of *The New Reasoner*, the first mouthpiece of the British New Left. While anti-Stalinist, the publication remained, more or less in spite of everything, within the movement of the Communist Party, qualifying itself as the journal of "Britain's largest unorganized party—the ex-Communist Party." It printed around four thousand copies and intended to regenerate Marxism.[34] MacIntyre returned to politics in the late 1950s, engaging in the Campaign for Nuclear Disarmament (CND), which was then in full swing. He joined the team of *The New Reasoner* and shared in its principal orientation: distrust of the Labour Party as well as of the Soviet Union. But he did not stay long.

In 1960, *The New Reasoner* merged with the *Universities and Left Review*, which was less tied to the pre-1956 Communist Party and more social democratic, with the goal of inciting a broad political movement. This would become the *New Left Review*. MacIntyre's name appeared in the first issue's editorial board but afterward disappeared. Even before its publication, MacIntyre made a point of distancing himself.[35] Did the merger imply confusion and by consequence a social-democratic "drift"? In France, a new left had gradually weighed down the two great traditional parties, waging intellectual guerrilla warfare on the periphery of the *Parti communiste français* (PCF) and finally breaking the *Section française de l'Internationale ouvrière* (SFIO) through the creation of the *Parti socialiste unifié* (PSU) in 1960.[36] MacIntyre quit the New Left's movement to avoid joining the British equivalent of the PSU. His engagement within the New Left was never exempt from ambiguities and doubts.

MacIntyre criticizes the very principle of reformism. "The expression 'revolutionary socialism,'" he writes, "is tautologous."[37] In his eyes, social security and economic planning pertain to an essentially capitalist mind-set and aim at tempering the perverse effects of the system, delaying their definitive failure. In abandoning every revolutionary goal, do not reformism and gradualism consecrate the viability of bourgeois institutions? After having for a time journeyed with the New Left, MacIntyre then separates from it to become a Trotskyist, and ironically discusses the New (!) Left.

In general, the members of the New Left had hardly any sympathy for the supporters of Trotsky. Many collaborators of *The New Reasoner* had belonged to the Communist Party and had kept a solid distrust toward them. MacIntyre himself, even though a Polish Trotskyist influenced him immediately after the war, had rather harsh words for Trotskyists, going so far as to write that they "share all the dogmatism of the Stalinists without any of their achievements."[38] This did not prevent him from joining their ranks a little later, to mark the distance that separated him from both the Labourites and the Stalinists.

In an article that he wrote at the same moment, MacIntyre distinguishes between three types of communist intellectuals. In the first place, there are those who become devoted Stalinists and "spell the death of the intellect." In the second place, there are those who leave the Communist Party for social democracy, proving by this the superficiality of their Marxism. Finally, there are those who leave the Party in order to remain revolutionaries and who "appeal to moral principle." A certain number of these, he adds, join the Trotskyists in founding the Socialist Labour League (SLL).[39] "The left reformist perforce acts as an unwilling liberal," writes MacIntyre; "he would [do] much better to become a conscious and aware liberal. Between revolutionary socialism and liberalism there is no third way."[40] MacIntyre therefore joined the doctrinal movement of Gerry Healy, in The Club, then in the SLL, which succeeded it in May 1959.[41] He wrote a pamphlet for the League and participated in its journal. Several months later, irritated by Healy's authoritarianism, he pulled away from the SLL and joined the Socialist Review Group, another Trotskyist organization, notably less orthodox and gathered around Tony Cliff. From autumn 1960, the group published its journal *International Socialism*, to which it owed its name starting from 1962—IS. MacIntyre's name appeared in the first issue. Starting from winter 1960, and up to summer 1962, he was the coeditor in chief of the journal and was sometimes presented as one of the movement's figureheads.[42]

The New Left, in fact, could never decide on a clear position vis-à-vis the Labour Party, fluctuating between hoping to instill good counsel and making a decisive break. Had Labour become a right-wing party playing into the hands of the dominant oligarchy? Or had it found sufficient elements to outflank the party staff's right-wing vector? For want of choosing between these two options, the New Left condemned itself to eclecticism. MacIntyre broke with the New Left, because it was unable to decide between revolutionary socialism and social democracy.

During the 1950s, the Labour Party, whose leaders unceasingly quarreled, lost its ground and remained out of power. Still, Harold Wilson's electoral success in 1966 gave birth to some hope. But what a disappointment! In the economic realm, MacIntyre judged Wilson's policies disastrous. He denounced the party's technocratic character on the BBC's airwaves, accusing the prime minister of fetishizing gross national product, and consequently of deliberately creating unemployment. For MacIntyre, Wilson seemed to be unaware of the simplest demands in the realm of moral conduct. But in fact, the Labour Party had veered to the right. MacIntyre wrote that the moral basis of English society, in particular that of the unions, had profoundly eroded. The action of the "right social democrats" became liberal, and "left social democrats" became "right social democrats."[43]

Whereas the Labour Party was veering right, the Marxist factions were veering left. In the spring of 1968, MacIntyre held the position of dean at the University of Essex, the most activist university in England. There he was confronted by his own contradictions. At the end of the month of May, MacIntyre took the floor at the demand of the university senate in order to calm spirits. Yet he was ridiculed. After MacIntyre eloquently expressed the noble mission of the university, a student asked him how he could reconcile his appeal to moderation with the article he had signed off on several days beforehand, which justified violence![44] Later, MacIntyre would be violently taken to task by the ultraleft.[45] He himself was not to be outdone. He condemned the voluntarism of Che Guevara and the intellectual mediocrity of Herbert Marcuse, to whom he devoted a cruel and entertaining pamphlet.[46] His pessimism fit poorly with student logomachy. Must one recall that neither Marx nor Lenin ever held leftism close to his heart? MacIntyre was a man of the first New Left, born after 1956, but not of the second. This second left blossomed around

1968; the passionate enemy of social gaps and of all rigidity, it desired to absolutize individual consent by hating all authority. If the second New Left had above all claimed individual autonomy as its theory of liberty, the first New Left called for a more substantial liberty (to the extent that the expression "New Left" unites these two movements, it veils this fundamental difference and is erroneous). Surpassed on his right by the Labour Party's drift to the right, and on his left by collective hysteria, MacIntyre was isolated. "Socialists," he wrote, "must now recognize that the labour movement cannot hope to win political power."[47] In the preface of *Marxism and Christianity*, which appeared at that moment, MacIntyre wrote that he has abandoned Marxism.[48] We sense then that he was unsettled, caught between two fires, isolated on his right as on his left.

The Congress for Cultural Freedom, which reunited anticommunist intellectuals even though they were often "on the left," then published the journal *Encounter*. MacIntyre pushed anti-Stalinism to the point of regularly collaborating with the journal, including after 1966, when it was proven that the CIA financed the Congress through intermediary organizations.[49] In the eyes of the New Left, such collaboration could not fail to pass as a provocation, if only because the leitmotif of MacIntyre's engagement then was "neither Washington nor Moscow."[50] The IS, to which he belonged, derived its name from the slogan "neither Washington nor Moscow, but International Socialism."

MacIntyre had tried to escape Gaitskell's Labour Party as much as the Stalinist Communist Party, wanting neither social democracy nor the Soviet Union. Thanks to the New Left, then thanks to Trotskyism, he had thought that he could loosen the vise grip. But the Labourites, whom he already judged to be too far to the right under Gaitskell, shifted more to the right under Wilson. So ironically, MacIntyre came to deplore the Labourites for abandoning social democracy. On the left, instead of the Stalinist Communist Party, factions more and more extremist and less and less intellectually rigorous flourished here and there. Far from being loosened up, the vise grip had in reality tightened up again.

The Hegelian synthesis was undoubtedly the philosophy par excellence of "modern times," to the extent that it strove to give the individual his due as well as the state and to give the market economy its due as well as the community. It seemed to fulfill the demands of those whom individualism leaves unsatisfied. But Hegel's official reign came to an end in 1848. In the political realm, Marx then took Hegel to task, while Kierkegaard, opening a second front, reproached Hegel for absorbing existence into concept, the individual into the system. Under the effect of this double incrimination, the Hegelian synthesis crumbled. In 1945, on the other hand, as Marxism and existentialism simultaneously triumphed, a synthesis seemed self-evident: "Marxist existentialism." Sartre put forward the existentialist themes from the young Marx, to save *Das Kapital* from its materialism and join it to a philosophy of freedom. He hoped to conserve the best from the philosophies of history and the philosophies of the subject, reconciling the individual and the state.

MacIntyre concedes to Sartre the pertinence of his questions, but not his solutions. *The Critique of Dialectical Reason*, where Sartre effects his most complete reconciliation of existentialism and Marxism, hardly convinces MacIntyre. In his eyes, Sartre gives himself over to a "permanent carnival of fetishized inwardness."[51] In fact, whereas existentialism represents the struggle of consciousness as eternal and starts from a dialectic of the solitary individual, Marxism relies on a social and historical dialectic and insists that work is the essence of man, and that man's relationship to nature takes precedence over man's relationship to God. MacIntyre feels hardly any sympathy for those "strange attempts to unite historical necessity and absolute freedom."[52] Marxist existentialists separate the very things that they had set out to reunite—the individual point of view and the political point of view. MacIntyre takes into account the Marxist and existentialist critiques of Hegel. But neither Marxist nor existentialist critiques succeed in escaping an instrumental conception of the social, and they do not succeed in showing how morality can be socially embodied.

In the 1960s, Freudianism replaces existentialism as the orthodoxy of the day. It is now the hour of Freudo-Marxist syntheses (in the manner of Herbert Marcuse), which reconcile political economy and the economy of desire through assimilating Freudian repression with social repression. MacIntyre replies: "If we start with Marx and the sociologists, we find ourselves seeing the individual as formed by socially prefabricated roles into which he has to fit. His private motives are only a shadow behind his public life. If we start with Freud and the psychologists, we find public life merely as screen on to which private motives project their images. . . .

Both taken by themselves are fatal to our understanding of human beings as human beings; and merely adding them together will not solve our problems."[53]

MacIntyre denounces the duplicities and incoherencies of Marcuse. He appropriates the questions of Hegel, without however adopting either his system or the different syntheses that followed in his footsteps.

MacIntyre was a Trotskyist in the late 1950s and early 1960s. But this Trotskyism was surely not so much a way for him to follow Hegel's descendants as it was a way to oppose both Washington and Moscow. Alexandre Kojève liked to emphasize that nothing important was written after Hegel—as a proof of the world's separation into right-Hegelianism and left-Hegelianism, into the United States and the USSR. Moscow sacrifices the individual to the community, and Washington sacrifices the community to the individual. MacIntyre's Trotskyism was a fallback position, conveying his dissatisfaction toward the Hegelian tradition. Thus MacIntyre sums up the nature of our epoch's political debates:

> These debates are often staged in terms of a supposed opposition between individualism and collectivism, each appearing in a variety of doctrinal forms. On the one side there appear the self-defined protagonists of individual liberty, on the other side the self-defined protagonists of planning and regulation, of the goods which are available through bureaucratic organization. But in fact what is crucial is that on which the contending parties agree, namely that there are only two alternative modes of social life open to us, one in which the free and arbitrary choices of individuals are sovereign and one in which the bureaucracy is sovereign, precisely so that it may limit the free and arbitrary choices of individuals. Given this deep cultural agreement, it is unsurprising that the politics of modern societies oscillate between a freedom which is nothing but a lack of regulation of individual behavior and forms of collectivist control designed only to limit the anarchy of self-interest.[54]

MacIntyre intends neither to ratify individualism or statism, nor consequently to ratify the attempts to combine the two.

De-Stalinization cast doubt on justice and truth within the socialist world. The bourgeois were not the only bastards. The Khrushchev report mentioned the violations of socialist legality, blind repression, collective deportations, and mass executions.[55] Up to 1956, everything was as if the Soviet regime embodied Reason. As victims of physical or moral torture in the show trials, the condemned were forced to avow imaginary crimes. The homeland of the proletariat, the USSR did nothing for which it could reproach itself; only individuals could be wrong. After 1956, the ceremonies of self-accusation ceased and the dissidents were recognized as such. Once some of Stalin's crimes were assumed by the state, the dissidents could plead their innocence. Soviet Russia was no longer necessarily at the vanguard of History. A whole world fell apart. MacIntyre seemed to have done everything to remain faithful to the most radical political ideal of the Enlightenment. A one-time Stalinist, he became Trotskyist to dissociate Marx from the Soviet Union and to reaffirm his fidelity to the modern epic and its ambition. But in the end he had to concede defeat. Sobered, he published in 1971 a book whose title expresses his disenchantment: *Against the Self-Images of the Age*. An event in the drama of the universal, the failure of Stalinism betrays if not the death of a god (*The God That Failed*[56]), then at least the end of the "Enlightenment project."

In the late 1950s and at the beginning of the following decade, MacIntyre led a struggle against social democracy within the British left. As the end of the 1960s approached and the ideological dissolution of the left intensified, he lost his natural milieu and discovered himself to be alone. A little after his arrival into the United States in the early 1970s, he separated from his second wife, as if he meant to mark a deep break with the past.[57] In terms of his political trajectory, he came, somewhat in spite of himself, to be reconciled with Locke, the theorist par excellence of tolerance and liberalism.[58] Faithful to the first New Left's reflections on the social bond and to its attempt to rediscover true socialism, MacIntyre became a revolutionary. But Marxist-Leninism also seemed to have lost its initial objective.

MacIntyre therefore rallied indirectly to liberal democracy—less, however, through preference and more through a kind of grudging resignation. We could insist that this is one of his most serious weaknesses. There is something in MacIntyre that prevents him from clearly recognizing the value of liberal democracy as a political regime, even though he offers no alternative. From another point of view, however, the principal orientations of his thought are not really won over to liberalism, and it would be curious if he called himself "liberal," even by default. He remains antiliberal and readily makes it known. He comes to understand or admit that liberalism triumphs over tyranny, but he remains faithful to his initial intuition, which I mentioned in my introduction. Society cannot merely flee from evil. It should make the good accessible to souls and nourish existence, without merely limiting justice to economics and to a purely formal freedom. The young MacIntyre had criticized the Old Left because it had forgotten that in its essence, socialism is a critique of the formal character of liberal democracy. But MacIntyre looks for what way society can teach about the good and make the good accessible to everyone, without holding to a systematic strategy that circumvents human nature.

II. From Marxism to Communitarianism?

MacIntyre is often compared with two other philosophers of his generation: Charles Taylor (born in 1931), whom I have already mentioned, and Michael Walzer (born in 1935). They are generally classified into the so-called "communitarian" school, which questions contemporary liberalism's individualism and atomism.[59] What is communitarianism? It is a reaction against the impoverishment of the human bond, a reaction against the limits of social democracy and the failure of communism. The dissolution of the social bond calls for a pendulum swing, a readjustment. It leads individuals to search for a less formal, less procedural freedom. Communitarians feel the separation of the private and the public as violence against them. To them, it seems too artificial to hold to a "neutral" public sphere that abstracts away from individual particularities. In their eyes, these particularities would stand to gain from public recognition. They should not be ignored, as the liberals would wish.

Even though the term "communitarian" would not come to be used in political philosophy until the 1980s, the kinship of the views of MacIntyre, Taylor, and Walzer goes back to the 1950s. Taylor's masterpiece, *Sources of the Self* (1990), takes up again the questions raised by the *Universities and Left Review*, with which he had once collaborated—namely, the enrichment of existence in commercial republics through culture. The title of a collection of texts that he devoted to Canadian politics, *Reconciling the Solitudes*, alludes directly to the questions that the New Left raised.[60] Additionally, it should be noted that Michael Walzer, a Fulbright scholar in England from 1956 to 1957, there discovered the British antistatist tradition and mingled in the milieu of the *Universities and Left Review*. Returning to the United States, he wrote his thesis at Harvard, where he participated in a circle christened the New Left Club, in an allusion to the British movement. In 1953, as a young student at Brandeis University, he met Irving Howe, a former Trotskyist who would soon found the magazine *Dissent*. Walzer joined the editorial board in 1959 and became its director in 1975. Disagreeing with the New Left on feminism and the Vietnam War, *Dissent* nevertheless played an important role in the genesis of the American movement: as in Great Britain, one of the magazine's starting points had been the question of mass culture, which is to say the end of class struggle and the emergence of the consumer society.[61]

Questioned about his youth, MacIntyre insists on the importance of "the local dimension" in his thought: "I was fortunate enough to be living in the east end of London, and to be confronted by the local Communist Party's critique of the local Labour Party. That critique was compelling in concrete terms, not in terms of large theories. As a result, I became convinced of the truth of some of the larger theories, for those theories appeared to explain and justify the local critique. But I started from that local critique, and I ended with that local critique."[62] The explanation is awkward, but significant. From 1953, MacIntyre had called for a new "community."[63] His critique of individualism can be described as a return to some of the favorite themes of Guild Socialism. His path is a reverse image of Cole's, with a fifty-year interval. The history of the origins of the New Left and the somewhat unsettling evolution of the author of *After Virtue* clarify each other. If Guild Socialism had transformed into the New Left, then MacIntyre had returned from the New Left to Guild Socialism. At the end of *After Virtue* (1981), he calls for a new St. Benedict and "the construction of local forms of community within which civility and the intellectual and moral life" could be practiced in an entirely new manner.[64] He expresses his esteem for a number of people—James McDyer, for example, who, in one of the poorest regions of Donegal, Northern Ireland, worked in the 1960s and 1970s to stem endemic unemployment and emigration. He taught young people a trade and organized cooperatives to give farmers and fishermen back some of their economic independence and pride.[65] MacIntyre advises societies that have lost their roots to rethink profoundly their local institutions and life, as well as to work on their collective memory—that of family, neighbor, city, or nation.[66] As individualism and utilitarianism progress, as traditional forms of sociability dissolve, as freedom contracts to the point of losing all content, a reaction proves to be necessary. Communitarianism is what remains of socialism after the failure of the welfare state to transform social relations. The disillusion caused by communism and social democracy pushes the contemporary heirs of socialism to call for "local communities." The sense that the social bond has dissolved calls for a return to more substantial forms of life. Individualism should be rebalanced by "communitarianism." The disappointments of the advanced version of the Enlightenment call for a reaction. They call for the rediscovery of the theories of freedom that relate freedom to truth, which the eighteenth century had vigorously undone. Communitarianism is what remains of communism after Stalin and Solzhenitsyn.

Neither MacIntyre nor Taylor was ever attracted to the theory of economic determinism. As young men, they looked to combine Christian freedom and Marxism. Today, their critiques of the theories of freedom as the absence of coercion start not so much from an analysis of property in the capitalist regime as from a moral philosophy. They consider Marx to have remained too dependent on liberalism and utilitarianism and to be wrong for placing his hopes in a "socialized Robinson Crusoe."[67] They remember Marx's deep sympathy for the Industrial Revolution. Individualism does not constitute the solution to Stalinism, because it is ultimately individualism (in its methodological form) that is responsible for the failure of Marxism! For communitarians, the first wave of modernity (Lockean, if we wish) does not reveal its true nature until it is completed and transformed by the second wave (Rousseauian or post-Rousseauian). The years 1688 and 1789 only make sense with 1793, 1848, or 1917. Should the failure of the Soviet Union be considered a victory for individualism? This MacIntyre denies. The "fear of 1984" must not be allowed to "revive the politics which glorified 1688," he wrote in the late 1960s.[68] Neither the failure of the welfare state nor that of Leninism legitimates the primacy of individual autonomy!

MacIntyre invites reasoning by reference to social forms and types of belonging. Individualism presupposes a social or common backdrop. The question of the social bond is also that of particularity. To what extent can a man realize himself directly at the level of the universal? To what extent does he need the mediation of the city? What should citizens hold in common? The starting point of the New Left, which we find again among the communitarians, is the conviction that it is impossible to dismiss these questions, for freedom is not so much about indifference with respect to the world as it is about a form of excellence and participation.

As individualism progresses, as societies "liberalize," a reaction is self-evident, which looks to give back substance and content to the social dimension of existence, to rediscover the meaning of the good that nourishes the soul. We cannot simply flee the bad; we must also look for the good. Communitarians make themselves the theorists and spokesmen for this rebalancing. They support regional movements and aboriginal minorities and look to re-create "communities." Since individual autonomy opens up abysses, we must look for anchoring points.

Communitarians criticize the idea that the law should be the same for everyone. They want the law to take into account the existence of specific communities, to "recognize" them. Communitarians believe that in the absence of positive discrimination, communities will not be accepted for what they are. Without always realizing it, therefore, they rediscover the Marxist critique of liberal democracy, a theory of alienation. With Marx, the liberal concept of liberty, linked to the formal character of the law and to the state's indifference toward civil society, comes to pose a problem: What is this "liberty" if it incites unhappiness and alienation? In the Marxist tradition, the individual is not satisfied until he is recognized in his particularity, in his singularity. Liberal equality, "formal" equality, equality before a law that abstracts away from singularity or from identity, is not satisfactory: we need therefore a "real" equality.

Inspired by Marx, yesterday's communists and today's communitarians rail against the liberal separation of the state and civil society. They rail against the formal character of a law that is the same for everyone and that notices neither poverty nor religion nor sex nor cultural identity. Hence the need for a logic of recognition that takes these differences into account. Like Marxists in the past, they call for a "real" democracy that gives life to authentic freedom, except that they concentrate less on poverty and much more on identity. In *The Jewish Question*, for example, Marx had criticized the liberal *separation*, the abstraction from the *contents of life*, and the essentially formal character of liberal freedom. The communitarian critique of proceduralism was akin to the purpose of *The Jewish Question*. In the 1960s and '70s, as Marxism's failure became more manifest, communists became communitarians and replaced one category of the oppressed (the proletariat) with another (cultures dominated by imperialism). In many respects the call for "community" is probably just the most recent disguise of the desire to abolish the separation between civil society and the state. The Marxist critique of "formal liberty" has found an unexpected legacy in the theory of "positive liberty," which some communitarians call for. "Negative" liberty is the mere absence of coercion, the freedom of the entrepreneur and of the consumer, the free use of their capital and their revenues, whereas "positive" liberty presupposes an end inscribed in social life.

The communitarian critique of national homogeneity also echoes another theme dear to Marxism: the critique of the nation-state. For Marx, the state is at the service of the bourgeoisie, and the nation pertains to a political illusion. The nation-state appears as a sham destined to hide the reality of class struggle. True unity is in fact social class and not the nation. Marx analyzes the nation-state as an illusion that obscures the reality of conflict between the bourgeoisie and the proletariat. As former Marxists, communitarians hardly take the reality of the national state seriously. Or, if they do take it seriously, it is to oppose it.

The nation-state tends to bring cultural community and political unity together. But historically, these political and cultural elements have more often been held apart, either because of the domination conquerors exert over nonnative peoples or because peoples driven by a fierce desire for autonomy have fragmented into politico-military units. Communitarians cast doubt upon the centripetal tendencies of the nation-state. As claimants for multiculturalism, they hardly appreciate either Jacobinism or "cultural" homogenization. They make themselves the spokesmen for minorities that they believe great modern nations either forget or oppress. Communitarians feel comfortable not in the nation-state but in vast federations. Michael Walzer is an American, Charles Taylor is a Canadian, and MacIntyre immigrated into the United States. Their critique of cosmopolitanism turns into a critique of the forms of national homogenization.[69] By the late 1970s, Charles Taylor, despite being crowned with all the glories of Oxonian university life, decided to return to Montreal, from which he never wanted to stray for too long.[70] His communitarianism corresponds less to the European nation-state and more to vast federations such as Canada. No other country creates such an impression of recognizing the diversity of its "communities." Questions of regional autonomy, minority representation, and language rights could be a Canadian specialty! Against the partisans of Quebec independence, Taylor shows the value of a multicultural Canadian federation. Against "hard" federalists, who refuse to admit the existence of identitarian demands, he emphasizes the legitimacy of a certain particularism.[71] As for MacIntyre, he has become all the more American, as he chose to become an American. Why did he leave Europe in 1969? Why would an intellectual immigrate into the United States? That a Marxist thinker—and, what is more, an antiliberal—should voluntarily install himself in the commercial republic most faithful to the Enlightenment—there's something to unsettle us! It seems that the America that he went to look for was, if not Jefferson's America, most attached to local life and to agriculture, at least the America that gives a certain pluralism its due: the "nation of nationalities" and the "social union of social unions." MacIntyre's America is akin to that which Madison describes in the *Federalist*, rather than that which Tocqueville analyzed: it is less threatened by conformism than saved by diversity. We often qualify the United States as an "imperial" republic; yet empires are more welcoming to minorities.

To understand the hostility of communitarians to the nation-state, we must remember the great lessons of historical sociology. The nation-state built itself by destroying feudalities and intermediary bodies. A formidable machine for equalization, the nation-state gradually transformed citizens into equals, which is to say into "atoms" and "look-alikes." Thus it destroyed numerous forms of life and modes of sociability. Historically, the nation-state constituted itself against regionalisms, against diversity of social forms, and thus weakened local forms of solidarity. The intermediary bodies that the communitarians defend have been gradually emptied of their substance by the modern state.

Scotland is perhaps the first country in the world to have knowingly and in relative freedom *chosen* integration into what was to become "the modern world." In 1707, should or should not Scotland have united with England to form the United Kingdom? Should Scotland have renounced its traditional Scottish forms of sociability for the benefit of integrating into global commerce? Was it possible to refuse? The debates that took place then prefigure even the most contemporary quarrels. Is the social bond based on interest as valuable as the social bond based on virtue? Is economic integration compatible with the maintenance of political identity? How to combine the universal and the particular? Is freedom as individual autonomy the whole of freedom? In *Whose Justice? Which Rationality?* (1988), MacIntyre devotes long chapters to these debates. Above all, he takes sides. With the Act of Union, Scotland lost her soul! Andrew Fletcher of Salton, the chief opponent of unification, is the hero of the book.

> Almost alone among his contemporaries Fletcher understood the dilemma confronting Scotland as involving more radical exclusive alternatives than they were prepared to entertain. For on his view at the level of political action either Scotland moved into the world of the modern large-scale state and large-scale economy and ceased thereby to be Scotland or it had to recreate itself within a form of government more local and more morally homogeneous than even the midseventeenth-century Calvinist Aristotelians had envisaged. And at the level of philosophy either the contending voices of the moderns could be studied, thereby producing institutionalized lack of agreement, or there could be a return to an education which relied upon Aristotle's *Ethics* and *Politics*. But neither at the level of political action nor at that of philosophy was there any third set of possibilities.[72]

Most partisans for unification believed that they could get rid of the bellicose temper of the ancients and appropriate the luxurious advantages of commercial civilization, without having to renounce traditional forms of sociability. One of the most successful chapters of *Whose Justice? Which Rationality?* is where MacIntyre finds the opportunity to deploy his great narrative talents. In pages filled with irony and indignation, he depicts the efforts of Hume to anglicize his name, his turns of phrase, and his manners. Like the Irish Burke, the Scottish Hume took the side of the enemy of his homeland; MacIntyre contrasts the assuredly deplorable example of these renegades with Fletcher's inflexibility.[73] He has, incidentally, long professed in private his sympathy for Irish republicanism and, more specifically, for the very violent Irish Republican Army (IRA).[74]

Communitarianism has achieved a real success today, for it strikes a chord. On the one hand, the process of "secularization" seems almost complete. In many parts of the West, Christian religion has lost its sway over society, and the meaning of life has not been clarified accordingly. Communitarianism gives a "cultural" response to the collapse of the authority of the churches. On the other hand, since the Enlightenment's universalism supports the centralizing work of the nation-state, the crisis of Enlightenment rebounds onto the nation-state. Most nation-states were formed by attracting local elites to a universalism superior to their own particularism. Why did these elites abandon their *patois* and their customs? In part because the national language gave access to literature, ideas, and a wider world—to "civilization," to "Enlightenment." It was also because the French National Assembly elected in 1789 declared there to be universal rights that it could be a fully "National" Assembly. Nation-states were formed through the conviction that the Enlightenment embraced and surpassed all particularism, that the Enlightenment replaced traditions with reason. But "modern" ideology is today in crisis. Reason is no longer unanimous, and the fashion is for "postmodernism." Questioning the advanced version of the Enlightenment (socialism or communism) rebounds on the Enlightenment as a whole. The idea of progress, which had enshrined an alliance between the people and their enlightened elites, is singularly criticized today. Communitarianism is the result of this crisis. It is the refuge of disappointed communists and socialists, a way of prolonging a little the great dream of a better tomorrow, a way of preserving their animosity toward liberal individualism without exposing themselves to the criticisms targeted at socialism and communism.

Why do communitarians, supporters of multiculturalism, want to get upstream from the unification wrought by the nation-state? They have inherited from Marxism a certain contempt for the category of politics: the *political* project of the nation-state leaves them indifferent or hostile.

But whereas Marxists reduce politics to economics, communitarians reduce politics to "culture" or to "identity." Correspondingly, proper concern for the nation-state, which looks to bring politics and culture together, appears to them to be senseless. The dream of cultural autonomy replaces the Marxist dream of the worker's freedom and the nationalist dream of political autonomy.

By his sensibility, MacIntyre is strongly attracted to communitarianism. He yields sometimes to an irritating rhetoric, longing for the renewal of communities of fishermen and craftsmen, in a vein of aging romanticism. He readily criticizes the nation-state. "Being asked to die for it [the nation-state]," he writes, "would be like being asked to die for a telephone company."[75] Against this malaise, MacIntyre counters less with civic virtue and more with moral virtue. He tends to sacrifice political philosophy to moral philosophy. Against the dissolution of the social bond and against the rule of manipulation, he counters less with patriotism and more with morally satisfying forms of life. His works pertain more to moral philosophy than to political philosophy. In this sense, his hostility to the nation-state appears to refer to a more general thesis: civic virtue can only constitute a limited response to the rule of utilitarianism and to the impoverishment of the human bond. The response to the prevailing malaise is less through political participation and more through subpolitical or transpolitical communities. In this respect, MacIntyre could remain faithful to the Marxist critique of politics.

Nevertheless, MacIntyre refuses to be considered a communitarian.[76] He only halfheartedly supports feminist, gay, and regionalist movements, as well as aboriginal or immigrant minorities. He is doubtful of the politics of affirmative action.[77] He writes, "It is therefore a mistake, the communitarian mistake, to attempt to infuse the politics of the state with the values and modes of participation in local community."[78] The concept of communitarianism is woolly and sometimes equivocal. Its meaning differs according to its interpreters and according to political traditions. In the French context the principal difficulty refers to the republican tradition. From the Anglo-American point of view, the debate that contrasts French republicans with French *communautaristes* (Basques, Bretons, Muslims . . .) is really contrasting two types of communitarians.[79] On the one hand, there is the communitarianism of the *communautaristes*, who claim rootedness in particular cultures. On the other hand there is the communitarianism of the French republicans, for whom negative liberty is insufficient: the state must promote certain types of life, help individuals to become rational and emancipate them from their "heteronomous" traditions, in particular through education. This state action falls within the framework of "perfectionist" liberalism. The "liberal" Anglo-American position, that of the primacy of negative liberty, does not really have a place in this debate. This says how much Anglo-American "communitarianism" risks being distorted in France. To hold to one defined conception, I shall not here distinguish MacIntyre's position from that of French *communautaristes* nor liken his position to theirs, whether they are republican or antirepublican. Rather, I shall envisage his position in relation to that of Charles Taylor and Michael Walzer, who consider themselves communitarians and who in the Anglo-American world are generally considered to be communitarians.

MacIntyre shares with them a restlessness about the nature of social relations and about the insufficiencies of the form of the nation-state. Like them, he affirms the importance of the social dimension of human existence; like them, he tends to reject any primacy of civic virtue as an answer to the malaise he analyzes. Unlike the communitarians, however, he does not believe that to resolve problems it is enough to "inject" a communitarian dimension into modern politics. More specifically, communitarians such as Taylor and Walzer tend to think that diverse identities can peacefully coexist with each other within a multicultural regime. MacIntyre has no sympathy for multiculturalism, for he is attuned to its paradox: multiculturalism is a kind of individualism. For multiculturalists, the individual can choose diverse identities and make them peacefully coexist in the same manner that, in today's great metropolises, we can choose to go to such and such a restaurant to taste such and such cuisine: French, Italian, Chinese, Japanese, Thai, and so on. Communities are subordinated to the choice the individual makes; the individual remains sovereign.[80] For MacIntyre, by contrast, it is not a question of putting multiple "identities" at the disposal of the liberal citizen, so that he can choose between them and combine them as he likes. On the contrary, it is a question of affirming the relative inertia of forms of belonging and the inelasticity of the logic of identity. A society worthy of the name is not a stopping house. It is within the framework of a given community, with relatively well-defined frontiers, that the individual develops, grows up, gains wisdom, and becomes free.

At the end of *Three Rival Versions of Moral Enquiry*, MacIntyre proposes reorganizing the universities. Rather than inviting universities to teach the "points of view" of different communities, MacIntyre recommends that they become the expression of a single community: that each university align itself with a single tradition of enquiry. Universities would thus compete on the basis of the unified projects that each one has taken hold of: for example, Thomist Catholic universities would compete against utilitarian universities. I am not sure if the proposal is meant to be put into practice, but it is thought-provoking. For MacIntyre, true intellectual formation comes not through mixing with diverse people, which would be immediately available to a cosmopolitan citizen freed of all roots. True intellectual formation comes through deepening a specific tradition. MacIntyre claims rootedness in an authoritative philosophical tradition. This is what leads him to criticize multicultural communitarianism, which tends toward relativism.

MacIntyre is not a communitarian, since communitarianism pertains to postmodern relativism. For communitarians, minorities ask to be recognized for their own sake, and not because they could contribute to society as a whole. Multiculturalism is a kind of relativism. Yet, as I shall show later on, MacIntyre unceasingly searched for an escape from relativism. Starting from a historicism barely compatible with the idea of moral truth, he gradually gave that up to reconcile the diversity of forms of life with the unity of humanity. For him, the question of political minorities raises first and foremost the question of the objectivity of truth: against the majority, how can a minority be *right*? Yet it is precisely this question that the communitarians, who reason not in terms of rationality but in terms of identity, neglect. As I shall have the opportunity to show later, the question in philosophy that unceasingly preoccupied MacIntyre is the question of the objectivity of moral life, of the existence of a true practical rationality. As I shall also have the opportunity to show, MacIntyre is very interested in the philosophy of religion as well. But this is less to contrast one religious "identity" to another and more to find, at the heart of faith, practical rationality at work. I shall add two criticisms of communitarianism that we do not find with MacIntyre.

Marx based his affirmation of the primacy of social classes on rigorous analysis, on economic determinism and principled internationalism.

Communitarians offer no comparable analysis to explain the primacy of the "community" over the nation. Communitarianism clashes against a second objection: it is uncertain if it is compatible with the democratic affirmation of equality. In practice, it is necessary to recognize the legal specificity of certain groups, granting them different rights according to different situations and knowing that all situations are to some extent different. This much is evident and cannot be denied, save by falling into a dogmatic individualism. But the demand for affirmative action implies a type of superiority incompatible with democracy. We cannot value equality and difference at the same time and in the same respect—that a community be simultaneously recognized as equal to other communities and as specific. For there to be equality, everyone must have the same rights. Yet the right to difference implies a hierarchy. Difference implies either a privilege or an incapacity, which is to say an inequality. In practice, the work of jurists consists precisely in reconciling the consideration of difference and the respect for equality. But jurists can only do this on a pragmatic basis; on a theoretical level, equality excludes difference. On the theoretical level, democracy can only be open to all on the following condition: that it ignores collective identities by considering the individual absent of any singularity and particularity. Within the egalitarian framework of "modernity," the only legitimate demand is for equal rights: to participation in civic life, benefits of the welfare-state, and so forth. Liberal democracy inevitably presupposes the "unencumbered" individual against which communitarians rail, for we can only consider human beings as equal on the condition that we *abstract* away from their differences. The "embedded" being is not only the one whose chances of success are unjustly low because he belongs to a despised ethnicity. More traditionally, it is also the Jew denied citizenship or the *ancien régime* aristocrat whose name is enough to legitimate his authority . . . Once imposed in the past as a mark of infamy, the ghetto is henceforth claimed as the sign of superiority, but justly so: a *superiority* with respect to white males, to Europe, and so on.

Marx, who simultaneously wanted difference and equality, was well aware of these difficulties. That is why he was not the supporter of a liberal democracy or of a formal liberty, but of a "real" democracy, a communist democracy. Marx teaches that real democracy is only possible on the condition that communism abolishes the private sphere. This is to say that it abolishes the difference between the private and the public, between civil society and the state. Without communism, without the proletariat revolution, "real" liberty can only remain as a pious wish. By contrast, Marx's theory confirms that in the absence of communism, difference is incompatible with equality. Yet communitarians, who no longer believe in either the possibility of communism or the possibility of revolution, nevertheless aspire for a "real" democracy, recognizing individual particularities. Marx would quite rightly say to them that they are not taking up the means to achieve what they call for. They want the recognition of individual particularities, which implies the abolition of the separation of state and civil society, while maintaining the separation of state and civil society.

We do not find this critique in MacIntyre, whose sensibility remains communitarian—that is to say, partially apolitical. But he is undoubtedly attentive enough to the very logic of Marxism to guess the weakness or incoherence of a rigorous communitarianism.

In 1960, *The New Reasoner* merged with *Universities and Left Review*. These two publications came from different horizons. The members of the journal *The New Reasoner*, with which MacIntyre was connected, were most often former members of the Communist Party. In this respect they were less inclined to turn social democratic than the editors of the other mouthpiece of the first British New Left, *Universities and Left Review*, who were very young, less working class, and who readily joined Bloomsbury with Saint-Germain-des-Prés. *The New Reasoner* was edited in Halifax, in industrial Yorkshire, whereas the members of *Universities and Left Review*, led by Charles Taylor, were more often students or fellows of Oxford:[81] "The ambivalence of the New Left is that it has not yet chosen between Prometheus and Adam. While Mr Charles Taylor hankers after a return ticket to Eden, there are others, like Mr MacIntyre, who plot to storm heaven."[82]

Contrary to the Old Left, the New Left considered Attlee's welfare state to be insufficient. It nevertheless judged it necessary and tended to see it as clear progress. While MacIntyre connects himself with the most anticapitalist elements of the First New Left and never ceases to mistrust "bourgeois" politics, Taylor, in his assessment of the New Left that he sketched in the late 1980s, concluded that it was necessary to abandon all references to Marx.[83] MacIntyre continues to feel a certain distrust toward the market economy, even if this distrust is henceforth less "revolutionary"

than potentially "conservative," for the regime that enshrines private property also enshrines private life, the instrumentalization of politics, and individualism. The list of "practices" around which MacIntyre organizes
moral life in *After Virtue* is so incongruous that it is less remarkable for
what it includes than by what it excludes—in particular, industry and bureaucracy.[84] Taylor's communitarianism, by contrast, is a relatively consen-
sual "multiculturalism." Taylor remains faithful to the culturalism of *Universities and Left Review*: he places himself on the field of "culture" rather
than "tradition." By contrast, in MacIntyre's eyes, virtue and wisdom are
more fragile than Taylor thinks. Whereas Taylor places himself within
"modernity" itself, MacIntyre rejects modernity and at the same time refuses to be considered a communitarian. MacIntyre's refusal of this label,
which Taylor never repudiates, refers to a more radical critique of individual autonomy and of the Enlightenment. Today, Taylor participates in the
political life of Canada, where he is one of Canada's most respected and
admired intellectuals, particularly for his moderation. MacIntyre, for his
part, has distanced himself from public life. We could not more strongly
contrast his activism in the years preceding 1968 with his political passivity
in the subsequent decade.

In terms of its criticism of liberal democracy's formal character, communitarianism takes up the central theme of communism, but in a tragic
mode: the necessary is akin to the impossible. In Taylor's work, this tragic
note remains almost inaudible; in MacIntyre, it is bellowed. MacIntyre
lends his voice to the postmodern "night of the spirit."[85] He writes, "For I
too not only take it that Marxism is exhausted as a *political* tradition . . . but
I believe this exhaustion is shared by every other political tradition within
our culture."[86] This constant leads him to break with the progressivism of
the Enlightenment at the same time as he breaks with politics itself. In this
respect, his reflection suffers from a serious handicap: his communitarian
sensibility professes too strong a tendency to disregard politics itself.

If they were to deepen some of their holistic premises, communitarians would perceive that they are looking for a response to religion's loss of
influence and the crisis of modern rationalism. This response involves a
certain conservatism, since conservatism has the function of moderating
liberal logic, of preventing liberalism from deepening to the point of turning against itself. MacIntyre ranks among those intellectuals who were on

the far left during the 1950s and who, horrified by the moral relativism of the 1960s, could today be passed off as "reactionaries"! The strangeness of his own intellectual journey perhaps clarifies here some aspects of communitarianism, as conservatism has assuredly one advantage over communitarianism: its classicism.

To orient ourselves in the world, it is not enough to belong to a liberal society. Do we, incidentally, "belong" to a liberal society? Liberalism coexists with the traditions by which people live, but in itself, liberalism probably does not constitute one of the traditions by which people can live. Liberal society depends on nonliberal forms of life, which it erodes and casts doubt on. So it is, for example, that individualism tends to cast doubt on the authority of Christian churches or the foundations of rational and objective morality, even though liberal democracy undoubtedly needs one and the other. Liberalism's founders (John Locke, for example) do not seem to have thought that liberalism could go without a religious dimension. In this sense, the affirmation of "community" is a legitimate reaction against the deepening of liberal logic to the detriment of liberalism itself. It is a question of giving substance to a society that has abused the liberal dynamic and, by consequence, no longer knows what it wants. But the conservatism that MacIntyre develops remains dependent on his communitarian sensibility: it is less "political" than "social."

III. A New Conservatism

Why are the New Left's intellectuals so sensitive to this rootedness of the individual in his community? Their first political initiation was sometimes through colonization and sometimes through the "frontier." Stuart Hall spent his youth in the Caribbean. Tom Nairn and Raymond Williams come from the Celtic fringe: one from the confines of England and Scotland, the other from the confines of England and Wales. Charles Taylor is an Anglophone Quebecois. MacIntyre is not exempt from this rule. We should recall here two important figures for his formation: Cyril Lionel Robert James (1901–89) and George Thomson (1903–87), experts in Marxism. C. L. R. James was Black, originally from the Caribbean, where he spent his youth. In his spare time he was an éminence grise, a colorful character, a novelist, journalist, Trotskyist, cricket specialist, maverick, and historian. He wrote extensively on racism, the colonial question, and imperialism.[87] As for Thomson, he was one of MacIntyre's favorite authors of the postwar years. Professor of Greek at Birmingham, he started by teaching Gaelic at Galway, on the west coast of Ireland. This left him with a deep admiration for the poetic character of this country. He contrasts the modern system of imagination with that of ancient Greece and rural Ireland. As a member of the Communist Party, he develops a critique of the Industrial Revolution that is imprinted with nostalgia for the culture that it swept out. Sometimes his critique seems to be founded less on hope for a better tomorrow and more on regret for a bygone past.[88] The parallelism between these two figures and the origins of some of the spokesmen for the New Left should be well noted. One can find the Celtic fringe and the United Kingdom's colonial empire in the same place. In mixing Marxism and reflections on acculturation, the books of C. L. R. James and George Thomson will have a decisive influence on MacIntyre. In the 1960s, MacIntyre and Taylor were very interested in ethnology and thought extensively on the way to account for the diversity of peoples and cultures. This reflection had an important political dimension, as one excellent observer, François Furet, noted—and not without irony:

> It took the dislocation of Marxist dogmatism between 1955 and 1960 for ethnology to fulfill a social expectation and meet a historical situation. Decolonization revealed to all the secrets of the ethnologists, those pioneers of anticolonialism: namely, that cultures are multiple, are equally worthy of respect, and manifest themselves in terms of permanence rather than of change. French colonization . . . claimed to place them in Western "time," putting them through European stages of progress whether they liked it or not. Now, however, there is perhaps a trace of expiatory masochism in the revaluation of these extra-European worlds. Furthermore, these exotic and impoverished worlds have the virtue of focusing all the distaste for, and rejection of, the "affluent society": even if they are no longer centers of revolution and are gradually sinking below the survival line, they are at least pure and innocent in the eyes of a Left that is at heart moralistic and

more Christian than it thinks. They remain a geographical refuge for the frustration with the historical immobility of a nonrevolutionary West.[89]

Tom Nairn and Raymond Williams did not hesitate to exercise their imagination, straining their genealogy to make themselves seem more foreign to England than they were. Likewise, MacIntyre likes to think of himself as Irish. Yet if his books owe nothing to the Celtic reveries of an Ernest Renan or a Matthew Arnold, nor profess a particular taste for eclogues, bucolic landscapes, or pastoral idylls, MacIntyre enjoys referring to Icelandic sagas, to the legends of St. Columban and to Brian Boru, to small, ideal fishing communities, and to immemorial oral traditions that he himself has collected.[90]

> My ancestors lived in small communities in Northern Ireland and
> in the West of Scotland—my father was one of the first generation
> of his family not to learn English as a second language. In other
> words, I come from the fringes of modern Western culture and
> have tried to give a clear voice to some of those people who do not
> belong to the dominant mainstream and cannot identify with
> it. But paradoxically, I was only able to do this, and I only became
> aware of the need to do so, because I myself spent most of my
> adult life in universities that belong to this mainstream.[91]

Sometimes a bit of a "poser," MacIntyre tends to define himself as a man from the West's periphery, on the margins of two radically different cultures. It is with regret that he has to concede a more banal truth—that he belongs to the modern world. At home, the New Left vilifies English imperialism and comes to the defense of Welsh and Scottish nationalism. Abroad, it denounces British imperialism. MacIntyre defends the European project, as a way to avoid a showdown with London.[92] He falls within this revisionist current, which exaggerates the democratic character of Scotland and Wales before their integration into the United Kingdom and readily discusses their immemorial identities without wanting to admit too much that Welsh identity, for example, probably owes its existence to English domination.[93]

Nostalgia for "community" is one of the dominant traits of the first New Left, and more generally, of British socialist milieus of the 1950s and 1960s.[94] The work of Richard Hoggart is imprinted with nostalgia for the working-class society of prewar Leeds, imbued with the working class's crisis of identity and the related sentiment of social atomization. In contributing to everyone's enrichment, capitalism removes the forms of dependence that compel people to help each other and form communities.[95] Such are the perverse effects of opulence. Despite his reservations toward Hoggart's conceptions, the editor in chief of *The New Reasoner*, E. P. Thompson, was himself influenced by William Blake's romanticism. While the philosopher Charles Taylor, the historian E. P. Thompson, and the literary critic Raymond Williams distance themselves from the most archaic forms of "community," they still feel some sympathy for the concept. Even though they refuse to replace class struggle with the ideal of an organically unified culture, and even though they intend to distinguish community from its idealistic forgeries by restricting it to the metaphorical realm, they also call for the creation of a new socialist "community."[96] In struggling against the economics of the Old Left, the New Left strives to struggle against the impoverished conception of freedom to which the Labour Party was unwittingly rallying. The failure of the advanced version of the Enlightenment leads some theorists of the New Left back to the most conservative dimensions of their own movement: to nostalgia for forms of sociability that the Industrial Revolution destroyed. The concept of a "practice" (which MacIntyre elaborates and to which I shall return later on) either evokes John Ruskin and his taste for craftsmen, or it evokes Guild Socialism, which proposes replacing the control of the banker with the control of the craftsman.[97]

The liberal nation-state is hardly conservative, for it destroys traditions, particularities, and social hierarchies. . . . By contrast, its adversaries tend to be conservatives. Supporters of community have a powerful concept to provide order: to be *rooted*—or, more precisely, to be *embedded*.[98] It is a question of rediscovering authoritative norms and traditions, of renouncing the illusion of a purely transparent and rational society. After the 1960s, the revolutionary perspective seems to give way to a thematic of rootedness and memory.[99] The Marxist critique of the formal character of law is transformed into a neo-Burkean critique of Enlightenment's abstraction.

MacIntyre denounces one of the fundamental articles of the liberal creed: the existence of subjective, universal rights. "But we need not be distracted," he writes, "for the truth is plain: there are no such rights, and belief in them is one with belief in witches and in unicorns."[100] MacIntyre thus echoes the threefold critique that Edmund Burke, Jeremy Bentham, and Marx targeted at modern natural right. MacIntyre has so little sympathy for the proliferation of individual or subjective rights that he goes to the point of denying their reality. By a singular detour, his denunciation of constructivism, his critique of individual rights, and his nostalgia for the "little platoon" dear to Burke make communitarianism akin to conservatism. Like the supporters of the counterrevolutionary school, MacIntyre tends to insist that reason, as an individual capacity, must rely on authoritative customs and traditions. As I shall explain below, he had learned the Wittgensteinian critique of the "private language" thesis, a critique that states that there are no innate ideas without acquired expressions and that reason's autonomy must be understood by reference to a received and transmitted language. Individual judgments must make resort to collective determinations. MacIntyre emphasizes that "the individual who reasons rightly does so *qua* member of a particular type of political society and not just *qua* individual human being."[101]

Marx and Burke agree on the critique of the abstraction of a certain liberalism. What remains of the Marxist critique of rights after the failure of Marxism? Burke? By way of "liberalizing," we have come to impose on society an indifference toward the subject of good and evil and true and false. This indifference rebounds onto everyone, leaving us with the misery of a freedom deprived of its object. MacIntyre invites us to reconstitute forms of life, institutions, and communities within the framework of which liberty can be built. The more we insist on the necessity of "liberalizing," of tolerating differences, of bringing about radical individualism, the more law becomes procedural, the more patriotism becomes "constitutional," the more we empty citizenship of any specific content, and the more we call for a reaction. This reaction rediscovers another kind of freedom at the level of communities, and these communities are not to be confused with the state. MacIntyre, this *zōon* viscerally *politikon* up to 1968, thereafter retires from public life.

MacIntyre is sorry to admit that he does not believe in the Marxist political alternative. He tends to reconcile himself with the liberal state, even though in many respects he remains illiberal and intends to leave Marx a place in his personal pantheon. Exaggerating somewhat, we could say that MacIntyre reproaches Burke for being insufficiently reactionary. Unlike Burke's conservatism, MacIntyre's is not a liberal conservatism but one that tends toward an antiliberal conservatism. MacIntyre reaffirms that we cannot *live* on liberalism. He grants no primacy to individual autonomy, and that is the reason why he remains attached to a provocative rhetoric. If he tacitly acknowledges the political legitimacy of liberalism, he argues against its social, moral, and spiritual value. He has resigned himself to liberal politics, but he denounces liberalism's *generalization*. Even though MacIntyre strives not to say it, I believe that he considers liberalism as a political solution, but *only* as a political solution, and as a solution by default. Freedom only remains alive if it is nurtured by the traditions that liberalism tends to destroy. "For liberal individualism a community is simply an arena."[102] The arena's circular enclosure symbolizes the city's ramparts: in throwing ourselves *into* the arena, we metaphorically throw ourselves *out* of the city—to the wild beasts. Community has vanished, and exodus has become our common lot. MacIntyre shares Hannah Arendt's analysis: the paradigm of modern politics is the refugee, the member of the political "minority," and the stateless person.[103]

MacIntyre's is a curious Aristotelianism. Undoubtedly, the struggle between the oligarch and the democrat is to Aristotelian politics what the struggle between the proletariat and bourgeoisie is to Marxism. To be sure, the Aristotelian democrat is not the proletariat of the *Communist Manifesto*, nor is the Greek oligarch a bourgeois. Nevertheless the insistence on class struggle, if we can use that shortcut, is one of the principal points in common between Marx and Aristotle. MacIntyre claims to be both Aristotelian and Marxist, yet he is barely attentive to the importance of the quarrel between the democrat and oligarch. He remains almost entirely silent about Aristotle's *Politics*, upon which he seems to have hardly reflected. Everything goes as if he draws Aristotle's politics not from the *Politics* proper, as we would expect, but from the *Nicomachean Ethics*. (Conversely, we could remark that Arendt privileges Aristotle's politics to the detriment of his ethics.) MacIntyre radically depoliticizes Aristotle's philosophical corpus. He neglects Aristotle's rich analysis of the city to make Aristotle into what he is assuredly not: a proto-Burkean theorist of tradition. At the same time, MacIntyre is right to find in Aristotle an analysis of the natural character of social life. Social order is not entirely the fruit of the will, of the human capacity to construct: it is in many respects already given. MacIntyre is a conservative in the sense that Aristotle is a conservative: through the critique of artificialism; through the desire to foreground the natural order of society, natural law; and through the natural desire to live in society (to which I shall return later). The human being is not an individual who must, through a contract, artificially construct the city in which he lives. In his book dedicated to human nature, *Dependent Rational Animals* (1999), MacIntyre explores the social character of human existence.

Here I shall readily refer to Simone Weil's book *The Need for Roots*, which was published in 1949 but written during the Nazi occupation of France. Like MacIntyre, Weil distrusts the nation-state, which she associates with individualism, with the destruction of intermediary bodies, and with Richelieu's Machiavellianism.[104] Like MacIntyre, she starts from the emptiness that modern societies create. Like MacIntyre, she is not "conservative," in the sense that she analyzes the impoverishment of existence and she is convinced that there is not much left to "conserve." Her book is motivated by a concern for reconstituting postwar France. It starts from an analysis of the exodus of May 1940 and echoes the Marxist critique of Hegel.[105] The German threat is insufficient for explaining why the French had so easily thought of abandoning everything, why France had renounced its sovereignty, and why it had committed political suicide. The exodus of May 1940 gives witness to the extent of uprootedness, in particular during the interwar period. Like MacIntyre, Simone Weil is less interested in examining rights and more interested in examining duties. She concludes the first part of *The Need for Roots*, on "the needs of the soul," with *truth*, which she describes as a need "more sacred than any other need."[106] Here, rootedness is not an unreflective attachment to the land, but a way of relating personal life to something beyond the political, of relating goods and practices (at the subpolitical level) with traditions of enquiry (at the transpolitical level), and of considering freedom in the light of the true and the good. The exodus of 1940 suggested that the French were too exclusively attached to the state and that their freedom was insufficiently rooted in traditions of enquiry that transcended the city. In abandoning all political engagement from 1971 onwards, MacIntyre wanted to show that the critique of individual autonomy implied not so much an abandonment of the liberal state as an invitation to root freedom in natural law and in faith.

To frighten the bourgeoisie, who were no longer tormented by the *Communist Manifesto*, MacIntyre declares natural law "subversive," and the virtue of temperance "seditious."[107] His provocation no longer relies on revolution, but on conservatism![108] Yet MacIntyre carefully avoids this word, out of fidelity to the radicalism of his youth and for fear of being identified with the ideologues of the US Republican Party.[109] He emphasizes what he still owes to Marx to show that we should not consider him to be a conservative. But in his case I believe the word and the concept to be indispensable. To rely on natural law theory, for example, is to emphasize against the positivists that law does not just owe its authority to the power of the sovereign, but that law must be maintained by mores. In calling for a philosophy of natural law jurisprudence, MacIntyre affirms the importance of habits and of customs that maintain the law, rendering it intelligible and rational for the many. In the late 1970s and early 1980s, MacIntyre's conservatism had taken an apocalyptic turn. It seemed to him that there was nothing left to conserve and that the West was only a field of ruins. At the end of *After Virtue*, he calls for a St. Benedict, as if there was nothing more to do but retreat from the world. This conviction has never really left him, but it is remarkable that in turning to Thomas Aquinas and the theory of natural right, he was gradually led to temper his pessimism.

MacIntyre's reflections refer to two political ideologies: the British antistatist tradition and Marxism, the British sense of "community" and the Marxist critique of formal freedom. But these two ideologies, eroded by the history of the twentieth century, have lost their revolutionary potential. Their "effectual truth" is henceforth akin to a critique of the primacy of liberty as the absence of coercion. We do not "immediately" belong to humanity: forms, institutions, and traditions are necessary to guide us toward wisdom and a sense of the good and the true. It is presumptuous of our own powers to believe that we can bypass these mediations. We must come to consider the dream of a technological state, perfectly transparent in itself, universal and homogenous, for what it is—a very bad dream.

MacIntyre draws a lesson from the unhappy communist epoch. The insufficiencies of individual autonomy should not ultimately lead to repudiating liberalism, but to anchoring positive liberty in something beyond the political, in traditions of enquiry that transcend the city and that inform and enrich existence. He responds to the totalitarian absolutization of the political by an effort to relativize the political. He thus, paradoxically, falls within a certain liberal tradition, but a tradition neglected by most contemporary theorists of liberalism. Individual autonomy has a political meaning, but it must be subordinated to truth, which reflects what is below and above the city. Without truth reflecting what is below and above the city, freedom is doomed to become poorer and poorer until it is completely bankrupt. It is this impoverishment that the postmodern school describes, without having a very clear awareness of it. MacIntyre probably remains too dependent on the Marxist critique of politics and the nation-state and takes too much at face value the individualist propaganda of a certain liberalism. But this defect makes his analysis all the more interesting. He truly takes modern ideals seriously and deepens them with rigor and sincerity. He falls into the trap of ideology, but that is what confers on his reflections all their acuity. His political thought is unilateral, and, truth be told, it is in many respects rather poor: he remains silent on war, rule of law, separation of powers, and civil liberties. This silence renders his thought singularly unbalanced, but this imbalance is in its own manner full of lessons. MacIntyre: a reactionary for our times!

MacIntyre opposes the "Enlightenment project."[110] Commentators have criticized this expression, denying the existence of a (unified) *modern* project. But they have perhaps missed the essential point: the existence of a modern *project*. The concept of a project refers to a theoretical hypothesis, a state of nature, and essentially abstract thought.[111] Following Wittgenstein, from whom he drew much inspiration, MacIntyre could oppose the conventional, the artificial, and the planned with what is natural, organic, and traditional.[112] A supporter of "rootedness," he sometimes seems to be mistaken as a disciple of Burke.[113] But he has deliberately distanced himself from Burke, and he is right to do so, up to a point. Unlike Burke, he is assuredly not a Whig. Moreover, and above all, MacIntyre's critique of abstract individualism and subjective right do not imply that he opposes "Reason" with "Tradition." Quite to the contrary, he unites them in "traditions of enquiry," traditions that are all the more compatible with a theory of natural justice because they are difficult to separate from it. The Burkean denunciation of political idealism rests in the last analysis on a type of empiricism that MacIntyre strives to escape, as we shall see later on. That is the reason why I prefer to speak here of "rootedness" rather than conservatism. It is also the reason why MacIntyre criticizes Burke.[114] For the most extreme conservatives, reason plays almost no role: practical reason is immersed in customs from which we can hardly ever separate it. For rationalist conservatives like MacIntyre, some customs perfectly articulate the demands of practical reason, but others prove to be dangerous and problematic. Reason enables us to improve and rethink customs and enables us to distinguish good customs from bad customs.

If we believe the progressives, attachment to custom or to established practices encourages unreflective lives, lives in which the most important questions are absent. Disorder and injustice are protected by the authority of the past. For conservatives, by contrast, practical reasoning requires a rich ensemble of traditions and practice. Moral and political reasoning presuppose shared customs. Philosophically, we can summarize the heart of MacIntyre's argument in the following way: individual reasoning is participation in collective reasoning, upon which it depends. Individual judgment is through collective agreement, through the institution of moral and political authorities that need to be justified. Reasoning presupposes a publicly recognized order. Practical rationality presupposes therefore a custom, a tradition, and a consensus. It is this conviction that simultaneously underlies MacIntyre's cultural pessimism (that there is no longer any consensus), his conservatism, and his rationalism.

MacIntyre does not model his thinking about "community" on the family. He does not write from nostalgia for tribal warmth. A great reader of Aristotle and Hegel, he exalts neither the land nor ethnocentrism. He does not suggest that we rediscover a socio-politics in utero or that we "reenchant" the world. By "community," he means less a specific "identity," fraternity, love, ecstasy, or orgiastic fusion, and more a shared intellectual tradition. MacIntyre likens Jane Austen to Aristotle. He finds in the author of *Pride and Prejudice* remarkable illustrations of what the *Nicomachean Ethics* describes as practical wisdom or prudence.[115] It is true that Jane Austen has a marvelous depiction of the relationship between moral life and social milieu—how much practical reasoning presupposes rooted-ness. But, in choosing the example of Jane Austen, MacIntyre shows that he is well aware of the sometimes unpleasant character of "community." For the milieus that the novelist describes are as charming as they are often hateful, as endearing as they are often cruel. The community that Mac-Intyre longs for is not necessarily an affair of the heart! He is guided less by a distrust of intelligence and more by a concern to save reason from the perils into which moral relativism and individualism plunge it.

MacIntyre learned from the first New Left that our liberties are con-siderably impoverished, since the primacy of economic rationality has led to the neglect of the question of the social bond. Yet this impoverishment calls for a reaction that becomes ever more necessary or inevitable: the re-discovery of other fields where life can become less abstract and liberty can become richer through the traditions that inform it. The history of ethics that MacIntyre writes establishes the parasitic character of liberalism. Lib-eralism only subsists thanks to the traditions that it destroys. The crisis of modern rationalism, manifest through Nietzsche and the postmodern school, bears witness to this collapse. By way of concerning ourselves with individual autonomy alone, we have come to isolate the individual from the moral resources that enable him to achieve freedom in the good. With the most important questions pushed back beyond social and individual conscience, existence has become sterile and desolate. The progress of se-curity must make us laugh and cry at the same time.

Deprived of its conflicting relationship with the objectivity of the human world, freedom is reduced to self-affirmation, to self-complacency. The deepening of certain traits of liberalism turns against true liberalism: that of a "liberal" education or of the "liberal" arts, which reflect what is above the city. Liberalism should not be confused with egalitarianism, and it does not exclude the consideration of virtue, which is to say a certain form of excellence. MacIntyre does not so much criticize the liberal regime as such, as he criticizes certain tendencies of liberalism: the tendency to-ward atomism, the tendency to associate liberty with license, and the ten-dency toward subjectivism, relativism, and skepticism. In response to dis-agreement over the essential (the meaning of life), this liberalism has been so good at bracketing off the essential that the essential ends up being for-gotten. It is a question, therefore, of redirecting liberalism to its noblest and highest sources, of reaffirming that liberty has no meaning except as the liberty to seek the truth and that politics refers to that which is beyond it. The laws of a liberal regime are not morally neutral; on the contrary. They refer to a morality that must be cultivated.

MacIntyre does not so much propose to overthrow the liberal regime as he strives to propose a reinterpretation of it. His conservatism is undoubtedly more compatible with the spirit of liberal democracy than he himself is disposed to admit. We find again here a point that I emphasized in the introduction: the critiques of liberalism studied here come *after* the failure of the great antiliberal waves: socialism, fascism, Nazism, and Marxist-Leninism. They do not cast down on liberal democracy as a political form or political regime. Liberalism imposes itself politically at the moment when its philosophical foundations are exhausted. A defense of liberalism is therefore necessary, which starts from a different philosophical approach. The question of minority rights is not principally the question of communitarianism or of collective identity, as is generally believed. It refers in part to the theologico-political problem, as I shall show in the third chapter of this work. It also refers in part to the status of rationality: how a minority can be "right" against the majority, how a small number that sees itself as just can triumph over the will of a larger number. MacIntyre questions minorities not by a taste for the local flavor, but by a concern to explore the nature of practical rationality.

We can distinguish two senses of liberty. The "negative" sense is linked to the question "What is the area within which the subject—a person or group of persons—is or should be left to do or be what he is able to do or be, without interference by other persons?" The "positive" sense is linked to the question "What, or who, is the source of control or interference that can determine someone to do, or be, this rather than that?"[116] On the philosophical level, the New Left's reflections bear on positive liberty, on the question of the status of the agent and on practical rationality.[117] Perhaps true freedom is achieved not so much through the absence of exterior obstacles as through the absence of interior obstacles. True freedom could presuppose a "positive" moment, a conception of the good and the true that enables us to remove these obstacles. The New Left has two origins: the critique of Stalinism and the critique of the Old Left. This twofold origin encloses MacIntyre in a dilemma. As an opponent of the

Soviet Union, he wants to be able to call upon conscience; as an opponent of the Old Left, he intends to rely upon community. One powerful voice guards against liberal individualism, and the critique of economicism leads him to turn toward a theory of positive liberty. Another voice, no less powerful, warns against Soviet cynicism; the critique of Stalinism leads him to ponder nature and the foundations of practical reasoning. His philosophical work is a response to a double tension: between the individual and the community, between rationalism and holism.

As a young man, MacIntyre was so attracted to the extremisms of his time that he occupied himself by combining them with each other. During the 1970s, he crossed into a period of profound uncertainty that led him to rediscover a sense of human finitude. His latest works give witness to an almost systematic effort to recover the constraints that wisdom imposes, or should impose, on action. MacIntyre comes to counter the crazed Reason of Marxism and of History with limits that we cannot cross and calculations that we cannot envisage: natural law and divine law, both understood by reference to the communities in which they are interpreted. MacIntyre ends by rallying to liberal democracy, but without ceding to certain forms of moral individualism that, he shows, turn against the individual.

Individualism and liberal agnosticism have impoverished our existence. For they have led us to neglect the desires that properly constitute human nature and give practical reasoning its content: the desire for excellence and for wisdom. Out of the concern to avoid discord, most contemporary theorists of liberalism bracket off virtue. But this comes at the price of mutilating moral, philosophical, and spiritual life, about which they take an insufficient measure. They reduce liberty to negative liberty, without realizing that practical reasoning is nourished on the good that it discovers in a social context.

TWO
Philosophy

Collective Reasoning

I. The Moral Critique of Stalinism

In this chapter dedicated to MacIntyre's philosophical journey, I propose to show that in MacIntyre's eyes, individual practical reasoning participates in collective practical reasoning or in a tradition of enquiry, for morality cannot be separated from politics.[1] Morality is not simply "subjective." The question of the relationship between morality and politics and the critique of individualism in morality has occupied MacIntyre from the 1950s— notably when as a young Marxist, he wanted to articulate a *moral* critique of Stalinism.

Marxism has been refuted by a tribunal it would find difficult to dismiss: History itself. Granted that it is no longer necessary to criticize Stalin, it is nonetheless important to remember the prestige he enjoyed immediately after the war. In 1945 the Soviet Union could bask in the glowing achievements of its armies and its ideas. With Marxist theory to propel it forward, it remained, or thought it remained, in the vanguard of the history it was bringing to a consummation. As the homeland of all workers, it incarnated or claimed to incarnate the future of a finally reconciled humanity. Several turns of events rapidly darkened this horizon. The Prague coup, along with several others, reminded all those who had not done everything in their power to forget them of the atrocities of the interwar period. In 1956, Khrushchev's denunciation of Stalin, followed by the bringing-to-heel of Hungary, deprived the Soviet Union of its remaining eschatological privileges. The misdeeds of Communism were being denounced on every side.

The political reasons for this denunciation were all too clear, but its philosophical bases were still uncertain. In his *Autocritique* (*Self-Criticism*), published in 1959, a former member of the British Communist Party summarized the nature of the contradiction in which Marxists who wanted to criticize Stalinism seemed to have become entangled:

> We knew how history plays fast and loose. We knew that history, as Marx said, progresses on its bad side. We knew that the road to hell is paved with good intentions and that, on the other hand, hellish methods can bring about progress. The cunning of reason! . . . We were naturally led to discredit any autonomous morality. Such a morality could only be sentimentality, subjectivism, a fear of the real. . . . "Abstract," "idealist" morality could condemn lies, bad faith, the police, murder. But real morality demanded that everything be subordinated to the enterprise that abolished man's exploitation by man. So morality was absolutely identified with politics. . . . Morality was thus the same as efficiency.[2]

Can efficiency justify the violations of socialist legality, the systematic lying, the terror inspired by blind repression, the breaking up of families at the behest of the police, a regime of state terror, mass executions— in short, the suppression of the elementary safeguards of justice? The Khrushchev report mentioned torture and minority genocide. The Communists had their pat answer: nothing is achieved in practice by bleeding hearts, and the protesting voice of one's conscience should be rejected as another useless scruple. But many Communists had rallied to the Soviet camp out of indignation against the complacency of the West, and reasons of conscience had not initially been foreign to them—quite the opposite.

Many of them consequently felt there was a contradiction between the motives for, and the reality of, their commitment. "The arrangement whereby the Communist intellectual sometimes stifles the voice of his conscience only works if we forget that this intellectual is a Communist precisely so as to obey the most imperious commandment of his conscience."[3] Can one flout morality in the very name of morality? Or commit injustice in the name of justice? Certain Marxists were profoundly convinced of the necessarily moral character of every action carried out by the Party and could not accept that there might be, within Communism itself, a conflict between ethics and politics. Others criticized morality for its formal, timeless, abstract postulates and prided themselves on not resorting to such postulates.

A few months after his denunciation of Stalin's crimes, Khrushchev ordered his tanks into Hungary. Morally discredited, the USSR wanted to send a clear message that it was still politically necessary. Even among the Communists most intent on turning a blind eye, there was increasing unease. Here, too, the ex-Communist mentioned earlier summarizes the situation well:

> My revolt remained too subjective in my view, and Stalinism remained too objective. I was too afraid I was merely setting my individual drama against History. I would never have dared think that this drama was the drama of history itself. . . . Morally, I rejected the system, but ideologically I rejected my morality. This contradiction fed into my anguish. Any effort to unburden myself of this anguish only intensified it, since it drove even wider apart my ideas and my demands, my theory and my life. I refused to be a "beautiful soul," but I couldn't resign myself to being an ugly soul. I was afraid that a moral rejection of Communism would lead me either into an ivory tower, or into "anti-Communism." My moral revolt struck me as individualistic, ineffectual, even though I'd already ceased to admire the system as necessary and rational.[4]

On the one hand, the Marxist is unable to reconcile economic determinism with human freedom. On the other, he has to learn to mistrust his own conscience and the residues of "bourgeois" mentality whose traces he might still carry around. Even if an action is criminal in nature, it can hasten the emancipation of the human race. Is not politics essentially a matter of violence, and is not violence endemic? Does not the "humanism of the future" demand "terror in the present"?

Is not the liberation of the human race worth getting one's hands dirty for, even if it means killing innocent people? In *The Rebel* (1951), Camus raised the problem of the ideological justification of violence and argued against the idea that the end justifies the means. Sartre wrote a reply to Camus, whose "moralism" he criticized, in *Les temps modernes* and came to the defense of Stalinism. He accused Camus of staying faithful to an "outmoded humanism," of wishing to keep his conscience clear, of living with only one foot in the real world, of affirming an empty ideal. Sartre denounced Camus as "the High Priest of Absolute Morality."[5]

> This Justice, that of some Stoic *grand seigneur*, this anachronistic conception of an Absolute Justice, is one so absolutely absolute that it would be a sin against it to try and bring it into play in the realm of the relative where, despite everything, men have to live and move. This noble demand, which allows real injustices to persist for fear of making them worse, and out of protest against some imaginary Injustice, should surely be characterized, rather, as a mania for absolute purity. The Just Man is the Pure Man: the one who has taken a vow of purity. He is *ipso facto* a naïve man, or an imposter.[6]

In urging Camus to bow to tactical and strategic necessities and to accept the ambiguities of all action, Sartre had an easy time of it in the postwar context influenced by Marxism. It is impossible wholeheartedly to reject politics for morality or morality for politics. Camus denied that he was moralizing and tried to defend himself by pointing out the dangers of a divinization of history and the cult of the fait accompli, with all the abdication of responsibility it implies.[7] Violence unleashed in the name of Progress can have no special status unless there is indeed a "meaning of history." But is one justified in considering the USSR as the instrument by which the Absolute is being realized?

The critique of Stalinism raised the issue of the nature of moral reasoning. The massacre of the Kulaks, the Moscow trials, the massive deportations, the Gulag, and the split between Eastern and Western Europe could all be defended in the name of the higher interests of humanity. From a Machiavellian or utilitarian point of view (utilitarianism being taken here in broadest and loosest sense of the term), the interests of the majority justify ignoring or immolating the minority. The moral critique of Stalinism focuses on Machiavellian utilitarianism, on the sacrifice of minorities for the ultimate well-being of the "majority": it asks, Does the importance of the human community justify one in sacrificing scapegoats on its behalf?

In the nineteenth century, the language of "interests" seemed more favorable to human freedom than did the language of rights. The comparative histories of the French and American revolutions could bear witness to this. The French Revolution let the concept of individual right slide to the point of favoring the Terror; the American Revolution often held to a respectable utilitarianism. While the language of interests managed to cast a veil over the abysses opened up by modern freedom, the language of rights encouraged the rashest explorations and the wildest and most overblown political promises. But, from the second half of the twentieth century onward, the situation has been reversed. On the theoretical level, what was needed to discredit totalitarianism was less capitalism than human rights. The Nazi and Communist tyrannies again raised the question of the viability of a utilitarian defense of liberalism.

If a calculus of the interests of the greatest number justifies torture, the genocide of minorities, and a regime of state terror, can one still rely, in the sphere of morality and politics, on instrumental rationality? The Soviet atrocities suddenly raised doubts in the minds of the British and Americans and seemed to strike a fatal blow at their habitual way of looking at things. Was not utilitarianism akin at least as much to Stalinist Machiavellianism (which they hoped to contain or discredit) as to capitalism (which they approved of)? The supporters of an individualist interpretation of utilitarianism came to realize that utilitarianism was not, perhaps, sufficient to condemn a tyranny that invoked a collectivist interpretation of utilitarianism. In the introduction to the first volume of *Philosophy, Politics and Society* (1956), Peter Laslett affirmed that political philosophy seemed to be dead. In 1962, in the second volume, Isaiah Berlin likewise wondered whether political philosophy still existed.[8] To put it mildly, these were strange questions. To be sure, political *science* seemed to be taking over, in the universities, from political *philosophy*, yet Hannah Arendt, Raymond Aron, F. A. Hayek, Michael Oakeshott, and Leo Strauss were just coming into their intellectual maturity. But these questions are significant all the same: the horror inspired by Stalinist utilitarianism caused consternation in an Anglo-American world that was itself traditionally utilitarian.

Classical utilitarian liberalism had rested on two main theses. On the one hand, human beings are equal under the law. On the other, this equality hinges on property, man being an economic animal, or *homo economicus*. Marx had shown that, if one stuck to the liberal interpretation, these two theses were at least partly incompatible. If man really is defined by his economic dimension, then we have to insist that the "formal" rights to which liberals appeal are not sufficient. Real rights are economic. Real equality includes equality of income and, in the final analysis, the communistic sharing of property. This radicalization, this Marxist way of taking things to their logical conclusion, starts out from economism or liberal utilitarianism, which it turns upside down so as to bring it more effectively to realization. But in that case, people must have wondered in the 1950s, How and why should we wage the Cold War, if it is in the name of utilitarianism that we condemn utilitarianism?

The success of John Rawls's neo-Kantian book, *A Theory of Justice* (1971), was part and parcel of these debates.[9] The neo-Kantian turn of Jürgen Habermas, who had at first been a Marxist, also falls in this context: Habermas did not turn toward liberalism until after the Soviet misadventures. Their respective Kantianisms put forward the justification of individualism made necessary by the apparent collapse of utilitarianism: Kant had developed the critique par excellence of utilitarianism by showing that action could be moral only if human beings were treated as ends and not as means. In considering the human world in light of utility or the quantity of happiness, we end by putting all human beings on the same level, without taking into account either the dignity proper to every human being or the incommensurable rights that are attached to this dignity. At its core, utilitarianism is not sufficiently individualist. Following Kant, Habermas and Rawls constructed vast intellectual edifices to argue that freedom cannot be sacrificed to equality, nor can individuals or minorities be considered as mere "means." Their philosophy offers perhaps less of a defense of social democracy, as we sometimes suggest, and more of a critique of the type of despotism made apparently defensible by utilitarianism.

Kant's philosophy constitutes a response to the major difficulty in every social contract theory. These theories postulate an essentially asocial man whom they transform into a good citizen, respectful of law and the common interest. These doctrines are vulnerable by virtue of their presuppositions, since it is difficult to show how one can move from pure particularity to a true meaning of generality, how man can find in his nature a reason to obey a law that is foreign to him, and how to deduce disinterest from the most inflexible egotism. This was the problem of which Anglo-American theorists suddenly became aware in the 1950s, before realizing that Kant had come up with a solution to this difficulty when he made law, which he associated with *respect*, the motive force par excellence of action—moral life implying an immediate relation to universality. This was an admirable solution, but its virtue came with a corresponding vice: the notion of contract relies on the social rootedness of moral life, which the Kantian sense of the universal does not allow. The categorical imperative focuses on man in his universality and does not take into account the particular political body to which the agent belongs.

Kantianism has been welcomed for its separation of facts and norms, of nature and freedom. It seems to offer an explanation of the failure of philosophies of history and revolution: attempts to unite nature and freedom, to "realize freedom," appear in retrospect condemned to the failure they suffered. More generally, the ahistoricism of analytical political philosophy, to which Rawls has given such a powerful impetus, responds to the sense that historical materialism has failed and to the disappointments that the communist hope left in its wake. The different schools (more or less obedient to Marxism), which explained that the Revolution worked a "synthesis" that would put an end to all contradictions, have been replaced by political philosophy of an analytical type, whose presupposition is, as its name suggests, the impossibility of any "synthesis." Or to put it differently, the failure of communism is the failure of political ideologies of "totality" or "totalitarian" political ideologies. This failure calls for a rediscovery of the importance of liberal separations (the state and civil society, politics and opinion, and so forth). This is to say that this failure calls for a return to the analytical spirit, another name for the spirit of separation.

Whereas the Anglo-American world was pondering the malleability of utilitarianism, which can give rise to both an antiliberal and liberal interpretation, German thinkers were pondering the malleability of the thought of Max Weber, the great German theorist of liberalism. The followers of Weber (a sincere liberal) questioned the consequences of his irrationalism and his appeals for a charismatic leader, and they brooded over that disciple of Weber who became a Nazi, Carl Schmitt. How could they rely on Weberian liberalism to castigate Nazism if the teachings of Weber on the ravages of instrumental reason and on the need for recourse to "charismatic" personalities were used to serve the cause of Hitler? The neo-Kantian philosophy of Jürgen Habermas started out from such debates, and via these Germanic detours it moved close to that of Rawls.

The solutions of Rawls and Habermas, which echoed that of Camus, did not please everybody, and they particularly displeased the "fellow travelers" who remained sensitive to Sartre's arguments and had no intention of rallying to liberal individualism, even of a Kantian type. These old-style Marxists—Trotskyists and mavericks of every kind—appropriated for themselves Sartre's critique of Camus, which was akin to Hegel's critique of Kant—namely, the following: the categorical imperative, which places man directly on the level of the whole of humanity, does not enable the understanding of action; the concept of rational will, insofar as it is the will of an individual, is ultimately empty; a universal morality is not sufficient to motivate an agent, as he fails to recognize in it his own particular self.[10] In the British context, the quarrel between negative liberty and positive liberty can be traced back not only to Isaiah Berlin, who knew German idealism very well, but even more so to the Neo-Hegelian "idealists" in the late nineteenth century.[11] Like Hegel, supporters of the primacy of positive liberty propose to reconcile critical consciousness with communal life and to surmount the conflict between subjectivity and law through an objective or concrete morality (*Sittlichkeit*). This unites the universal and the particular in such a way that the individual is satisfied in recognizing the universal as law and in taking the community as an end. For Hegel, as for the communitarians, the work of mores should teach human beings to realize themselves by giving themselves to the whole. MacIntyre chose to start his philosophical work with a critique of theories of action that put practical life in a direct relationship with humanity, without the mediation of a particular city. We could note incidentally MacIntyre's unceasing interest with Hegelian philosophy of action.[12] He counters abstract universalism with a concrete universalism. "Loyalty to that community, to the hierarchy of particular kinship, particular local community and particular natural community," MacIntyre writes, "is on this view a prerequisite for morality."[13] Rawls's solution leads back to the uncertainties of the ex-Communist whose *Autocritique* I mentioned earlier: How can one understand politics by starting from the "individual"? Hegel's critique of Kant found too attentive a hearing among Communist Party sympathizers for Rawls's or Habermas's neo-Kantianism to rouse any of their enthusiasm. But the fact remained that after 1956, the realization of Absolute Spirit could no longer be taken for granted, either in its Hegelian or its Marxist form. Already for some time, modern political rationalism had been in a state of crisis. The heirs of the most advanced version of the Enlightenment could no longer take refuge in Moscow—not even in thought.

Lenin distanced himself both from the economic determinism of *Das Kapital* and the democratic spirit of Marxism itself. His political voluntarism had justified the confiscation of power by a minority of professional revolutionaries, who in theory had a clear understanding of the "meaning of history." The more the leaders of the USSR insisted on political voluntarism, the more they found themselves forced to insist on a dictatorship of the proletariat, as revolution was not the result of a spontaneous realization, among the working class, of the state of economic forces and relations. In 1939, Trotsky no longer had any illusions about the Soviet Union. To save Marxism from Stalin's tyranny, he fell back on the language of economic determinism, which he implicitly contrasted with that of political voluntarism. But in availing himself of this language, he took the risk of invalidating the Marxist philosophy of history. While the 1929 crash seemed a final confirmation of Marx's somber prophecies, giving support as it did to the thesis of the inevitable crisis of capitalism, the progress made by the consumer society during the thirty years of the so-called Golden Age (1945–75) could be explained by Marxism only with the greatest difficulty.

Marx's predictions could not be postponed forever. If the phenomenon of Stalinism were merely a passing anomaly, a marginal phenomenon, it was necessary to remain in solidarity with the USSR, the first workers' state. But if this phenomenon constituted a new form of exploitation, then Marxism had to be revised and perhaps abandoned. In a 1939 essay, "The USSR at War," written shortly before his death, Trotsky raised the possibility of a new form of oppression. He asked himself whether the Soviet Union was not the first state to represent a completely new type of organization, neither capitalist nor socialist, and whether there might not emerge, alongside bureaucracy, a new exploitative class that would owe its position less to the economy than to politics—which would in turn throw doubt on Marxist determinism.

> Either the Stalin regime is an abhorrent relapse in the process of transforming bourgeois society into a socialist society, or the Stalin regime is the first stage of a new exploiting society. If the second prognosis proves to be correct, then, of course, the bureaucracy will become a new exploiting class. . . . If the world proletariat should actually prove incapable of fulfilling the mission placed upon it by the course of development, nothing else would remain except to recognize that the socialist programme, based on the internal contradictions of capitalist society, ended as utopia.[14]

The group Socialisme ou Barbarie, which sprang from a split within the French section of the Fourth International, owed a great deal to the disillusioned Trotsky of the end of the 1930s. Claude Lefort and Cornelius Castoriadis, the main figures in the group, took from him a number of their reflections on the nature of the Soviet Union and on bureaucratic society as a radically new social formation.[15] They maintained that the revolution had either to be abandoned or to be rethought. Via the mediation of Socialisme ou Barbarie, postmodernism owed much to the Trotsky of the period before World War II. Jean-François Lyotard, the author of *The Postmodern Condition*, the first manifesto of the genre, was for a long time closely associated with their group.[16] In his preface to a reprint of the articles he had written for Socialisme ou Barbarie, Lyotard observed that "already [in 1960], there was a dawning suspicion, shared by a significant number in the group, that politics was, or was on the point of, ceasing to be the main arena in which intractable reality showed its presence. We spoke of a 'depoliticisation'. . . . This was more or less what I tried to designate, clumsily, by the term 'postmodern.'"[17] Once Marx's predictions on the decreasing rate of profit, the pauperization of the proletariat, and the inevitable worldwide crisis of capitalism turned out to be false, Marxists were tempted to sacrifice the mechanistic and positivist dimension of Marxism to its "ideological" dimension. Wishing to affirm their own political voluntarism as against the determinism of *Das Kapital*, the new-style Marxists, reputedly "postmodern," foregrounded the "cultural" elements that Marx had deliberately left in the background. But by underlining the importance of this "ideological" dimension that Marx had resolutely subordinated to the economic infrastructure, they gradually lost Marx's materialist sheet-anchor and preferred the "will to power" to class struggle. The correct response to Stalinist utilitarianism was not the neo-Kantianism of Rawls but a critique of Enlightenment Reason. Marxism, based on the glorification of rationalism, was abolished in favor of political irrationalism. No longer Science, but Life! No longer Reason, but Will! No longer "Marx," but "Nietzsche"!

The USSR for a long time concealed a voracious and tyrannical imperialism behind a theoretical universalism: universality (reason) and particularity swapped their attributes, and Reason was toppled from its pedestal. "How can a transnational entity, the international organization of workers, have a historical-political reality when it ignores national proper names?" wondered Lyotard, before discussing "the difficulties then and thereafter encountered by the workers' movement and its ultimate failure through its collapse back into national communities (at least since the socialist vote in favor of war budgets in 1914)."[18] Tracing the story back from socialism to the French Revolution, Lyotard denounced "the authority which the representatives of the French nation arrogate to themselves by speaking in the place of man." There is a "differend" or incommensurability at work in the politics that emerges from the Enlightenment—an incommensurability that shakes it to its very foundations. Meditating on the Soviet experience, Lyotard eventually came to affirm the existence of irreducible forms of incommensurability. Abandoning the Enlightenment's universalism, he came to abandon rationalism itself. How can one behave rationally? For a long time, socialism and communism seemed to provide an answer, by taking the fullest advantage of the premises of the Enlightenment. But after 1956? Did not the despotic regime in Moscow condemn the political ideologies that drew their resources from the eighteenth century? The so-called postmodernist school, born in reaction to Stalinism in the 1960s and 1970s, replied to this question with an apparent clarity. "We have to abandon the Enlightenment, and thus reason, which is fundamentally authoritarian," it exclaimed in enthusiasm and despair. Marx had described the human world as essentially contradictory, but he announced an end of history that would abolish these contradictions. A century later, having ceased to believe in the possibility of a revolution, his disciples preserve only the first component of Marxist theory: the world is contradictory, their own philosophy is contradictory, and it is because of this that it is true.

"Postmodernism" constitutes in certain respects an extension of the logic of individual rights—in other words, of "modern" politics itself: in this regard, it is "on the left." And yet, the indeterminate darkness of postmodernism can take two contradictory political forms: the one is liberal and even libertarian (authority is bad in itself), the other quite authoritarian (if man is bad, why grant him the freedom to be even worse?). Is Nazism political Nietzscheanism? The postmoderns strenuously deny this. If the Enlightenment has been sullied by its communist heritage, postmodernism must not be sullied in advance by disgraceful political consequences. So the postmodern school of thought carefully distinguishes between Nazism and the Nietzschean critiques of socialism, democracy, liberalism, and civilization.

For fear of falling into "ideology," Marx had put dialectical and historical materialism before a concern for justice. By rediscovering the "ideological" element, twentieth-century Marxists and, later, the theorists of postmodernism could have returned justice back to center stage. On the whole, they did not. For they considered that their critique of the rationalism of the Enlightenment swept away with it every theory of rational or natural justice. A theorist of economic determinism, Marx hardly gave any place to initiative or to the will. To the extent that his predictions were invalidated, his disciples were led to revalorize elements of the will, of consciousness, and of ideology. But the more they deepened these elements, the more the economic dimension itself appeared as ideological. By a curious chance, then, they came to align themselves with Nietzsche. Nietzsche, however, had not hidden that egalitarianism and a concern for social justice inspired his contempt. At the moment, after 1956, when these new-style Marxists lost their hope in the revolution, nothing was left for them except an essentially relativist theory that served to denounce the human world as a "construct," without offering an alternative: the enthusiasm for critique, but the despair of changing nothing.

A third philosophical trend, neither neo-Kantian nor postmodern but neo-Aristotelian or even neo-Thomist, also attempts to come to terms with the problem of the moral critique of Stalinism. Like most of the postmodernists, Alasdair MacIntyre considers that it is no longer possible to be a Marxist. Himself an ex-Trotskyist, he takes his inspiration from the Trotsky of 1939, rather like the theorists of Socialisme ou Barbarie. "A Marxist who took Trotsky's last writings with great seriousness would be forced into a pessimism quite alien to the Marxist tradition, and in becoming a pessimist he would in an important way have ceased to be a Marxist. For he would now see no tolerable alternative set of political and economic structures which could be brought into place to replace the structures of advanced capitalism. This conclusion agrees of course with my own."[19]

Following Trotsky, MacIntyre turns historicism against Marxism. How can one still be a Marxist after the failure of most of the predictions made by the ultradeterminist Marx? This difficulty, raised in the late nineteenth century by Eduard Bernstein, has become insurmountable, even for the very people who have done everything, or forced themselves to believe everything, in their effort to remain Marxists, revolutionaries, and worshipers of history. In Nietzsche, the most resolute and perhaps the most profound critic of the emancipatory project of the Enlightenment, the author of *After Virtue* finds the diagnosis that enables him to account for the Communist catastrophe: MacIntyre belongs to the same generation as Gilles Deleuze, Michel Foucault, or Jacques Derrida. But their analyses and conclusions are different. *After Virtue* consists of eighteen chapters. The first nine chapters end with a question, "Nietzsche or Aristotle?," to which chapter 18 replies: "Nietzsche *or* Aristotle, Trotsky *and* St Benedict." MacIntyre champions Aristotle to avoid being a postmodernist.

"Essentially, the situation today is as it was at the end of the nineteen fifties," writes Castoriadis in the 1990s. "It is true that, during the nineteen-sixties, different movements (of young people, women, and minorities) in France, the United States, Germany, Italy and elsewhere seemed to go against this analysis. But from the mid-seventies onwards, it started to become evident that all this represented one last great upsurge of the movements that had begun with the Enlightenment."[20] We can here illustrate this remark of Castoriadis by showing that contemporary political philosophy proceeds in a large measure from this "dirty hands" problem, which was raised in the 1950s with a very particular acuity and presented three different ways to articulate morality and politics: neo-Kantianism (modern rationalism), neo-Nietzscheanism (postmodern irrationalism), and neo-Aristotelianism (premodern rationalism).

In an essay that originally appeared in the winter of 1958–59, MacIntyre criticized the Polish revisionist Leszek Kolakowski, often considered one of the heroes of 1956. Deploying, probably without being aware of it, some of the arguments that Sartre had already leveled against Camus in *Les temps modernes*, MacIntyre argued:

> The reassertion of moral standards by the individual voice has been one of the ferments of Eastern European revisionism. But, because of the way in which it is done, this reassertion too often leaves the gulf between morality and history, between value and fact as wide as ever. Kolakowski and others like him stress the amorality of the historical process on the one hand and the moral responsibility of the individual in history on the other. And this leaves us with the moral critic as a spectator, the categorical imperatives which he proclaims having no genuine relationship to his view of history. One cannot revive the moral content within Marxism by simply taking a Stalinist view of historical development and adding liberal morality to it.[21]

MacIntyre counters abstract individualism with the image of a human being fully "set" within his environment. He thus opposed Kolakowski, to begin with, but also, twenty years later—in a context that was not greatly different—he opposed Rawls.[22] The moral critique of Stalinism, in the manner of Kolakowski, had left an impotent individual wrestling with a tyrannical state. The direction taken by MacIntyre's later works was already here in a nutshell, for at this point he took stock of the impossibility of a morality based on an abstract universal. He argues that the individual cannot place himself directly on the level of humanity as a whole without the mediation of some form of particularity—party, city, or church. At the same time (and here lies the rub), one has to ensure that one has the means of criticizing the community if it happens to go astray—hence the problem of the moral critique of Stalinism. It may have been necessary for Sartre to criticize Camus's pamphlet; but Camus assuredly had good reasons not to yield to Soviet propaganda. It is not enough unilaterally to affirm the importance of community. It still has to be shown to what extent man cannot be reduced to his forms of belonging. MacIntyre belongs to the school that, from the 1950s onwards, has reflected on the modern forms of tyranny and, foreseeing the individualist reaction to which the phenomenon has given rise, has judged that reaction to be inadequate. He warns both against totalitarianism and against the indefinite multiplying of the rights of the individual.

It is useful to compare the reactions of MacIntyre and Jürgen Habermas to the events of 1956. They belong to the same generation, being born in the same year (1929). Both strove to remain Marxists in spite of Stalinism, and indeed managed to do so until the middle of the 1960s. But the student revolts, far from filling them with enthusiasm, made them fear the worst. Habermas came to a somber conclusion: Marxism did not enable him to say whether the students were on the extreme left or the extreme right. Marxism, which until recently had been the politician's infallible guide, no longer allowed one to distinguish between saints and sinners. Habermas denounced "left fascism." Around 1970–71, the ideas of MacIntyre and Habermas changed course perceptibly so as to avoid the postmodernism that they sensed was in the offing. At the very moment when people started to suggest that we were entering postindustrial society, a "society of knowledge," they both offered an analysis in terms of *logos koinos*, of a common language, in place of one in terms of "interest."[23] Having entered their forties, they gave a new impulse to their intellectual life. But Habermas moved toward neo-Kantianism, whereas MacIntyre became a neo-Aristotelian.

By developing the thinking of the Trotsky of 1939, MacIntyre became in his own way a "postmodernist," but he finally called for a more radical reaction: a return to the philosophy of Aristotle. According to MacIntyre, the collapse of the Enlightenment project, largely a polemic against

Aristotle, pointed to a return to classical rationalism. In *Three Rival Versions of Moral Inquiry* (1990), MacIntyre maintained that today, we have the choice between three possibilities: postmodern Nietzscheanism, a return to the Enlightenment, and Thomist neo-Aristotelianism. This book could be described as an analysis of the post-1956 situation, since the failure of the Soviet Union left open three possibilities. The failure of the second wave of modernity (the wave of Rousseauism and Marxism) leads one to call for either the first wave (Locke and Montesquieu) or the third wave (Nietzsche). MacIntyre turns to the ancients to escape from the most commonly contrasted alternative today: between a rationality of the neo-Kantian kind and the subjective irrationality of the postmodern kind. MacIntyre no longer "believes" in Absolute Spirit. Following the crisis produced by the denunciation of Stalinism, the great hope of a reconciliation of humanity with itself, as embodied in the progressive wing of the Enlightenment, had ended up losing any real substance.

After 1971, MacIntyre implicitly rallied to liberal democracy, but without enshrining the primacy of the individual. Such a primacy, in effect, would suppose that it is possible to conceive (individual) morality independently of politics and would suppose that we can separate the right from the good, while MacIntyre's efforts consist in showing at once the necessity and the possibility of a *moral* critique of *political* Stalinism, a critique that precisely joins together the right and the good. If morality is in the last analysis an individual affair, is it truly possible to propose a *moral* critique of Stalinism, a critique that rationally joins morality to its political dimension, and politics to its moral dimension?

Habermas and Rawls appeal to a separation of the right and the good (or a priority of the right over the good) to clarify the moral neutrality of the liberal state: on the one hand, the good man; on the other, the just citizen. They do so without any classification of regimes relating the right and the good to each other, in the way of Aristotle. Rawls and Habermas do not deny that individual freedom has to be related to a truth or a metaphysics. But for them this truth and this metaphysics can and ought to be separate from political life. Anxious to reach a minimal consensus, they want to prevent moral disagreement from creating political discord. But MacIntyre insists on the inevitability of disagreement. The right is inseparable from the good, and if there is a primacy, it is the primacy of the good.[24]

The history of the twentieth century is that of hyperbolic wars and of immoderate ideologies. MacIntyre answers it by an effort to rediscover the limits of action through a philosophy of natural justice. These are the limits that no society ought to cross, fundamental laws that no society ought to violate. Laws have a moral component. MacIntyre's intellectual journey, which has led him from Marx to Thomism, is intelligible only in the light of an ever-deeper concern to question the Machiavellianism from which Marxist doctrine provided no escape. It is intelligible only in light of his desire to join together the right and the good, justice and morality.[25] This desire presided over the moral critique of Stalinism; it presides over the naturalism to which MacIntyre ends up aligning.

I return to the question that I raised in the introduction and that constitutes the guiding principle of these pages. The Machiavellian and Hobbesian schools separate the right from the good: they start from evil and from the fear that the primacy of the good plays into the hands of tyranny. The Aristotelian and Thomist tradition starts from the fear that a too-exclusive concern over evil only comes to impoverish existence, depriving it of goods. MacIntyre does not ignore the danger of tyranny: he makes a point of criticizing Stalinism. But it is remarkable that he does not deduce from this some primacy of evil, as if one must start from the state of nature of a Hobbesian type. On the contrary, he deduces from it the necessity to start from a natural law oriented toward the good. Why, in his eyes, is the moral critique of despotism so important? Because it constitutes the decisive test: if it shows that we can start from the primacy of the good to triumph over tyranny, then it suggests that the fears of the Machiavellians and Hobbesians are empty.

We can distinguish two reasons to come back to the theory of natural justice. One reason is based on the belief that modern reason has a self-destructive character. The other derives from the critique of democratic individualism. MacIntyre orchestrates and links these two themes. The concern for finding a balance between absolute democracy and a sense of excellence, or between consent and wisdom, leads to a theory of natural justice that combines the rights of conscience with the rights of truth. In *Whose Justice? Which Rationality?* he compares different theories of natural right and defends premodern theories of natural right simultaneously against modern or individualist approaches and against the adversaries of natural right as such—sophists, positivists, and irrationalists. Even though Mac-Intyre prefers to express himself in terms of prudence rather than "law," the book's title could equally well be *Which Natural Law?* It offers a theory in search of that from which he started, thirty-five years before. The work relates in a systematic way moral philosophy and the theory of justice, in showing that different moral philosophies correspond to different theories of justice. But in the last analysis, it is Thomist Aristotelianism that enables us to relate ethics and politics in the most satisfactory way.

MacIntyre denounces one of the fundamental articles of the liberal creed: the existence of subjective universal rights. He opposes subjective rights just as he argues against the primacy of individual autonomy. However, if MacIntyre opposes modern natural rights jurisprudence, he is not opposed to natural right as such. He rails against an individualism that supposes one can separate morality and politics, but not against the natural law itself. Today, he is perhaps even one of its principal supporters. As natural law reconstitutes nature, it differs from legal positivism by its reference to morality, a morality that is inseparable from the community in which it is embodied. Whereas the positivists repudiate every custom and tradition in the name of the free will of the sovereign, natural law jurists emphasize that the interpretation of the natural law is achieved by established norms, by a moral accord incarnated in social and political life. Unlike the positivists, who only put forward the importance of strong and stable power, the theorists of the natural law insist on the importance of mores and of socially established practices for the right understanding of what justice requires.

The disagreement between positivists and their Aristotelian or Thomist adversaries notably bears on their attitude toward the future. The positivist argues against every tradition: Bentham, for example, does not recognize any normative value to the common law. The positivist is in a sense authentically revolutionary: he is disposed to take risks, to act in an apparently immoral way in light of new results and new consequences that he hopes are good. The natural law jurist is more pessimistic. He thinks that in violating received moral traditions, in entering into evil, in the long run we have a high chance of inviting sinister consequences; we build a lair for evil that it can take over. To the positivist (and utilitarian) who proclaims that "we do not make an omelette without breaking eggs," the natural law jurist answers with a warning: Do we truly know which omelette we are preparing? The natural law presupposes a principle of continuity, but the positivist puts forward discontinuity. MacIntyre's conservatism proceeds in this sense from the moral critique of Stalinism. Practical reason does not fully develop except in the framework of customs; or more specifically, in "practices" and "traditions of enquiry."

The young MacIntyre asked how to articulate a *moral* critique of Stalinism and how to join together morality and politics. This investigation had two components. On the one hand, MacIntyre looked to establish that politics could only be understood by reference to morality. On the other hand, and correlatively, he strove to show that morality is not an essentially "individual" affair. It is only intelligible by reference to political life and, more specifically, to socially established practices.

II. Moral Life and Socially Established Practices

The last several decades have witnessed a renewal of Aristotelianism, in Germany but also in Great Britain and the United States, brought about by growing dissatisfaction with neo-Hegelian, neo-Kantian, and positivist solutions. In Germany, the disciples of Husserl and Heidegger—Hans-Georg Gadamer in particular—have seen in the Aristotelian theory of practical reason a means of avoiding the trap of positivism, without thereby yielding to the charms of postmodern irrationalism or nihilism. In Great Britain, those who have reread Aristotle in the light of Wittgenstein have argued that the *Nichomachean Ethics* was capable of renewing a moral philosophy that had become anemic. Some philosophers related the questions raised by ancient philosophy to the problems studied by analytical philosophy. Among the figures prominent in this movement, Elizabeth Anscombe was one of the foremost.[26] Anscombe was one of Wittgenstein's closest students and the executor of his will (today, their graves are side by side in a Cambridge cemetery). She proposed an antiskeptical and antirelativist interpretation of Wittgenstein. This interpretation is hardly unanimous amongst Wittgenstein's commentators, but we nevertheless find it in MacIntyre.

MacIntyre criticizes individualism, relativism, and moral subjectivism. At the same time, he places moral life back into a particular social context, a context that presupposes a theory of justice. He succeeds in combining these two demands by developing two concepts that join together contextualism and objectivity: a "practice" and a "tradition of enquiry." Against positivism, "practices" and "traditions of enquiry" join the question of morality with that of social life, the question of the good with that of justice. This section is dedicated to "practices"; and the following section is dedicated to "traditions."

Against positivism, MacIntyre insists that we cannot understand human behavior by only referring to "causes." The positivist thesis, that we must systematically ignore the "reasons" we give for our actions, is false. We cannot give an account of action without starting from "reasons," which is to say from our deliberations. Positivism, which on principle separates (causal) science from morality (the world of our "reasons" for acting), in fact reflects a specific moral philosophy, an irrationalist moral philosophy. In separating "facts" and "morals," positivism tends to exclude values from the field of science or reason. It leaves morality with a monopoly on "values." These refer only to the subjective choices of individuals and exclude the whole conception of practical rationality around which social life can be organized.

MacIntyre reserves some of his harshest barbs for emotivism, a theory forgotten about today, even in Great Britain, where it had its moment of fame in the late 1940s.[27] Emotivists analyze ethics in terms of interjections. "This is good" means "Hurrah for this!" whereas "This is bad" means "Damn!," "Bother!"—which is also why we sometimes call it the "Boo! Hoorah! Theory." Emotivists cite the "Hear, Hear" by which British parliamentarians, at Westminster, express their approval.[28] Upon analysis, "You *should* behave like this" turns out to be an order that does not admit to being an order. "This is good" should be understood to mean, "I approve of this, do so as well." As its name indicates, the emotivist school considers that our "reasons" or our "intentions" are only disguised emotions. A belief is a feeling of approval whose object is a proposition. MacIntyre grants emotivism great importance, for the doctrine seems to show the kinship between individualism and irrationalism. In considering beliefs to be thinly veiled emotions, emotivists reduce moral judgments to desires, the cognitive to the affective. They maintain that reasons for acting disguise emotions. They deny that there are true "reasons" or "intentions" worthy of the name. Philosophically speaking, MacIntyre's work is an effort to refute the theories of the emotivist school and to show that practical rationality is only understood by reference to socially established practices. To do so, he is first and foremost inspired by Wittgenstein.

In the late 1950s and early 1960s, MacIntyre conducted research at Oxford. Wittgenstein, who died in 1951, never taught there, but his students spread his gospel. One collection, *Logic and Language*, was published at that time. The articles were collected according to a very simple criterion: they had to be among those most frequently recommended to university students. Wittgenstein's students wrote seven of the nine articles.[29] In the journal that Taylor edited, *Universities and Left Review*, MacIntyre defended Wittgenstein's line of thinking against one of its principal critiques.[30] Most of the debates in which he then took part bear Wittgenstein's mark: the critiques of methodological individualism, Cartesian dualism, the "myth of interiority," and "unencumbered" reasoning are at the heart of the theory of individual autonomy.[31] One of the first books that MacIntyre wrote was under Wittgenstein's influence: he dedicated *The Unconscious: A Conceptual Analysis* (1958) to the critique of Freudian philosophy of action.

The problem that MacIntyre tackled from the 1950s onwards, and which he never abandoned, is that of the nature of practical reasoning. How do we account for action? To what extent is human behavior intelligible and rational? What place should we confer on reasons for acting, on intentions? Following Wittgenstein, MacIntyre shows that we cannot reduce explanation in terms of reasons (those that the subject gives to justify his act) to explanation in terms of causes (what makes the subject act). Conversely, neither can we reduce explanation in terms of causes to explanation in terms of reasons.[32] We can explain an action by indicating a cause (he went to sleep because he was exhausted) or a reason (he went to sleep to recover his strength). By "cause," we must understand a natural correlation between two events, a way of envisaging action as a simple behavior observable from the exterior, without reference to lived experiences. By "reason," we must understand the intention that falls within the framework of practical reasoning, of a teleological structure—motives, meanings, and the point of the view of the agent himself.

Positivism defines science by the rupture with ordinary language, with agents and their intentions. Whether it is under the form of behaviorism, rational choice theory, and neurobiology, or even certain forms of anthropology, positivism replaces ordinary discourse with a causal theory. Conversely, positivism's adversaries tend to absorb the human sciences into ordinary discourse, privileging explanation in terms of reasons to the detriment of causal explanation. Wittgenstein's solution, which inspires MacIntyre, consists in maintaining that the two explanations are not mutually exclusive. It is not necessary to choose between the two theses. We need neither to reduce reasons to causes nor to reduce causes to reasons. Causes and reasons prove to be partners who get along and complement each other very well. Wittgenstein surpasses and dissolves a pseudoalternative.[33]

MacIntyre had started by studying Wittgenstein's philosophy of action in his little book on the theory of the Freudian unconscious. Since the notion of deliberative conduct is much narrower than that of voluntary conduct, the Freudian theory of the unconscious tries to bridge the distance between them. But by referring exclusively to "causes," it does so in too unilateral a way. The "unconscious" does not cause such and such an action and cannot be considered as an "entity" capable of being invoked to explain certain phenomena. MacIntyre explains that if "unconscious" can be an adjective, an adverb, or a noun, its use in a substantive form remains unjustified. He proposes an analysis of the concept that takes up the best of Freud and enlarges its adverbial meaning, without falling into (causal) determinism.[34] In a similar vein, Taylor suggests in his first book (*The Explanation of Behavior*, 1964) that the concept of psychological behavior is teleological. We cannot reduce explanation in terms of the goal to an explanation in terms of the antecedents, which is to say we cannot reduce it to a mechanism. The concept of intention receives its content by an ordered subordination of the means to the end.[35]

Following Wittgenstein, and particularly Elizabeth Anscombe, MacIntyre maintains that the difference between causes and reasons is "grammatical."[36] It is a distinction "of reason," not a "real" distinction. It is a necessary distinction, because every cause of an action is not a reason, and because we must separate actions that we undertake and the things that happen to us. But it is not a distinction between two specific and separated entities. Intention is not "another thing" apart from action. "Reason" is the action described in its mental aspect. Rational explanation is a form of causal explanation. Reasons can be causes. In an explanation of action, what constitutes a reason remains relatively undetermined. The relation between intention and action is a relation between two aspects of the same reality, action. Numerous philosophers have gotten into the habit of separating action from intention, of divorcing action itself from the mental state of the subject, as defined by its internal constitution. But this divorce raises more difficulties than it solves. This is at least what Anscombe shows when she writes, "We can epitomize the point by saying 'Roughly speaking, a man intends to do what he does.' "[37]

This philosophy of action is the basis for a moral philosophy, revolving around virtue, which MacIntyre analyses by reference to two concepts: (1) a "narrative concept of selfhood" and (2) the concept of a "practice."[38]

(1) To consider this narrative concept of selfhood, a brief detour through literary theory is useful, where we contrast between realist and dualist theories of narrative. The dualists bluntly separate causes and intentions. They consider that literature describes the world of reasons for acting, but it does not bear on causal reality. They are "formalists." The formal or dualist analysis of narrative closes literature in on itself and imposes a rule of immanence. It relativizes the representative dimension of literature. Its supporters, occupied with tracking down textual artifices, recall that our business is with a text and not with "reality." They emphasize the work of transformation and transposition that is effected, as well the artificial character of the resulting narrative. The world of the novel is pure artifice and presupposes no "cause" and no "fact." The alleged representation of reality is in the last analysis only a simulation by means of processes destined to create illusions (epistolary novels, supposedly collected testimonies, fictitious memories . . .). Literature confuses discourse, which has its proper laws (the short story, for example), and representation of a "referential" reality. Faithful to Wittgenstein's teaching, MacIntyre criticizes this dualist theory. He explains that we dream, hope, believe, learn, hate, and plan in narrative form. Stories are lived before they are recounted. "Narrative is not the work of poets, dramatists and novelists reflecting upon events which had no narrative order before one was imposed by the singer or the writer; narrative form is neither disguise nor decoration."[39] Tragedy, comedy or farce, and literary genres are not the affairs of conventions independent from life, if only because many aspects of existence are unintelligible except in tragic or comic terms.

Narrative gives the diversity of intentions its due, which cannot be reduced to simple causal laws.

One example will give the measure of the contrast between MacIntyre and dualist theories of narrative. Tzvetan Todorov, in a work that has as its slogan the necessity of "treating literature as literature," proposes to understand the quest for the Grail as a narrative quest.[40] Relying on phrases like "But here the tale ceases to speak of Galahad, and returns to Sir Gawain" or "But here the tale ceases to speak of Perceval, and returns to Lancelot, who had stayed at the good man's home . . . ," Todorov maintains that the quest does not refer to concrete human existence, but to literature alone, to the world of representations; or to take up again the vocabulary used above, the world of reasons. The narrator is not a person, but the tale itself, so the fundamental theme is less the alleged quest for the Grail as that of the narrative. MacIntyre, by contrast, interprets the medieval notion of the quest as expressing one of the most important aspects of human existence. The quest shows man as tending toward a good, toward an end. Far from being enclosed in literature alone, the genre of the quest claims the right to clarify "real" life.[41]

MacIntyre invites us to start from opinions and to take narratives, which is to say intentions, seriously. The formalist theory presupposes the existence of two heterogeneous planes: the plane of concrete action and the narrative plane properly speaking. Issuing from positivism, formalists explain that as a purely conventional affair, literature only refers to itself, the real being only what is empirically observed and scientifically described. Realists, by contrast, insist that literature is a cognitive power, that it is a mode of knowledge. In *After Virtue*, MacIntyre suggests that the attribution of an action only has meaning by reference to the principle of narrative intelligibility.[42] He therefore argues against the existence of these two heterogeneous planes and therefore against the pertinence of dualism. Wittgenstein had remarked that the verbs that serve to describe intentional activities do not signify an isolated state, but form a conceptual system and call for a narrative context. In a Wittgensteinian vein, Anscombe's analysis contrasts to mentalism. Her analysis (what some call "historical" or "biographical") does not hold to internal states and takes into account an agent's conduct in the context of his past activities and the milieu of his life.[43] The narrative is analyzed as the mode of rationality proper to an

agent. Man is a story-telling animal. We find again here the Wittgensteinian critique of "theories" that propose to redescribe human action on the
theories' own terms. These theories do so by means of concepts supposedly more appropriate than natural language, replacing illusory "apparent
reasons" with real "causes."

(2) As Anscombe emphasizes, "What is so commonly said, that reason and cause are everywhere sharply distinct notions, is not true."[44] "Reason" (intention) is not only a mental event confined to "interiority," for it
falls within an objective structure. In the wake of Anscombe and Aristotle,
MacIntyre insists on the difference between the theoretical syllogism
(which terminates in a theoretical conclusion) and the practical syllogism,
whose conclusion is an action. To escape from a "practical problem," it is
not enough to reason: one still must act. The plane of deliberation and the
plane of action cannot be separated. We cannot maintain that an action is
reducible to movements (that it is only "caused"), if only because the same
movement can be described in different ways, according to the context. Action is not made of up primitive actions, of isolated segments. It is a structure where the elements are inseparable. Just as in philosophy of mind, the
unity of meaning is not the word, but the proposition or the "language
game," so in the same way the unity of meaning is not the action (the primitive, isolated action), but the "form of life" or the "practice."[45] The attribution of an intention presupposes a context of institutions and customs. An
action accomplished within the framework of a practice is not intelligible
independently of that practice, since the end it serves and the norms that
it obeys are defined within the framework of the practice and are internal
to the practice. As Wittgenstein remarked, it would be impossible to say
that someone has an intention to play chess, for example, if there was not
a practice of the game of chess.[46]

MacIntyre analyzes action in light of "practices" that he defines by
reference to their internal relations. "By a practice," he writes, "I am going
to mean any coherent and complex form of socially established cooperative human activity through which goods internal to that form of activity
are realized in the course of trying to achieve those standards of excellence."[47] What is the type of relation between causes and reasons? Not an
external relation but an internal relation. An internal relation is a relation in
which the related terms cannot be defined independently of the relation.

There is an internal relation between A and B if in the absence of B, A cannot remain A. Correlatively, there is an external relation between A and B if in the absence of B, A remains A. According to MacIntyre, the good can be used in different types of categories and does not have a univocal use, clearly determined in its type. This is contrary to what the emotivists maintain, who are the theorists par excellence of the external character of the good.[48] "Good" does not always describe the same characteristic. It is important to distinguish between attributive and predicative terms. "White" is predicative. From "x is a white house," we can infer that x is white, that x is a house. "Large," by contrast, is attributive. From "x is a large house" we can infer that x is a house, but not that x is large—x is large if it is a house, small if it is a palace. The adjective "good" belongs to the class of attributive terms. "x is a good book" by no means implies "x is good."[49] We cannot understand what the adjective "good" signifies without knowing to what it is attributed. The good is internal to a practice. Action A is only intelligible by reference to a certain action or a certain context B, which is to say in the context of a practice or narrative that relates A and B. With the same steps, MacIntyre defends an internalized theory of the good and a narrative concept of selfhood.[50]

MacIntyre draws inspiration from Wittgenstein to show that action is only intelligible by reference to socially established practices. Atomist doctrines that first and foremost start from the individual, as placed outside the world or as essentially "autonomous," presuppose a dubious dualism. Moral life falls within a social context, which we cannot abstract away from.

Consider two anecdotes. One is about Anscombe. The other is about Richard Hare, whose externalist theory of good, strongly influenced by emotivism, is unceasingly attacked by the partisans of the structural theory of action. Richard Hare, who subscribes to the Oxford tradition that Anscombe denounces, was strongly marked by his internment in Japanese camps at Singapore and in Thailand. "In the artificial community of the prison, he came to realize that nothing was 'given' in society, that everyone carried his moral luggage in his head; every man was born with his conscience; and this, rather than anything in society, he found, was the source of morality."[51] This captivity constituted for him a formative experience, from which he believed that he had to deduce that "values" in the end stem from the individual and from him alone. The second anecdote, also linked to Asia and the Second World War, offers a sharp contrast. In 1956, the University of Oxford decided to award a doctorate *honoris causa* to President Truman. Resolutely opposed to the use of the atomic bomb and anxious to denounce Truman's responsibility for the bombing of Hiroshima, Anscombe wrote a pamphlet against awarding him the degree. Did Truman *himself* have to have *physically* pushed the button to have *acted*? Or is the fact of having given the orders enough to establish his responsibility? Action does not necessarily presuppose bodily movement, and most actions are of the cooperative type. It is not necessary that Caesar physically participated in the construction of a bridge so that we can say or write: *Caesar pontem fecit*. Anscombe elaborates a theory of action that enables her to integrate the agent into his social context.[52] Whereas Anscombe strongly links practical reason to social life, Hare strives to detach them. On the one hand, we have a philosopher concerned to show the link between a decision taken in Washington and an action that took place over Japan. On the other hand, we have a philosopher who wants to show that ethical bonds between men who live together day and night for many months, within a few dozen square meters, do not exist.

In their defense, Stalin and his supporters could explain that they did kill innocents but without having the *intention* to kill, their only intention being the salvation of humanity. From another point of view, they could admit to having had the *intention* to kill innocents, but insist at the same time that intention, unlike consequences and "objective" results, does not matter. Deepening the moral critique of Stalinism, then, implies pondering the place of intention in the explanation of action. For Anscombe, the critique of Truman was the equivalent of MacIntyre's reflection on Stalinism. It is, incidentally, following this pamphlet against Truman that she examined the notion of intention, to the end of clarifying her views on the responsibility of the president of the United States. She dedicated her course to it, out of which came *Intention* (1957). One could justify the use of the atomic bomb in a utilitarian manner, by emphasizing that the horror roused by the death of many innocent civilians forced the Japanese government to surrender. From this point of view, the *intention* to kill innocents should not be taken into account: only the global welfare that would result with the end of the war mattered. Anscombe's book looks to prove the opposite, by showing that action proves to be unintelligible when it is separated from the intention that underlies it.[53] Therefore the quality of the intention is of utmost importance, even if it is not sufficient to exhaust the nature of the action. Means and ends have an internal relationship.

MacIntyre connects action to a structure and proceeds in three stages. First, he offers an analysis of the good as a good internal to a practice. Second, he connects action to a narrative. Third, he defines virtue by reference to these two concepts: that of narrative unity and of an internal good. "A virtue," MacIntyre writes, "is an acquired human quality the possession and exercise of which tends to enable us to achieve those goods which are internal to practices and the lack of which effectively prevents us from achieving any such goods."[54] The goods pursued by the virtuous man cannot be characterized independently of the practice that enables him to pursue these goods. Virtue is a form of excellence that is only understood within the framework in which it is exercised. "Chess, physics, and medicine are practices": the excellence of a chess player or the excellence of a doctor (their virtues, as such) is only intelligible within the framework of a chess game or of the *practice* of medicine.[55] MacIntyre places professional achievements at the heart of what Hegel calls concrete morality.

MacIntyre looks to shatter every instrumental approach toward the world and human beings and to shatter every moral philosophy of Machiavellian or utilitarian inspiration. For utilitarianism, means relate to ends in a contingent or external manner, whereas for critics of utilitarianism, this relationship is often necessary or internal. "We are now able to specify one crucial difficulty for *any* version of utilitarianism," writes MacIntyre. "Utilitarianism cannot accommodate the distinction between goods internal to and goods external to a practice."[56] Can innocents be sacrificed to the higher good of society and humanity? In making reference to internal goods, MacIntyre shows the limits of a utilitarian reasoning that leads to sacrificing such individuals to the interest of the greatest number. We cannot rationally give ourselves over to these kinds of sacrifices, for in MacIntyre's eyes we cannot compare or measure what is incomparable (or internal). No calculus enables us to explain why, in moral matters, it would be rational to add the utilities together. In critiquing Stalinism, MacIntyre intends to escape both from utilitarianism, which seems to him to have contributed to the complacency of numerous communists, and from moral individualism, from the positions of Camus and Kolakowski. The reasons are henceforth clear: neither utilitarianism nor emotivism (which seems to him to constitute the essence of moral individualism) takes into account the true nature of action.

MacIntyre insists on the existence of internal goods, but he admits the existence of two external goods: power and money. These are not linked in a necessary way to specific practices. Such a distinction enables him to distinguish between two types of relations, cooperative and competitive relations. In the matter of internal goods, progress in the good benefits everyone. The deepening of a practice is beneficial for all those who take part in a practice. They transform a person for the good, and all can be transformed. Internal goods thus naturally call for cooperation, concord, and unity. External goods, by contrast, call for a form of competition and division. What someone gets in terms of power or money deprives another. *After Virtue* joins together two theses, the internality of the good and the limits of individualism. But in reality they are one thesis. A contrast with Hobbes can clarify this point. For Hobbes, there are only external goods. It follows that human relations are essentially competitive and non-cooperative. The state of nature, where man shows himself as he is, is a state of war. Man is therefore not a social or a political animal, but an autonomous individual. By contrast, MacIntyre rediscovers the Aristotelian thesis: internal goods exist, and man is a social or political animal. Common life must not be essentially envisaged as a potential menace (even though it might be so). It must also, and above all, be understood as a form of cooperation and emulation for the good. Internal goods are by nature common goods, and we obtain them within the framework of common life. The human richness of a social life is measured in light of the internal goods that are cultivated in it. Moral life is enacted less through autonomy and more through participation in traditions of enquiry, which take up and rank practices.

MacIntyre at once affirms that individualism is false, unreal, and without a hold on social reality and at the same time that it is poisonous, too real, and too much of our social reality. Some liberals appeal to an atomistic ontology of the social. Others, more historicist, rely on an idea of the progress of liberty—such as in "Whig" historiography. MacIntyre fights these two types of liberalism in turn. Consider two book titles: *Against the Self-Images of the Age* and *After Virtue*. The first title refers to the image people make of themselves and denounces its chimerical character; as for what is essential, the question remains on the plane of knowing, of knowledge. The same cannot be said about the second title, which is more ambiguous in this respect. Has virtue disappeared "in reality" or "in minds"? Has it disappeared *in fact* because it disappeared *in law*? The evil that *After Virtue* denounces goes beyond self-knowledge alone. Individualism appears not just nor even primarily as abstract, but also as *deadly*. MacIntyre thus combines two refutations of individualism: one metaphysical, and the other practical. One presupposes that man remains eternally what he is, which is to say social, and that atomism is abstract. The other presupposes that man can decay, lose his social character, and make liberal atomism the reality. How do these critiques cohere? Are they even compatible? MacIntyre criticizes liberalism both from the point of view of nature and from the point of view of history. Does he pursue these two lines of thought simultaneously, without coming to choose between them, without wanting too much to realize that they are incompatible?

We must distinguish two periods in his philosophical trajectory. In the 1970s and up to *After Virtue*, it is the Marxist, historicist version that triumphs. Starting from *Whose Justice? Which Rationality?*, the Aristotelian version tends to impose itself. But how does liberalism tend to impoverish existence? That was, we recall, the theme of this book's first chapter. Fundamentally, the problem of liberalism is that it does not cultivate virtue, because it tends to sacrifice "the good life" to life tout court. In one sense, this comes back to saying that liberalism subordinates virtue to consensus, to concord. Nevertheless, according to MacIntyre, by neglecting the practice of virtue, liberalism challenges social life itself. It dissolves the human bond, gradually returning us to a prepolitical state. This insistence on the naturally social character of human beings does not imply, in itself, a critique of liberal democracy: it only implies a reformulation of its philosophical presuppositions and the abandonment of liberalism's most individualist and relativist forms.

Who is MacIntyre's adversary par excellence? In his description of the implicit Cartesianism of the Americans, Tocqueville gives perhaps the best analysis:

To escape from the spirit of system, from the yoke of habits, from family maxims, from class opinions, and, up to a certain point, from national prejudices; to take tradition only as information, and current facts only as a useful study for doing otherwise and better; to seek the reason for things by themselves and in themselves alone, to strive for a result without letting themselves be chained to the means, and to see through the form to the foundation: these are the principal features that characterize what I shall call the philosophic method of the Americans.

If I go still further and seek among these diverse features the principal one that can sum up almost all the others, I discover that in most of the operations of the mind, each American calls only on the individual effort of his reason.

America is therefore the one country in the world where the precepts of Descartes are least studied and best followed.[57]

"Without letting themselves be chained to the means"? The theory of internal good directly addresses this trait. "To take tradition only as information"? The theory of the "tradition of enquiry" that MacIntyre proposes condemns this attitude. "The individual effort of his reason"? As he lingers over the importance of what is common, MacIntyre seeks precisely to establish that the individual is not sovereign. Descartes is Wittgenstein's adversary par excellence, as well as that of numerous neo-Aristotelians, notably Anscombe and MacIntyre. For Descartes begins by dismissing opinions, instead of making them his starting point. Thus he founds the point of view of the "unencumbered" subject, which his critics counter with the "embedded" agent. The condemnation of Cartesian dualism is inseparable from the condemnation of the primacy of the ego, this dualism constituting the matrix of modern individualism. The Cartesian self effects the repudiation par excellence of traditions of enquiry, starting by abstracting away from everything that the self has received to leave only the *cogito*, the only evidence of the self and its existence.

Duties are determined by one's place within a community, within the framework of a tradition. Practical reason depends on a substantial context. Tradition is the source of norms. It is *qua* father or mother of a family, prince, citizen, craftsman, that I know what it is I ought to do. MacIntyre's virtue ethics go in the opposite direction of individualism by relying on the normative character of social practices and traditions: if we consider ourselves as "individuals" and act like that, we disregard the traditions to which we belong, and we lose the foundation of practical rationality.

By separating justice and morality in the name of positivism, by separating freedom and truth in the name of individual autonomy, we end up losing practical rationality. The indefinite deepening of individualism or subjectivism has come to ruin the social forms and traditions that true freedom presupposes. The subjective character of autonomy must be compensated for by the objective dimension of the organization of communal life and the nature of the good. Liberal dissociation presupposes association or, better still, community. Here we find again the arguments elaborated during the critique of the Old Left. Liberalism is not a self-sufficient doctrine. "Modernity" depends on "premodernity," and modernity destroys the social bond that it presupposes. It has a *parasitic* character. If making autonomy absolute implies the dissolution of practical reason, it is because we are first and foremost *social animals*. MacIntyre counters the abstract "individual" of a certain liberalism with the "rooted," human being "embedded" in his environment. Detached from all sense of a "truth" inscribed in "practices" and in "traditions," the individual is condemned to the impotence of ideality. Without a substantial context, autonomy does not exist as an ethical reality but only as an internal possibility. "Human beings cannot be understood in detachment from their necessary social context, that setting within which alone rationality can be exercised."[58] Action refers to forms of life, to institutions that develop within a community and a tradition. "It is in general only within a community that individuals become capable of morality."[59] As another philosopher, who is sometimes likened to MacIntyre, writes: "Liberalism teaches respect for the distance of self and ends, and when this distance is lost, we are submerged in a circumstance that ceases to be ours. But by seeking to secure this distance too completely, liberalism undermines its own insight."[60] The liberal critique of politics presupposes the politics that it criticizes.

Modern and contemporary moral philosophies often prefer to envisage duty only in the abstract, independent of all traditions. Most often they propose to show how people can recognize their very humanity in each other. These philosophies offer different versions of the immediate recognition of the humanity of another. The pairings of "man-woman," "master-slave," "young-old," "friends-enemies," and "believer-unbeliever" would thus be replaced by the pairing of "ego" and "non-ego." Every individual is supposed to question by himself and for himself. In his quest for the true and the good, man cannot hope any longer for the support of a tradition. He is now reputedly "free." Modern moral philosophy has turned away from the question of *one's position* and *the duties of one's station* to envisage action in the abstract, independent of all traditions. MacIntyre, by contrast, insists that these duties of one's station are important for moral life. He insists on the difference between the duty that flows from one's position and the obligation that flows from a contract.[61] He analyzes social function as one of the roots of moral life in general and of duty in particular.[62]

> Hence *qua* member of this or that particular community I can appreciate the justification for what morality requires of me from within the social roles that I live out in my community. By contrast, it may be argued, liberal morality requires of me to assume an abstract and artificial—perhaps even an impossible—stance, that of a rational being as such, responding to the requirements of morality not *qua* parent or farmer or quarterback, but *qua* rational agent who has abstracted him or herself from all social particularity, who has become not merely Adam Smith's impartial spectator, but a correspondingly impartial actor, and one who in his impartiality is doomed to rootlessness, to be a citizen of nowhere.[63]

"Duty" should not be considered in the abstract, but in relation to the function occupied in society, for each function brings specific duties. MacIntyre examines our roles, which enable us to go from facts to values. We can infer from "he is a sea-captain" that he ought to do whatever a sea-captain ought to do. "He gets a better yield for this crop per acre than any farmer in the district" implies "He is a good farmer." Reason teaches us how to act not as an individual, but by reference to a tradition capable of explaining what is a "good farmer" and a "good man."[64]

MacIntyre proposes a kind of virtue ethics. But it is remarkable that he has relatively little to say about the virtues themselves: temperance, courage, and moderation. In this respect, his own ethics hardly resembles the *Nicomachean Ethics*, from which he draws much inspiration. His philosophical effort bears not so much on the different virtues but on the forms of life that they require, and on the type of apprenticeship, education, and authority that is associated with them. This is one of the reasons why he condemns emotivism, which we could characterize as a denunciation of all moral authority based on practices or established mores. MacIntyre writes that every practice necessarily involves "standards of excellence and obedience to rules as well as the achievement of goods. To enter into a practice is to accept the authority of those standards and the inadequacy of my own performance as judged by them. It is to subject my own attitudes, choices, preferences and tastes to the standards which currently and partially define the practice. . . . If, on starting to listen to music, I do not accept my own incapacity to judge correctly, I will never learn to hear [it]."[65]

The examples chosen—here that of music, that of medicine just before—are strange: to which virtue or virtues do they directly relate? MacIntyre's goal here is neither to propose a new catalogue of the virtues, nor even to compare the respective merits of different catalogues of the virtues, nor to rank the virtues in different ways. His goal is rather to establish that moral life presupposes an apprenticeship comparable to that which medicine or music requires. Practices offer an objective framework for developing the right kind of desire. MacIntyre intends to emphasize that moral education does not necessarily or even primarily start from individual subjectivity: good practices fashion subjectivity and teach it to desire the good. These practices, not reducible to subjective dispositions, fashion subjectivity to orient it toward the true good. Moral life presupposes an authority and therefore a hierarchical community in which authority can be exercised. There is no dualism between the individual (his subjectivity) and the rest of the world. Moral reasoning is inseparable from habits, mores, and social practices that are embodied and taken up in an authoritative tradition of enquiry.

Individual reasoning is participation in collective reasoning, upon which it depends. Individual judgment is enacted through collective agreement, through the institution of moral and philosophical authorities that must be justified. Reasoning presupposes a publicly recognized order. It intimately joins together this justice and this morality, which positivism would keep separate. Practical rationality presupposes a custom, a consensus that tightly joins together these "causes" and these "reasons," these "facts" and these "values," which positivists mistakenly separate. The positivist separation of justice and morality only ends up rendering values arbitrary, "individual," and "subjective." In the last analysis this separation is condemned to emotivism. MacIntyre contrasts this separation with a concept of "practice" and "virtue," which is an endorsement of the impossibility of rigorously maintaining these separations. MacIntyre argues against moral relativism at the same time as he places moral life in a particular context: that of "practice," but also that of "tradition of enquiry."

III. The Philosophy of Tradition

In 1971, MacIntyre published a collection of articles with a largely negative tone. Eloquently entitled *Against the Self-Images of the Age* and subtitled *Essays on Ideology and Philosophy*, he combined an ideological approach and a more analytical approach, a Marxist part and a Wittgensteinian part. He intended to relate these two parts together and draw a politics from Wittgenstein's apolitical book *Philosophical Investigations*. But as he wrote in the introduction, he had to recognize that he did not know "how to tie these arguments together into a substantive whole."[66] *After Virtue*, published in 1981, is in this respect more satisfying: "*After Virtue* took more than eight years to write. . . . My plan had originally been to write two quite independent books: one on the fate of morality in the modern world, another on the philosophy of the social sciences. But the argument of each book turned out to require the argument of the other."[67]

After Virtue therefore ensures the synthesis of these two points of view, since the chapters on the social sciences (chaps. 7, 8, and 15) are mixed together with the chapters on moral philosophy (chaps. 2, 3, 4, and 17). In *Whose Justice? Which Rationality?*, published in 1988, MacIntyre completes his enterprise. By its title alone, the book announces the completion of the program that he set for himself. The political dimension and the moral dimension are at last put in parallel and reconciled: Wittgenstein and the critique of modern rationalism. Against the skepticism and the atomism that are the basis for the primacy of individual autonomy,

MacIntyre counters with a rediscovery of the concept of nature, which he owes to a realist interpretation of *Philosophical Investigations*. As we shall see, this interpretation enables him to escape on the one hand from the "modern" theory of abstract universalism and on the other hand from the "postmodern" critique of this universalism. He thus intends to take into account and reconcile the diversity of forms of life (particularism) and the unity of humanity (universalism and rationalism). He intends to show that individual reasoning is participation in collective reasoning. As I explained in the preceding section, moral life is enacted through socially established practices, and justice cannot be entirely separated from morality.

In the domain of the philosophy of social sciences, MacIntyre strives to draw lessons from Wittgenstein's *Remarks on Frazer's Golden Bough* and its criticisms of the great positivist anthropologist James George Frazer. Frazer describes the beliefs of the people of Asia, Oceania, and Africa as scientifically meaningless. These peoples still belong to humanity's infancy: their mentality is not "positive," but is well and truly "primitive" and prelogical. Frazer is a positivist. A contemporary of imperialism, he tends to believe in the possibility of unifying the world around the single rationality of the Enlightenment. He never ceases to ask why the savages do not perceive the inefficacy of their magic. He analyzes primitive rites as a sort of technology founded on inept scientific theories. Whereas empiricists or positivists denounce myths as unaccomplished forms of science, Wittgenstein's supporters emphasize that myths have their proper rationality—on the subject of the universe, people pose different questions and answer differently. Whereas positivists claim an omnipotent Reason, a single reality that we can describe in a logically perfect language, that of scientific causality, Wittgenstein's supporters put forward the irreducible diversity of the human world and the diversity of motives and intentions. Does science not prove itself incapable of entirely articulating the nature of art, languages, games, rituals, and legal, social, and religious institutions? We stand to gain by completing the causal explanation of Galilean science with the Aristotelian teleological explanation (with reasons for acting). Neither mathematical certainty nor the subjection of phenomena to causal laws can be the only ideals of perfection. It is a question of rediscovering the richness and specificity of human existence through taking into account the reasons of agents.[68] Against the primacy of causality, Wittgenstein's disciples counter with the meaning of the diversity of human motives. They rediscover the pretheoretical world or the irreducibility of the study of society to biological or physical nature. In a scarcely different context, we find the question of "causes" and "reasons" that I raised above. It is henceforth a question about the philosophy of the social sciences rather than moral philosophy. But the problem, in the philosophy of action, is the same.

MacIntyre follows in the footsteps of those in the twentieth century who work to correct Frazer's views. First Bronisław Malinowski insists on the necessity of taking into account the point of view of the natives, their reasons for acting. E. E. Evans-Pritchard, his student, takes the next step in extending the theory to the method. Against Frazer, Evans-Pritchard emphasizes that by taking into account the presuppositions and the representations at work in the studied culture, we uncover a true rationality. Upon analysis, the "primitive" or "mystic" mentality proves to be complex and coherent. The collection of data must avail itself of a theoretical perspective. Evans-Pritchard does not, however, completely abandon the positivist field. In his study on the Azande, he insists on the rationality of their belief in the efficacy of oracles and the reality of sorcerers, even though he maintains that these beliefs are simply false. But MacIntyre's position was developed above all in a fruitful dialogue with Peter Winch. Winch (1926–97) was the student of Rush Rhees, who studied with Wittgenstein in the mid-1930s and who was, as Wittgenstein's literary executor, his heir.

Winch completes the evolution that Malinowski starts and that Evans-Pritchard deepens.[69] He agrees with these last two to recognize the importance of a description of the world in the terms and categories of the studied populations, but he denies these two the right to judge the truth of beliefs. The science of empirical verification, the analysis in terms of causes, is only one language game among others. Winch criticizes the universality and superiority of a causalist science, which seems to him linked to a specific historical context and based on the normative consensus of one scientific community. The beliefs of the Azande obey rules, like our science, but they are different rules. Without going so far as to allege the existence of incompatible logics, Winch considers that what is rational in one culture can prove to be irrational in another. According to Winch, the ethnologist must, as far as possible, abandon his own categories of thought and prefer those of the population that he is studying, so as not to truncate his description. The rationality of the observer must strive to step aside before the rationality of the observed.

Winch counters the empiricism and causalism of most ethnologists with a holism that he borrows from the author of *Philosophical Investigations*. Against empiricalist or positivist epistemology, he puts forward the plurality of practical rationalities. Each type of society has its own specific form of rationality, so much that it is impossible to pronounce on the nature of behavior in a given culture without learning its languages and ways of thinking. Any action must be understood by reference to the norms in force. Yet these norms vary from one society to another.

Causalists are mistaken when they believe they can abstain from relating action to a set of mores, habits, laws, as if there were "basic actions," autonomous from the point of view of meaning. Frazer, in casting the cold eyes of a gentleman upon the practices most alien to British culture, could not fail to associate their exoticism with the epitome of irrationality. Rather, it is important to integrate oneself into the society in question: to adopt its codes and assimilate its usages and customs so as to understand behavior and reasons for acting, as the natives themselves would do. However savage the barbarians may appear to be, their actions nevertheless obey rules.

MacIntyre partly approves of Winch's critique. But he relies on another, nonrelativist interpretation of Wittgenstein, closer to Anscombe's interpretation. He maintains that the criteria of coherence and contradiction are everywhere the same, writing:

> There is once again no question of being able to distinguish between *our* criteria of rationality (the anthropologists' or sociologists') and *their* criteria (those of the agents whose culture is the object of study). Rationality is nobody's property. It is necessary to re-emphasize this point in order even more clearly to discriminate the position defended in this essay from that of the Victorian defenders of reason, and in order to show that a rationalist standpoint is not merely (as Winch takes it to be) the ideological standpoint of a Western culture which aspires to be the judge of others without being judged itself. The argument of this essay implies the possibility of ascribing irrationality to modern Western culture on precisely the same grounds as we should make this ascrip-

tion elsewhere. . . . The community of shared rationality to which I have argued that all recognizably human societies must belong must of course also be a community of shared beliefs to *some* extent. For there are some commonsense beliefs (about day and night, the weather and material environment generally) which are inescapable for any rational agent.[70]

"Rationality is nobody's property." The ethnologist must therefore have recourse to the category of rationality, to that of causality, and remain faithful to one of the aspects of Victorian anthropology. For MacIntyre, Winch forgets that the point of view of the actors is never perfectly satisfactory. Only by observing from the outside can certain elements of Azande society, which escape the Azande themselves, appear. Winch abandons the ideal of explanation for that of description. Yet a good description calls for an explanation and often implies the manifestation of irrationalities or contradictions about which the natives are unaware. What meaning can Winch confer on the work of a Christian missionary, explaining to a certain tribe that its beliefs are idolatrous and that, because they do not exist, idols can "cause" nothing? What meaning can Winch confer on the real practice of an ethnologist who starts from observed beliefs, but not without reformulating them into his own terms, into his own categories of thought?[71]

MacIntyre reckons that Winch makes a big step forward in taking into account the norms of each society, but he stops too soon. Starting from the interdependence of language, rules, and rationality, Winch rightly emphasizes the nonexistence of a practical rationality that could abstract away from social context, but he is too quick to deduce the incommensurability of forms of thought. In effect, once the rules of the game are known, we can distinguish the talented players from the less talented, as well as detect the cheaters. If Frazer dooms certain cultures to the hell of primitivism, Winch's epistemological abstention seems to be no less paradoxical in dooming them to perfect rationality. Must we choose between ethnocentrism and relativism?

MacIntyre and Winch pursue the same goal: the "preservation of a humanist sociology, the retention of the human image of man. . . . They wish to save *the anthropomorphic image of man himself*."[72] They propose to rediscover human life, inasmuch as it is not reducible to the science of causes. They propose to grant an essential place to the reasons of agents, against the reduction of human action into simple "observable behavior" or "natural fact." However, MacIntyre considers that Winch goes too far and that he comes to forget that alleged motives are often false. MacIntyre starts from the privileged place of the agent to explain the agent's own action, all the while recognizing that some elements can escape the agent. The agent's honest admission and his reasons for acting retain ultimate authority, but not without taking into account the fact that there are people notoriously incapable of recognizing their ambitions, their jealousies, and their passions.

According to MacIntyre, a comparative science is possible, provided that we neither neglect nor exaggerate *the depth of the social*. MacIntyre deplores the relativist consequences of Winch's theses, without however sharing in the empiricism of Evans-Pritchard. It is important neither to privilege the observer in relation to a supposedly unaware native, nor a native supposedly omniscient in relation to the observer.[73] A balanced approach imposes itself. This happy medium presupposes taking into account rules and institutions. Eurocentric ethnologists ignore them through their individualism and positivism; Winch takes cultural depth to be obscurity. The spectacle of the rationality of the natives leads Winch to recognize a form of truth in their beliefs, whereas Frazer, in inferring their irrationality, judges them scientifically doubtful. One is too quick to associate rationality with truth, the other too quick to associate irrationality with error.

Undoubtedly, myths pertain to science, literature, and theology simultaneously. In envisaging them under our habitual angles, we risk disfiguring them, and it is ridiculous to contrast myth to reality, as if myth aspires to "represent" reality.[74] We cannot begin evaluating the rationality of a practice and its related purpose without knowing to which genre it pertains. Let us imagine, for example, Martians observing humans playing chess. If they did not know what it is "to play," they would not necessarily have a bad description: they would not even be able to identify the action that they want to explain. They cannot explain that the players follow the rules, nor whether they fundamentally master the secrets of the game or do not know them. Yet a good explanation of these movements requires this type of appreciation. Action is only intelligible by reference to the social institutions and practices within which reasons for acting are developed. To render the actions of agents intelligible, it is necessary that "we *understand* their self-descriptions. We may, indeed often must, take account of their confusion, malinformation, illusion; but we make sense of them if we grasp *both* how they see things *and* what is wrong, lacunary, contradictory in this." So writes Charles Taylor, whose reflections follow a parallel course to MacIntyre's.[75]

Victorian ethnology excessively privileged the point of view of the observer over that of the observed: the rationality of the primitives is assessed in light of causality alone. The representations of the agents are considered as secondary, the nominal and the real separated without nuance. In reaction against this dualism, Winch comes to reduce the physical to the mental. At the risk of exaggerating, we could maintain that Winch is less about getting rid of empiricism than about reversing it. Empiricists privilege causes ("facts") and subordinate reasons ("representations") to causes, ignoring that laws do not reflect reality but organize it. Winch, for his part, tends to suck facts into representations. Following Wittgenstein, MacIntyre proposes to show that human reality is situated between two extremes. Practical reason is linked to a context: it is neither reduced to a context, nor is it enclosed by a context.

Initially, MacIntyre was more historicist and attached to a certain historical relativism, going up to the point of maintaining that "moral concepts change as social life changes,"[76] and of taking up the Hegelian thematic of the historicity of concepts. He discussed the history of virtue as that of a concept wandering through time. But at the same time, it is remarkable that he did everything to escape his own relativism without renouncing the type of holism that is dear to him. The historicist element has now almost disappeared from his reflections.[77] Even though MacIntyre was an Aristotelian in 1981, he refused to take into account what he then called Aristotle's "metaphysical biology," which is to say the manner in which he combines "nature" in the biological sense of the term with "nature" in the metaphysical sense of the term. Nevertheless, in *Dependent Rational Animals* (1999), MacIntyre relates human nature to animal nature, biology to metaphysics. Henceforth he uses the concept of nature. MacIntyre ends up by placing the historical dimension, to which he had been attached, within the nonrelativist framework of an authoritative tradition.

MacIntyre establishes that individual reasoning is participation in collective reasoning, elaborated within the framework of a given community. But this thesis does not imply relativism. The question of the relation between cause and intention is also that of the relation between practical rationality and relativism. MacIntyre posed this question in five different forms that we can, for convenience, associate with each of the decades of his intellectual life. In the 1950s, he envisaged this relation under the angle of the relation between theology and philosophy; tempted by the position of Karl Barth, he was nevertheless concerned to leave a place for natural theology. I shall return later to this aspect. In the 1960s, he was interested in the philosophy of social sciences and strived to show, against Peter Winch, that one can be Wittgensteinian without being a relativist. Starting in the mid-1970s, he examined the history of the sciences.[78] In the 1980s, he expressed himself in terms of a "tradition of enquiry" and treated the problem under the angle of incommensurability and translatability. Against a model too linguistic or too drawn to reduce culture to a theory, he countered with an anthropological model, a language game presupposing practices and forms of life; we can compare the work of the anthropologist to that of the translator but on the condition that we do not neglect idioms.[79] In the 1990s, he continued to express himself in terms of "traditions," but he envisaged these questions anew, from a different angle, attaching himself this time to the problem of the nature of truth and in particular to the relation between criteria of coherence and adequation.

The debates with Winch still preside over what MacIntyre develops in *Whose Justice? Which Rationality?* and *Three Rival Versions of Moral Enquiry*. In these texts, MacIntyre strives to demonstrate the existence of conceptual schemas that are not reducible to each other and nevertheless are partially commensurable. He strives to take into account both the variety of reasons for acting and the existence of a worthwhile practical rationality, both the diversity of forms of life and the unity of humanity. If we had to divide the late Wittgenstein's legacy in two, with one part being relativist and the other part not, we could consider Winch as the spokesman for the first, and Anscombe as that for the second. As a disciple of Wittgenstein, MacIntyre identifies with Elizabeth Anscombe's interpretation.[80] His principal articles on the realism of truth were published in anthologies: one in honor of Peter Winch, the other in honor of Anscombe. This is no mere coincidence. For MacIntyre, the rejection of "private language" does not imply renouncing the notion that language refers to causes that are themselves independent from language. Even though practical rationality falls within a given social context, it presupposes a certain universalism—a "form of the good."[81] With Winch, MacIntyre considers that it is impossible to relate to an autonomous, positive, causal "reality," which would be known independently of a society's representations. But against Winch, MacIntyre refuses to condemn cultures to autarky and incommunicability. It is as if he were taking up the objections with which Wittgenstein countered private language to shatter the thesis of cultural solipsism. Reality is not socially constructed. The rules that we follow are only the established usage of a community, and normativity is nothing other than this conformity: the consideration of "reasons" does not exclude taking "facts," which is to say "causes," into account. We cannot separate our behavior (subject to "causes") from our intentions (our "reasons").

The rootedness of practical rationality in communities does not imply relativism, but it does presuppose a tight relationship between a society's ways of life and ways of thought. Up to a certain point, different ways of life imply different ways of thought, an incapacity to understand one another. The internality of this link results in the incommensurability of traditions of enquiry. With our thought dependent upon our way of life, it is inevitable that essentially different ways of life lead to disagreements that are difficult to overcome. The history of the "ought" as a taboo bears not so much on *facts* as on conceptual problems. The adhesion to certain values is constitutive of modes of life. MacIntyre criticizes the view that freedom can be located on an empirical ground that is either theologically or metaphysically "neutral."[82] Hence this curious phrase to find in a philosopher: "I too must have been and will be speaking as a partisan."[83] Answering the objections that are made against him, MacIntyre writes by way of a preamble: "I do not expect my critics always to be convinced by my replies. Often of course they will be unpersuaded simply because of the inadequacy of those replies. But it is also worth noting that, if the central theses in favor of which I have been arguing for nearly twenty years are true, then we should expect them to be rejected by the most articulate and able representatives of the dominant culture of modernity."[84]

Most of MacIntyre's works and a large part of his articles open with the question of disagreement, since for him, disagreements reflect the qualitative leaps that one must make from one order to another, in order to understand certain things. We believe that, with complete "independence," and so to speak, with complete "exteriority," we *choose* certain goods and we *select* certain ends in a "neutral" way. But "practices" are not good because they are desired: they have in themselves a normative character, for the desire itself. It is more accurate to say that these goods and these ends precede us and constitute us. Our decisions and the way we formulate them reflect our identity. We do not *choose* such and such a habit, community, or religion: more often, it would almost be more accurate to say that such and such habits, communities, or religions are *internal* to our deliberations and choose within us.

For MacIntyre, the most successful tradition of enquiry must be capable of offering the most satisfying interpretation of the strength and limitations of other traditions. As Taylor explains,

> The superiority of one position over another will thus consist in this, that from the more adequate position one can understand one's own stand and that of one's opponent, but not the other way around. It goes without saying that this argument can only have weight for those in the superior position. . . . Thus, in the sciences of man in so far as they are hermeneutical there can be a valid response to "I don't understand" which takes the form, not only "develop your intuitions," but more radically "change yourself." This puts an end to any aspiration to a value-free or "ideology-free" science of man.[85]

Taking up a theme that he started to develop with his critique of behaviorism, Taylor adds—in a vein very close to MacIntyre—that the social sciences "cannot be *wertfrei*; they are moral sciences in a more radical sense than the eighteenth century understood. Finally, their successful prosecution requires a high degree of self-knowledge, a freedom from illusion, in the sense of error which is rooted and expressed in one's way of life; for our incapacity to understand is rooted in our own self-definitions, hence in what we are. To say this is not to say anything new: Aristotle makes a similar point in Book I of the *Ethics*."[86]

The circularity that is at work here is, properly speaking, virtuous, for the more virtuous we are, the more we understand the precepts of practical reason. Incommensurability points to the limits of self-knowledge; by contrast, commensurability points to self-knowledge. Commensurability is possible from the points of view of the agent or of a tradition whose habits are most satisfactory, most rational, most virtuous, and wisest. Before we declare such and such a behavior to be irrational, we must ponder the limits of our own habits and prove that we have some wisdom. This hermeneutic can lead to the Aristotelian figure of the *spoudaios*, who *is* the moral standard.[87] It is in the last analysis by reference to the wisdom of the *spoudaios* that MacIntyre reconciles both the consideration of the diversity of cultures and the unity of humanity.[88] We are "culture-transcending rational animals."[89] Here, the moral virtues come to the rescue of the intellectual virtues. It is important to reintegrate the "human" sciences with what was once called the "moral and political" sciences.

I noted earlier, in the context of the moral critique of Stalinism, that MacIntyre intended to escape both from modern rationalism and postmodern irrationalism. Frazer's position falls under the former, and Winch's position falls under the latter—his theory of incommensurability could be akin to Lyotard's. MacIntyre intends to show that true freedom unfolds within the framework of traditions or communities that give meaning to our reasons for acting. He denies that the Enlightenment, in making us escape from the world of traditions and in detaching us from our forms of belonging, has emancipated or freed us through making us access the world of causality. He denies that the Enlightenment, in making us into "autonomous" individuals proud of the absence of their "prejudices," had made us access "universal" truths that hitherto escaped us. For both the "modern" partisans of universal commensurability and the "postmodern" partisans of incommensurability, the life of reason and social life are strangers to one another. For "moderns," every society is particular: a mere set of prejudices that we must surpass through individualism and cosmopolitanism. For "postmoderns," the very status of reason is doubtful. Neither for the former nor the latter can there be any *rational (or natural) desire to live in society.* For both, man is essentially an individual, and society is ordered toward satisfying the individual. MacIntyre strives to find a middle position, which presupposes the existence of such a desire. Social life is the point where the universal mixes with the particular to become concrete. The desire to belong to a society is not in itself the effect of prejudice, superstition, and unreasonable traditionalism.

MacIntyre escapes from the theory of universal commensurability because he emphasizes the importance of belonging to a society. He escapes from the theory of incommensurability because he emphasizes that social life is not foreign to human nature: it is the place where human nature is fulfilled. Societies can therefore relate to each other, because they all presuppose an idea of human nature, which tends toward a more or less correct appreciation of what human nature demands. The natural character of social life implies therefore that societies are neither constructs wholly foreign to each other (the thesis of incommensurability) nor constructs that remain on the surface of individual life (the thesis of commensurability). The affirmation of the natural character of social life does not imply a natural law that would be a kind of abstract universalism, but a natural law that is understood and interpreted within the framework of different social forms.

If individual reasoning is participation in a common reasoning, in a tradition, then social life is a good in itself. Here we must come back to the question that I raised in the introduction: avoiding evil, desiring the good. For the Machiavellian and Hobbesian schools, social life is not a good in itself. Nor, therefore, do traditions and customs linked to social life constitute goods in themselves. They do not necessarily contribute to social harmony. They are by no means indispensable to practical rationality—practical reason incidentally does not have great importance, because it is the authority of the prince or sovereign that matters. Positive law is independent of traditions, and justice is conceivable independent of morality. By contrast, for the Thomist-Aristotelian school with which MacIntyre aligns himself, social life is a good, and the traditions that are linked to it are equally good in themselves. Positive law is intelligible by reference to natural justice, which takes substance in the form of traditions that are inseparably moral and political. MacIntyre shows that, far from excluding practical reason, traditions help develop it, help give it substance. MacIntyre therefore presupposes that life in society is a good in itself, that man is a social animal, that there is a natural desire to live in society. Man is a social animal because he needs a socially embodied tradition to reason justly.

Law is not entirely separable from morality: the demands of common life that express the law reflect the demands of individual conscience.

There is no opposition between nature and society. Society is not essentially artificial, and law is not only or even principally a construct. Law does not impose itself only or even principally as a mere convention, from the outside: it is the expression of human nature itself. It responds to human desire. MacIntyre suggests that the concept of an internal good (to which he is very attached, as we saw above) was first developed by Plato in response to the sophists, who are the adversaries par excellence of any conception of natural justice.[90] Developing Wittgenstein's arguments in a direction Wittgenstein himself carefully avoided, MacIntyre comes to affirm the existence of natural justice and even a natural law (even though Mac-Intyre's repugnance to express himself in terms of natural "laws" refers precisely to Wittgenstein). Society is not an artifice: there is a natural desire to live in society. For Hobbes, for example, men do not have a natural desire to live in society. Men are wolves to men. Natural law is therefore minimal: it has survival as its object, not common life. For MacIntyre, human *will* cannot *decide* what is just and unjust, good and evil. This is, in the last analysis, the answer that the moral critique of Stalinism calls for: a natural law that cannot be reduced to subjective rights. Additionally, MacIntyre's critique of the state and of cultural homogenization, which forms the basis for his conservatism, points to his refusal of the positivist idea of sovereignty. It is not for the state to "produce" social life. The social bond is not artificial, and the social order is in many respects received.

For MacIntyre, the type of liberalism that foregrounds autonomy to get rid of the partiality of "traditions" is itself a "tradition," with its own conception of the good and its own substantial ends. Empiricist and dualist liberalism proves itself to be incapable of accounting for its own nature and its own history. Despite their denials, they are erecting the scaffolds of a tradition:[91] "No institution, no social practice can be inspired solely or even mainly by liberalism; and every institution or social practice that claims to be so inspired—such as the 'liberal' university or the 'liberal' state—is always a fraud."[92]

Society has not ceased to depend on the operation of power. It merely ignores this dependence. Liberalism is a tradition, in the sense that it implicitly relates practical reason to a conception of the good, without however accepting that it does. MacIntyre develops the concept of a tradition to show that any conception of justice or law refers to a conception of morality. As there can be different conceptions of morality, there can be different conceptions of justice, which enter into conflict and which we have to decide between. But there is no conception of justice that can be entirely separated from a conception of morality; there is no moral neutrality. Legal positivism, which claims to separate the law from morality completely, is not philosophically tenable.

When they concern themselves with the question of the good, theorists of liberalism tend to separate two spheres: a political sphere and a moral (private) sphere. They thus suggest that it is up to the individual to choose his own conception of happiness and to look for the good. Then they suggest that the city can and should merely avoid evil and that it benefits from sticking to limited objects—comfort and security, for example. This separation is in many respects useful. But does it offer a mere practical orientation, a maxim among others? Or does it call for a real wall of separation, a difference of principles? Can this be rigorously maintained? MacIntyre works to show that it cannot. In the last analysis, the separation between (private) morality and politics is untenable. The true or the good that nourishes freedom is not discovered by individuals detached from all social and historical contexts, but by individuals rooted in forms of life and traditions of enquiry that enable them to reason and judge. To relegate the search for happiness to a private domain conceived independently of social life and the life of faith is, in fact, to renounce it.

Political science cannot isolate itself from moral philosophy, from the question of "character." Following in the footsteps of the Aristotelian classification of regimes, MacIntyre relates political life to moral life. In his eyes, nothing represents Victorian England more aptly than the figures of the Explorer, the Engineer, and the Headmaster; and nothing is more characteristic of Wilhelmine Germany than the Prussian Officer, the Professor, and the Social Democrat. The twentieth century is represented, in his view, by the bureaucrat and the psychoanalyst.[93] MacIntyre relates politics to anthropology, and the organization of city and state to certain human types. Freedom is not only the right to do anything that does not harm another, nor is it even individual autonomy. It is more profoundly participation in the good or the truth—positive liberty. There is no freedom without character or virtue. There is no theory of justice without moral philosophy and without the idea of the good.

Against the theorists of negative liberty, who want to account for action without reference to ends, MacIntyre insists on the necessity of taking into account reasons for acting, intentions that refer to goals and therefore to a theory of positive liberty. Liberty is analyzed not only as the absence of coercion but by reference to an end that gives it meaning. The theory of liberty as the absence of coercion clashes against a powerful objection: from holding to sensible experience alone, to the field of causality alone, it is very difficult to explain how we differentiate important obstacles from negligible obstacles, how we circumscribe externally the domain of coercion, how we rigorously distinguish influences that are coercive from those that are not. It is uncertain if we can hold up the causal, empirical sphere without referencing intentions. To save individualism from this difficulty, we can have recourse to "autonomy" as a "positive" ideal. That is notably the Kantian solution. But is individual autonomy enough to ground morality in reason? That is what MacIntyre denies.

Unlike classical liberalism, which called for limiting the state, contemporary forms of liberalism tend to call for "neutralizing" the state. The state is supposed to be neutral with respect to the values of each. Contemporary forms of liberalism demand that the state place itself above moral differences. Political principles must be conceived independently of morals or of final ends. No matter what, the state must not favor a particular "conception of the good." This is the dominant idea in Anglo-American political philosophy today. But, in the last analysis, this theory pertains less to the liberal tradition than to a certain legal positivism, for which Hobbes offers the classical illustration and H. L. A. Hart offers the modern illustration. It is the essence of legal positivism that it separates the definition of law from all moral authority. By contrast, it is the essence of the natural law jurisprudence that MacIntyre calls for to relate the interpretation of the law to moral truth.

In going from "cultures" analyzed by anthropology to "traditions of enquiry," MacIntyre gradually redirects his own enquiry, but without changing the object. In his debates with Winch, it was the nature of practical reason that held his attention, and he looked to relate the specificity of social forms with a specific interpretation of practical reason. In his reflection on traditions of enquiry, it is again the nature of practical reason that interests him. The traditions of enquiry that MacIntyre analyzes relate moral philosophy to a theory of justice. Contrary to the individualist, neutralist, or positivist thesis, morality is not essentially individualist, nor is justice fundamentally separable from morality. At the most fundamental level, the diversity of forms of social organization refers to different customs, to different ways of articulating the demands of justice, but also, and perhaps even above all, to different moral philosophies.

If we define man as an individual rather than as a social animal, we insist that man does not need the city to be fully human. He can already be human in the state of nature, distinguished from the social state. In this schema, the city is wished for as a tool destined to accomplish specific functions, foreign to the proper good of the soul: to bring, for example, comfort and security. By contrast, if we define man as a social animal, we presuppose that man cannot become fully human except in a social context; only animals and gods can pass society by. It therefore follows that the city cannot be understood as an instrument to a limited end. The city has for its object, whether it wants it or not, the good life, that which renders men virtuous and happy. The city cannot be neutral towards goods reputed to be indifferent to the city. For it is in the context of the city that men become what they are. Positive laws shape the soul of a social and political animal, which is only accomplished within the framework of the city. Positive law does not only have for its object an order exterior to the human soul, and it is not only a matter of morally indifferent conventions. Positive law influences the soul itself. It can be just or unjust, and it can echo natural justice or contradict it.

Liberals, who are inspired by Hobbes more often than they are aware, generally consider that the "natural" world is, if not chaotic, at least not human. Natural order (or disorder) implies no social or political order. It is for human beings to decide their own ends and laws, to order their world and invent the rules that they need. To humanize the world is to escape from nature's empire, to *flee* it. Since nature is coercion and oppression, liberty is defined by the absence of coercion, which is to say by flight, by negation. For the theorists of the primacy of this negative liberty, nature is a state of war; it divides men and is intolerable. The end is not that toward which man naturally tends, but that toward which nature forces him. To survive, man artificially constructs a society, based on an "unsociable sociability." Nature therefore only tends toward freedom indirectly, through a sort of cunning of reason. Freedom comes less through submission to a complete and perfect nature, and more through the conquest of a nature, which we must transform. Man must invent for himself the "ideals," "values," "culture," or "civilization" that nature (that ungrateful mother) refuses to grant him.

According to the Thomists, the world is not chaotic, and values are not simply created artificially. Some desires have a permanence and can give consistency to the moral life. These desires define human nature. They ensure the convergence of traditions of enquiry and their commensurability and are the basis for practical reason. In his *Treatise on Laws* (*Summa Theologiae* Ia-IIae), Thomas Aquinas proposes a list of desires: (a) the preservation of life and reproduction (our vegetative and animal nature) and (b) life in society and knowledge of God (our human nature).

(a) While utilitarians tend to reduce man to his animality, Kantians isolate humanity from its animality. MacIntyre rediscovers Aristotle's point of view through Wittgenstein: man is a rational animal. He is also an animal. There is no discontinuity between instinctive behavior and rational behavior. We are not as distinct from intelligent animals as we sometimes think. "In transcending some of their limitations we never separate ourselves entirely from what we share with them."[94] Some ("animal") desires are also rational. The Wittgensteinian thesis on the continuity of causes and reasons fundamentally refers to a philosophical anthropology: man is not on the one hand an affective being and on the other a rational being. These capacities are correlative and not opposed. Man develops his capacities, which include rational or affective elements that we cannot always separate.

(b) MacIntyre insists above all on what is proper to man, on life in society (I neglect for the moment the knowledge of God, which I shall come back to later). While liberalism's founders insist on the fundamental solitude of the human being, MacIntyre analyzes social life as a good that human beings naturally pursue. Social life is one of the goods that we must look for in order to become free. As MacIntyre shows in *Dependent Rational Animals*, we naturally need others. This dependence defines us, and, as the title indicates, it is the correlate of our rationality. We need family, friendship, diverse associations—in short, "communities." In this argument,

MacIntyre joins together the first New Left's nostalgia for community, socialism, the Marxist critique of liberal individualism, his interest in the social sciences, and his reflections on Wittgenstein.

The social bond is not reducible either to the desire to escape a violent death or to the desire for comfort. Freedom does not consist only in fleeing from evil (oppression, coercion); it also consists in living in the good, and social life is one of those goods. True freedom does not consist in rediscovering the autonomy threatened by the perverse effects of contract but by obeying the law that teaches us and renders us free. To affirm the natural sociability of the human being is not to yield to naïveté. It is not to believe that human beings systematically prove their courtesy, gentility, and their devotion, and it is not to discount that human beings are capable of being aggressive or criminals. It is to emphasize that the goal of society is not only comfort and security and that we cannot understand social life from an essentially instrumental perspective. For MacIntyre, to define man as a social animal is to affirm that there are internal goods and that these internal goods must be common goods by nature, things that are just by nature. We find again here the great Socratic discovery: the good is the common good.

The partisans of the Enlightenment, MacIntyre writes, consider that "such abstraction and detachment is defensible, because it is a necessary condition of moral freedom, of emancipation from the bondage of the social, political and economic *status quo*."[95] But they then lose the sense of social life as a good. MacIntyre writes: "E. M. Forster once remarked that if it came to a choice between betraying his country and betraying his friend, he hoped that he would have the courage to betray his country. In an Aristotelian perspective anyone who can formulate such a contrast has no country, has no *polis*; he is a citizen of nowhere, an internal exile wherever he lives. Indeed from an Aristotelian point of view a modern liberal political society can appear only as a collection of citizens of nowhere who have banded together for their common protection."[96]

Acting according to nature implies acting within the framework of the polis; virtue consists in imitating nature, and man is *naturally* political. MacIntyre adds: "This time however the barbarians are not waiting beyond the frontiers; they have already been governing us for quite some time."[97] Is it important to become citizens of the world? Or should we rely on the wisdom of the Greeks, who despised the *barbarians*, which is to say those who belong to no city?

To summarize, MacIntyre wants both to shatter moral relativism and to show that practical rationality unfolds in the context of a particular community. He comes to reconcile these two apparently contradictory demands by developing *a philosophy of tradition*. Tradition is a social environment in which conceptions of justice hinge on moral conceptions; tradition offers a particular context in which practical rationality is developed and enriched. The positivist attempts to separate the right and the good ignore the reality of moral life as political life. This was fundamentally the problem that MacIntyre had posed when he asked himself how to criticize Stalinism, how to articulate a moral critique of injustice.

MacIntyre proposes to report on the limits of individualism and to establish that we can belong to a community without having to reduce ourselves to it. To take up the title of one of his books again, man is an animal at once "dependent and rational." "Dependent," he falls under a particular community; "rational," he can escape the magnetic field of the social. Thus MacIntyre rediscovers Aristotle's teaching, which defines man by the *logos* that at once constitutes him as a rational animal and a political animal. The *logos* that makes the human being a political animal calls for overcoming itself in the science of *logos*, in contemplation, whether it be philosophical or theological. MacIntyre is haunted by two themes: God and society. He is also haunted by a question: How does the social cohere with the divine? If he criticizes liberalism, it is in the end to breathe life back into two definitions of human nature that are neglected today: man is a social animal, and man is a creature made in the image of God.

THREE
Theology
The Community of Believers

I. Are Wars of Religion as Dangerous as Secularization?

MacIntyre maintains that action falls within the context of a community. But what happens when the duties of one's station conflict with each other? How do "communities" relate to each other? What place does MacIntyre grant to international relations? What should we do when communities decide to come to blows? Most often we can rank their demands— for example, subordinating the family to the city, or the county to the region. However, this is not always the case, particularly when it is a question of church and state. This question is all the more important as it is at the heart of the thought of Hobbes, who is the great theorist of atomism and sovereignty. MacIntyre refers to a theory of natural law, thus suggesting that a set of norms transcends cities and enables arbitration over conflicts. But this forgets the gravity of the tensions that go with religions. Machiavelli, then Hobbes, devoted the essence of their reflections to these tensions. Faith introduces into the city an absolute that disorients and knocks awry the course of civic reasoning. The believer cannot compromise without

111

fearing that he compromises his reasons for living. The disagreement between communities quickly degenerates into civil war, for neither "good sense" nor "interest rightly understood" always fulfills its function when salvation and eternity are at stake. In considering that each individual is both unique and of an infinite value, in choosing a God who is both personal and absolute, Christianity proposes a synthesis of the universal and the particular. From a political point of view, however, this synthesis is not without its weaknesses. The wars of religion showed churches preaching war and anathema, exalting their own particularities in the very name of charity and truth. Churches of universal ambition and incompatible credos are condemned to clash with each other. They take up a combative stance, which is to say, a particularist stance.

The religions that preoccupy us, particularly Christianity, are universalist, and MacIntyre himself is concerned to take the unity of humanity into account. Nevertheless, to the extent that religion presupposes a singular faith and revelation, it cannot be confused with the pure universalism of reason. When compared to the Enlightenment's overblown universalism, Christianity seems like a particularism, and consequently, like fuel for division, like a troublemaker. By way of answering these troubles, the Enlightenment's cosmopolitanism proposes to remedy the difficulties raised by the distinction between God and Caesar, and by the wars of religion. MacIntyre claims a certain particularity, which is in the last analysis the particularity of the Church, but it could just as well be that of the chosen people.

What happens when the duties community life calls for come into conflict with one another? Above all, what do we do when several communities make contradictory demands? Certainly, we can rank the spheres and subordinate the demands of the family to that of civil society, and these in turn to the state; we can also, through patriotism, rank the different communities. But there are two that we cannot rank so easily: church and state. It was once asked who was supreme, the pope or the emperor. The solution that seventeenth-century political philosophy brings to the theologico-political problem is to reduce politics to the quest for security and to *separate* it from the rest: in the first place, from religion, then from the economy and society. Separation of the state from civil society, separation of man and the citizen, separation of church and state . . . In placing each man on the level of humanity, in making each believer and each citizen an "individual," the Enlightenment offers a response to the theologico-political problem. Following Hobbes, who was himself hardly a liberal, the theorists of liberalism call for the sovereignty of the individual and of the state. Thanks to the nation-state, these same citizens conceive an identity that is no longer essentially confessional. Thanks to individualism, these same citizens come to conceive of themselves as relatively independent from their church, whatever it may be. If Hobbes develops a radical individualism, it is in order to isolate man from the duties of his station, in order to offer a solution to the conflict between church and state.

Concerned to join together the right and the good, MacIntyre criticizes the liberal separation thereof. The *artificiality* of Hobbes's Leviathan and its legal positivism contrasts with the idea of a community ordered around *natural* law, as well as with the *supernatural* community (the Church). To the extent that MacIntyre is a theorist of the rights of minorities, which is to say a critic of individualism at the same time as being a critic of the positivist idea of sovereignty, Hobbes is his adversary par excellence. On what do they disagree? On the importance, the existence, and the significance of the theologico-political problem.

The theorists of liberalism often return to the question of the wars of religion, as if it were liberalism's deepest source, because there they find a justification for their universalism. By contrast, their adversaries tend to neglect the theologico-political problem, to better denounce liberal universalism. Marxist Christianity, with which MacIntyre was for a long time aligned, thus seems to presuppose the natural harmony of (Marxist) philosophy and (Christian) theology. Marxist Christianity inherits the Hegelian synthesis of Christianity and modernity. The Hegelian theory of objective spirit relies on a theory of Absolute Spirit, which reconciles or encompasses God and History, which is to say church and state. Does God not save human beings throughout history? Is not reading the newspaper a kind of morning prayer, and history a kind of theodicy? In the early 1950s, MacIntyre reproached modern Christianity for its apolitical nature, its tendency to want to build the kingdom only in heaven. Marxism, desiring to build the kingdom on earth, seemed to him to offer happier perspectives, provided that faith was associated with it. At the end of his intellectual journey, referring to St. Benedict, he leaves to monasticism the privilege of symbolizing the successful articulation of the city of God and the city of men. In both cases, the tension between church and state is singularly absent. More generally, this tension is hardly the driving force of MacIntyre's work. The ancient community can receive two interpretations, which, if they are not contradictory, are at least different—one as *polis* and the other as *ecclesia*. The liberal figure of the individual was invented in the seventeenth century as a means to escape conflicting allegiances. At the end of the millennium, MacIntyre believes that this conflict is no longer the order of the day. MacIntyre falls within the British tradition of scholars such as Ernest Barker, Francis MacDonald Cornford, Eric Havelock, and Arthur W. H. Adkins, who understand Plato much more as an enemy of the sophists than as an enemy of the poets.[1] He thus suggests that the poets (the theologians of pagan antiquity) and the philosophers can (and should) make an alliance against the sophists (the liberals).

The theorists of liberalism tend to insist on the individual character of practical reasoning. Most often, they repudiate every authority and every tradition. The Church, inasmuch as it represents an authority and embodies a tradition, appears to them to be essentially irrational: hence the "theologico-political problem." By contrast, MacIntyre looks to show that individual judgment relates to collective reasoning, taken up in an authoritative tradition. Thus the Christian tradition does not fuel irrationality: as a tradition, it potentially offers a powerful contribution to practical rationality itself. At the most fundamental level, the theological and the political spheres prove to be less incompatible and more complementary. Once a Christian Marxist, now a Thomist, MacIntyre is not overly concerned with the tension between reason and revelation—even though he takes care to distinguish between the reason of the Enlightenment (in conflict with faith) and medieval philosophy (compatible with the faith). A former Barthian and an antiliberal, he is sensitive to the tension between the Church and the world. But in his eyes the theologico-political problem does not have the importance or the meaning that liberalism's founders ascribe to it.

Historically, the wars of religion called for a fourfold reaction: liberal individualism, the theory of state sovereignty, the cultural homogenization of the nation-state, and the abandonment of the Aristotelian theory of the mixed regime. Each time, the same goal was pursued and wisdom sacrificed to consent. Each time, it was a matter of circumventing the question of community and truth. MacIntyre, for his part, opposes the sovereignty of the individual with the individual's forms of belonging, and the sovereignty of the state with the existence of a kind of natural right and (up to a certain point) the rights of minorities. He criticizes national homogenization and takes up the theory of the mixed regime, by proposing to temper consent with wisdom.

I hope my reader will excuse a rather long quotation, but the lines below are all the more important as they open MacIntyre's first book, *Marxism: An Interpretation*, and thus they mark the general orientation of his works from 1953 onward.

> The division of human life into the sacred and the secular is one that comes naturally to Western thought. It is a division which at one and the same time bears the marks of its Christian origin and witnesses to the death of a properly religious culture. For when the sacred and the secular are divided, then religion becomes one more department of human life, one activity among others. This has in fact happened to bourgeois religion. From Monday to Friday one is occupied with earning one's living. On Saturday and Sunday one relaxes and, if one is so minded, fulfils any religious obligations. Politics, industry, art—this is the kind of list to which religion can be added. But religion as an activity divorced from other activities is without point. If religion is only a part of life, then religion has become optional. Only a religion which is a way of living in every sphere either deserves to or can hope to survive. For the task of religion is to help us see the secular as sacred, the world as under God. . . . Likewise if our religion is fundamentally irrelevant to our politics, then we are recognizing the political as a realm outside the reign of God. To divide the sacred from the secular is to recognize God's action only within the narrowest limits. A religion which recognizes such a division, as does our own, is one on the point of dying.[2]

The fear expressed in these lines is clearly that of the end of religion, threatened by liberal separations. What is properly religious is unceasingly further isolated, further restricted, and further eliminated. MacIntyre designates liberal individualism as the root of secularization.[3] It seems to him that, under the guise of taming the Church, the liberal tradition comes to make the Church disappear. His starting point is the threat society poses to faith. Yet the starting point of liberalism is exactly the opposite: the threat faith poses to civic peace. Liberalism responds less to the danger that society poses to faith than to the danger that religion poses to the city.[4] If the anguish of liberalism's founders is religious warfare, the young MacIntyre's anguish is secularization, the loss of the difference between good and evil. If the custom of decorating books with frontispieces remained, it would be a good bet that some scene of disagreement would illustrate *After Virtue, Whose Justice? Which Rationality?*, and *Three Rival Versions of Moral Enquiry*. Most of MacIntyre's works and a large part of his articles open with this theme.[5] Whereas liberals start with disagreement as a *fact*, MacIntyre starts with disagreement as a *problem*. Disagreement is the political form that philosophical skepticism takes. This skepticism, which numerous liberals take as basic, tends to appear to the believer as a difficulty, or even a defeat and an error. If individual reasoning is participation in collective reasoning, as MacIntyre maintains, then agreement on a custom or tradition proves to be indispensable to practical rationality.

We find here the questions raised in the book's first chapter. Whereas liberalism considers that forms of belonging threaten the individual, MacIntyre considers that the erasure of forms of belonging threatens the individual. Whereas liberalism protects the person from the state and from tyranny, MacIntyre recalls the importance of participating in something greater than oneself. The insistence on "community" is a reaction of believers against utilitarianism and emotivism as much as it is a reaction against the agnosticism of liberal democracy.[6] In MacIntyre's eyes, the same individualist danger threatens faith and practical reason. In neglecting his forms of belonging in certain rich traditions, the agent loses subtlety and finesse, and impoverishes his reasoning to the point of reducing it to brute emotion. In turning away from the sacred, the "individualist" believer ends up wrecking the substance of his faith, reducing it to some edifying principles, and becoming agnostic without even perceiving it. Both reason and faith pass through wisdom rather than calculation. Both reason and faith presuppose that man considers himself called to step outside of himself, to be concerned with something greater than himself. If liberalism starts from the conflict between faith and reason, between the sacred and the profane, and between religions themselves, MacIntyre starts from the common danger that individualism poses to the believer and to the citizen: the enclosure in a self reduced to almost nothing and the loss of the sense of the sacred, the meaning of good and evil. From the 1950s onward, MacIntyre's restlessness is located in two spheres: one profane, the other sacred. In the profane sphere, it is the progress of "the consumer society" that has led him to analyze the emptiness of a society reduced to commerce and to ratify the description of society that the postmodern school proposed. In the sacred sphere, it is the process of "secularization" that has retained his attention. Since liberalism domesticated the Christian faith too well, people no longer set goals for themselves.

If MacIntyre relativizes the importance of the theologico-political problem, it is to develop and privilege the interrelatedness of Augustine's two cities.[7] In *The City of God*, Augustine answers certain accusations. Christianity is not responsible for Rome's decline, for it combats the vice and corruption that are the real sources of decline. In his eyes, the city of God refers to the perfect city of Plato, except that Plato held his city to be practically nonexistent, and Augustine shows it realized, or on the way to realization. The Church is the divine instrument that leads civil society to virtue and that ensures the fulfillment of pagan philosophy. Augustine contrasts the city of men to the city of God, but he also shows how closely the two cities are associated: how some of the virtues that the city of men encourages can also help build the city of God, and how the virtues that grow within the city of God improve and strengthen the city of men. MacIntyre follows in Augustine's footsteps. Against liberalism, which proposes to escape discomfort, anarchy, and tyranny, he counters with the perfection of the soul. He counters the flight from evil with the search for the good.

An activist for the first New Left and a Christian Marxist in the 1950s, by the end of the twentieth century MacIntyre is nostalgic for medieval and neo-Thomist communities. In his intellectual journey, MacIntyre thus replicates a classic schema from the early twentieth century, except in reverse. The same body of doctrine can be reached from opposite directions. Reactionary slavophilia matures into revolutionary Leninism; Guild Socialism matures into the New Left; and the kind of Christianity most hostile to change matures into the communist mystique.[8] Revolutionaries often reversed the politics of their reactionary progenitors, while preserving their hatred of the bourgeois, of liberalism, or of the West, and their refusal to accept and adapt to the present. Sometimes chronological turning points sketch intellectual boundaries. Very often, the reactionaries of 1910 were the forefathers of the revolutionaries of 1945. The condemnation of liberalism by the *Syllabus* of 1864 paradoxically favored Marxism. Before Marx, Maurras was considered the champion of the "Christian recovery."[9] The "red" Dominicans of the 1950s and 1960s had as their masters the Royalist and reactionary Dominicans from the early twentieth century. The worker priests were raised in the school of *Action française.* The postwar Christian Marxists were grateful to the communists for their hostility to representative democracy. Had they not, as good monarchists, learned to hate it? Rome's condemnation of the worker priests in 1953 answers its condemnation of *Action française* in 1926. In France, Christian Marxism is, if not the spiritual son, then at least the prodigal son of neo-Thomism. Here I shall only note the name of Maurice Montuclard, who between 1942 and 1945 shaped the journal *Jeunesse de l'Église.* While the first volumes echoed Maritain, the last came to consider Marxism the "immanent philosophy" of the working-class world.[10] Christian Marxists sought to baptize Marx, just as St. Thomas had in his time baptized Aristotle. Thus those nostalgic for medieval guilds became partisans of the New Left, and the Thomists of *Action française* became Christian Marxists.

MacIntyre, for his part, takes up this path in reverse, undoing between 1950 and 2000 the work completed between 1900 and 1950. To be sure, British Dominicans did not share all the political passions of their Continental brothers. But we should note one exception, one who happens to have played an important role: the Dominican Herbert McCabe. Like MacIntyre, McCabe was at the University of Manchester in the early 1950s. McCabe had long been one of the dominant figures in *Slant,* a journal of the Catholic left. Both Marxist and Thomist, he effects MacIntyre's transition from Marxist to Thomist. It was notably under McCabe's influence that the fifty-four-year-old MacIntyre, after spending a year at Oxford delivering the Carlyle Lectures, converted to Catholicism in 1983 and reconsidered the objections with which he had countered Thomas Aquinas in *After Virtue.*[11]

The sources of Christian Marxism lie in the conviction that "the modern worker, in order to enter into a Christian sphere of life, is not so much stopped by the spiritual leap from unbelief to faith, as by the sociological disorientation to which the average lifestyle of pious Christians calls him." The author of these lines, Emmanuel Mounier, edited the journal *Esprit*, which effects a political turnaround at the end of the Second World War, not unlike that of the Dominicans.[12] Following 1945, the Church seemed ill. Is this not the same argumentation that links the Church to a peasant sociology, a reactionary politics, and an Aristotelian philosophy? Is that not what Louis Althusser, then still a Catholic, wrote at the time, in the journal Montuclard edited?[13] Mounier borrowed his conclusions from the little book by Frs. Henri Godin and Yvan Daniel, *La France, pays de mission?* (1943); the Paris Mission, which was at the heart of the worker priest movement, wanted a response to their book. The fashion for the expression "France, mission country," generally attributed to Fr. Godin, in fact dates back to the 1890s.

The same fear of de-Christianization is found in the origins of the Thomism of *Action française*, Christian Marxism, and MacIntyre's approach. The starting point of the Thomism of *Action française*, Christian Marxism, and a fortiori MacIntyre, is the threat that society poses to faith.

What is a "community"? MacIntyre merely says: neither an empire nor a nation. But that is not enough. Is it a tribe, a mafia, a *polis*, a chosen people, or a church? This "community" does not seem to correspond to any *political* form. Properly understood, the communitarian school's reflections could have as their object *the community of believers*—Israel or the Church—insofar as it is not actually confused with humanity, in the abstract sense of the term. Taylor and MacIntyre are Catholics.[14] Michael Walzer is Jewish—as is Michael Sandel, Rawls's most systematic critic. Contrary to what most communitarians suggest, the debate over communitarianism in fact bears on the theological-political problem. Whereas only yesterday liberals defined themselves in relation to the great democratic revolutions of 1789, 1793, 1848, and 1917, today's liberals increasingly tend to focus on the wars of religion. "Multiculturalism" takes liberalism back to these origins. Incidentally, the contemporary problem is not really that of "multiculturalism," because one does not really fight or die for one's "culture": a "culture" is not properly speaking an authority. One dies as a hero for one's country, one dies as a martyr for one's faith. Cultural differences, which are readily exalted today in the name of "identity," are of very limited interest. "Culture" is a residual phenomenon, what remains of patriotism when the law has disappeared. "Culture" will not do: because if all differences are recognized to be on an equal footing, then those differences are emptied of their content. They become flat, banal, and trivial.

It is noteworthy that none of the principal communitarians who are usually likened to MacIntyre belong to a religion that is the political majority in their country. Neither in Britain, Canada, nor the United States could Catholicism and Judaism claim that status. It is significant that it was an American theologian who was one of the most influential supporters for religious freedom at Vatican II.[15] The contemporary renewal of the Church relies on her awareness of forming a counter-society within society itself.[16] Communitarians belong to religious minorities. As such, they take a certain cultural and religious pluralism for granted—at least from a human point of view. They start from the absence of consensus in liberal regimes, the absence of a recognized authority in moral and religious matters, and the necessity to deal with this absence in other ways than through individualism, relativism, and skepticism.

Why did MacIntyre leave Europe in 1969? Why did he need to immigrate into the United States, into the most liberal of the commercial republics? Beyond the Atlantic, MacIntyre discovered the possibility *of not being of his time*. European homogenization entails an imperious demand for presentism. Yet, in its origins, America was intended precisely as a land where different temporalities could coexist without melting together. MacIntyre can only align himself with "the liberty of the Ancients" against "the liberty of the Moderns" by refusing to share in the obsession about anachronism that is Benjamin Constant's theme, in a vein of thinking specific to the old continent. He finds asylum in North America. For there, one can profit from the liberal separation of the state and civil society to critique liberalism, and one seems to be able to deepen the demands of faith without fear of restarting wars of religion. MacIntyre found a nation where the theological-political problem had received an apparently satisfactory response. His theory of the primacy of traditions presupposes liberalism's success: it comes *after* liberalism.

Following the Pilgrim Fathers, MacIntyre found in the United States the possibility of escaping the European demand for homogeneity, a land of faith rather than a land of civic-mindedness. His criticism of the Act of

Union of 1707 refers to the malaise that he feels before the spectacle of uniformity in European nation-states. MacIntyre can only align himself to a St. Benedict and St. Thomas—who in his bizarre logic are *subversive*—because he inserts himself into the American political tradition.[17] A good illustration of this is the admiration he bears for Andrew Lytle and Wendell Berry. They are poets and farmers, Christians and proud of it. "Rooted" in Tennessee and Kentucky, respectively, they define themselves as "agrarian traditionalists."[18] MacIntyre's America is the same as that which gave asylum to the Puritans of the seventeenth century: the territory not ruled by the treaty of Westphalia.

Here we touch at the heart of the question of minority rights, or of communitarianism. To foreground these rights is to presuppose that the nation-state, the theory of sovereignty, and cultural homogenization have no objective. It is therefore to say that the problem of religious war, civil war, and war between nonstate communities does not arise.

MacIntyre's America is the America founded by the Puritans, who from their arrival formed self-governing, self-disciplined religious communities, thus combining the democratic dimension (self-government) and the religious dimension.[19] For this reason, it is America that has never needed to consider that democracy must become secular or anti-Christian in order to be established. Unlike Europe, America remains Christian and practical. North America could be MacIntyre's political *Nunc dimittis*. We do not stand to gain if we understand the allusion to St. Benedict, which concludes *After Virtue*, as referring either to Joachim de Flore, who dreamt of a harmonious city and an "age of the Spirit," or as referring to Nietzsche, who often dreamt of a new Port-Royal-des-Champs, for which he would have been St. Cyran. We should understand the allusion to St. Benedict as referring to the Puritans, who founded the United States. There is room for a geography of ideas alongside intellectual history. Is it a coincidence that MacIntyre immigrated to the United States and Taylor returned to Canada? In North America, they found nations where the theological-political problem received a satisfactory enough answer to dispense them from further thought.

MacIntyre's works respond to this new situation, to the existence of antimodern communities within the most modern country. Does not liberalism, in its American version, ensure the durability of traditional forms of sociability, the permanence of particularisms within the most universalist nation? Since "separation" is only possible in the most liberal regimes, it is in the country organized around the thought that is least compatible with his own that MacIntyre seems to have found a form of inner peace. His St. Benedict is not so much the patron saint of Europe as the spokesman for antiliberal religious communities within the very heart of a liberal state. MacIntyre demands a renewal of community life with even more eloquence because he seems to be able to count on the achievements of liberalism. That is why he finally rallied, as if in spite of himself, to liberal democracy. His reflections bear less on liberalism as an art of ensuring coexistence than on contemporary liberalism's moral and spiritual consequences. He comes to sacrifice the political community to a community of believers that is not and cannot be its substitute.

Does MacIntyre really think of man as a *zōon politikon*? His theory of *internal* goods, which is to say goods that we cannot really compare, seems to appeal to an architectonic theory of politics. This theory understands the political art as the art of comparing these goods, of articulating how one relates to another, and of establishing which goods are equivalent in spite of their heterogeneity. But while Aristotle follows this route and considers politics as the architectonic framework within which ends are ordered, MacIntyre leaves only a limited role for civic life. Internal goods are understood in terms of ethics rather than politics. MacIntyre remains indifferent to the neo-Aristotelianism of German origin, which, in particular with Hannah Arendt, Eric Voegelin, and Leo Strauss, looks to the Stagirite's political thought. MacIntyre draws his inspiration from the neo-Aristotelianism of analytical philosophers such as Elizabeth Anscombe, who are mainly interested in the philosophy of action.

Aristotle makes mores depend on the law: the change of regime or political form is a radical change, which leaves almost nothing as it is. MacIntyre insists that the liberal political system remains dependent on preliberal provisions. It presupposes the mores that it progressively destroys. For him, therefore, political *form* does not absolutely supersede political *matter*. His definition of man as a "dependent" animal invokes less of Aristotle's "political" animal, and more of Thomas Aquinas's "social" animal. It represents the Christian diminishment of the city of men, and the universalism of the city of God. MacIntyre aligns himself with a tradition that has never placed politics at its center. I will not ask here whether this tradition is true, which is quite possible. I shall merely remark that this tradition insufficiently confronts the questions that the founders of liberalism raised.

Communitarians appeal all the more readily to the community of believers when they know it is weakened. From this point of view, their thinking is linked to a specific context. Outside this context, their remarks would be either obvious or an absurd call to restart wars of religion. Politically, their remarks have a limited bearing. Communitarians can only allow themselves to ignore the theological-political problem by taking the results of liberal democracy for granted. Politically, their considerations are important only for societies that have lost all sense of truth and need to rediscover it. Their considerations are not for societies threatened by fanatics too convinced of their rectitude—these fanatics should be reminded of the importance of civil peace.

It is important here to contrast two generations of philosophers: those born around 1900 and those born between 1925 and 1935. Inasmuch as Raymond Aron, Karl Popper, Arendt, and Berlin pondered the Cold War and the *political* criticisms of liberalism, so Foucault, Derrida, Bernard Williams, Deleuze, Jean Baudrillard, Walzer, Taylor, and MacIntyre neglected the problem that the division of the world into two antagonistic parties raised. For this second generation, the pressing enigma was not so much the conflict between East and West as the spectacle of the consumer society within the very heart of the Western camp. Politics is here but a relatively secondary preoccupation. Foucault's work is typical in this respect. His analyses of "micro-powers" and his studies of asylum and prison reveal forms of oppression more subtle and perverse than those that Marx denounced. His work, in this sense, responds to the feeling that behind the appearances of liberal freedom and of class reconciliation under the aegis of the welfare state, a more radical alienation is at work. Foucault's or MacIntyre's antiliberalisms are rooted in a virulent reaction to the climate of their youth and to the questions raised by the critique of Stalinism. This leads them to argue that "for modern thought, there is no possible morality."[20]

As a young man, MacIntyre wanted to be both a Marxist and a Christian. "If the Christian hope is to be realized in history," he wrote in 1953, "it must assume the form of a political hope. . . . Marxism is in essence a complete realization of Christian eschatology."[21] Marxism is a kind of political maximalism, and Christianity a kind of ethical maximalism. Christianity has its highest ambition for the person, at the same time as it has a tendency to subordinate civic life. Marxism, by contrast, nourishes the highest hopes on the subject of society, but has hardly any esteem for the individual. With Christian Marxism, which adds the utopianism of the city of God to that of the city of men, MacIntyre adopts the utopia par excellence: more impatient than Christianity, more perfectionist than Marxism.

The Marxist critique of the category of politics can be read in two ways—one revolutionary, the other abstentionist. As a Marxist and Christian, MacIntyre had combined two expectations; having become an Aristotelian and Thomist, he comes to combine two kinds of contempt. Behind his "subversive Thomism," his "St. Benedict and Trotsky," it would hardly be difficult to discern the now-somewhat-rusty sign of Christian Marxism, if MacIntyre had not shifted his emphasis. As he came to despair of the Enlightenment, "politics" seems to have disappeared from his horizon. If we no longer believe in the revolutionary ideal, abandoning politics may be the only way to remain in some manner faithful to that ideal. By abstaining from participation in political life, MacIntyre paradoxically remains faithful to Marx's teaching, even though it is a Marx who has suddenly become pessimistic. In MacIntyre, we find a "politics" and a "philosophy"; I am not sure that we find a "political philosophy."

The European nation-state looks to combine cultural community and political unity, to build a community in which human beings can fulfill their own humanity. Why does MacIntyre have hardly any sympathy for the nation-state? He has inherited from Marxism a certain contempt for the category of the political, in the sense that he is indifferent to the *political* project of the nation-state. But while Marx reduced politics to economics, MacIntyre tends to reduce politics to religion.

Although MacIntyre is an Aristotelian, he hardly makes any reference to Aristotle's *Politics*, to the dialectic of democracy and aristocracy. Far from relating wealth, magnanimity, and virtue together, as Aristotle does, MacIntyre suggests that virtue refers not so much to aristocracy as to humility and democracy. Even though Aristotle never professes any particular esteem for craftsmen, even though Socrates speaks less *to* craftsmen than *about* craftsmen, MacIntyre, who claims to be an Aristotelian, tends to give the place of honor to craftsmen.[22] He rediscovers the Christian admiration for "simple people" and the democratic taste for work in contrast to the aristocratic taste for leisure. "The peculiar excellences of the exercise of craft skill and manual labor are invisible from the standpoint of Aristotle's catalogue of the virtues," he writes melancholically.[23] He writes his books in a style that he claims is pleasant, to the end of popularizing philosophy. This is true of *After Virtue*, but even more so of *Against the Self-Images of the Age*, which deliberately mixes highly technical articles with articles destined for a wider audience. When asked about his audience, he replies:

> I hope to be listened to exclusively by those whose activities are considered marginal by those who occupy the dominant positions in today's societies. Small farmers, fishermen, teachers who refuse to become bureaucratic civil servants; all those who preserve, in manual work as in intellectual work, the ideal of the craftsmen: members of cooperatives dedicated to the relief of hunger or lack of housing: they are the ideal public readership for my works. I should add a few small businessmen, some professors, and a certain type of doctor. By contrast, one could hope, and I hope, that the majority of lawyers, bureaucrats, business school professors, and the ambitious, the powerful, and the rich in general, will not read me.[24]

Here we find what is at the heart of the alliance between Christianity and Marxism: the opposition between on the one side "small" farmers, "small" traders, and on the other side those who occupy the "dominant" positions—the ambitious, the powerful, the rich. The use of the adjective "small" echoes the societies and economies of "small" size that alone find favor in the eyes of the author of *After Virtue*. MacIntyre hardly feels the philosopher's contempt for the *vulgum pecus*. Under the influence of Christianity, Aristotelianism underwent a transformation, for the Greeks did not regard humility as a virtue. From a Christian point of view, the individual autonomy of the "magnanimous man," to which Aristotle gives an important place in *Nicomachean Ethics*, bears a strong resemblance to pride. Refusing to bring nature and grace into conflict with each other, MacIntyre refuses to bring the self-sufficiency of nature and the virtue of humility into conflict with each other. When he evoked Aristotle's magnanimity in the early 1960s, it was as "this appalling picture of the crown of virtuous life," and the concern to give humility its due distanced him from Aristotle.[25] Thirty years later, in *Dependent Rational Animals*, he develops an analysis that follows in the footsteps of St. Thomas rather than the Stagirite. Nature does not so much call for a proud autonomy with respect to the gods or to others as it calls for a sense of solidarity and our deep *dependence* on others, which MacIntyre analyzes in detail. Yet "plain persons" (in MacIntyre's vocabulary) have a better sense of their dependence on nature and on grace. The soft pillow of luxury does not isolate them, nor do they live with the illusion of their autonomy, in the element of pride and abstraction. MacIntyre retains a sympathy for democracy that owes more to Marxist Christianity than to Aristotle's political reflection.

MacIntyre comes to rely on community and tradition as illusory substitutes for political life. But this "community" does not seem to correspond to any *political* form. Yet concern for the soul or the Church does not justify neglecting the demands of the city. MacIntyre's thought offers a typical illustration of the theological critiques of liberalism. They are profound critiques, often justified, but they do not sweep liberalism itself away as far as they tend to believe. A community of believers can be recognized as specific and having rights of its own, but only to a limited extent, so that the liberal background is not challenged and different communities can peacefully coexist.

MacIntyre makes himself the spokesman for communities that, discharged of the burden of politics and war, could finally circumvent modern political philosophy (by presupposing it). The combat between liberalism and communitarianism is unequal. For it is liberalism that provides the active principles for our development, and communitarianism is doomed to *react* against it. The struggle between liberalism and communitarianism is only the expression of the process originally induced by the liberal political formula.

II. The Absence of Liberal Spirituality

MacIntyre's critique of modern moral philosophy and his defense of Aristotelian morality rely on the socialist and Christian idea of humanity's corruption through commerce. At the end of *After Virtue*, MacIntyre calls for "a new St. Benedict." We can interpret this call by reference to the fact that the asceticism and work of medieval monks contributed to their own enrichment, which gradually moved them away from their initial poverty. This made successive reforms necessary, the most important of which was undoubtedly the Cistercian reform. In an analogous process, Protestant asceticism incited capitalism. But without the equivalent of the Cistercian reform to correct it, the success of the Puritan ethic comes to destroy the faith from which it was originally inseparable. Benjamin Franklin's generation bequeathed to the following ones a good conscience for enriching themselves. It is in the light of these considerations that one must understand on the one hand MacIntyre's lack of sympathy for Franklin[26] and on the other the appeal that concludes *After Virtue*. There is no doubt that the apostle he longs for is called to repeat the work of St. Bernard, so that the spirit of accumulation does not take precedence over faith.

According to MacIntyre, Europeans lost all widespread agreement on the way to live together, then refused the authority of the Church. "It is not the case that men stopped believing in God, and in the authority of the Church, and then subsequently started behaving differently": it is the opposite that is true.[27] The change in moral dispositions is chronologically prior to the loss of belief.

In the 1960s, MacIntyre gives an account of secularization by means of the history of moral philosophy. He criticizes the view that "moral capital" had been accumulated in times more religious than ours.[28] He implicitly takes up and develops Weber's thesis. "Religion must necessarily produce both industry and frugality, and these cannot but produce riches. But as riches increase, so will pride, anger, and love of the world. . . . So, although the form of religion remains, the spirit is swiftly vanishing away."[29] Protestantism favored the expansion of capitalism, which ended up destroying religion. Victorious capitalism no longer needs the support of the forces that created it. Weber writes that capitalism "no longer needs the support of any religious forces, and feels the attempts of religion to influence economic life, in so far as they can still be felt at all, to be as much an unjustified interference as its regulation by the State. In such circumstances men's commercial and social interests do tend to determine their opinions and attitudes. . . . These are phenomena of a time in which modern capitalism has become dominant and has become emancipated from its old supports."[30] In order to combine two theses that he holds close to his heart, the rootedness of practical reason in life forms and the impoverishment of freedom under the influence of individualism, MacIntyre looks to compose and tell stories. I would briefly like to repeat one of them, taken from *After Virtue*.

"Does moral philosophy rest on a mistake?" asks one British philosopher, H. A. Prichard, in a 1912 article bearing that title.[31] Some philosophers, he writes, insist on the intrinsic value of right action. Others emphasize its beneficial effects. But in one way or another, everyone has assigned himself the task of justifying duties. Yet this task is meaningless, for it omits the sui generis character of obligation. The word "ought" refers to actions and actions alone. The duty is immediate, not derived; it is characterized by a form of obviousness that is incompatible with the search for proofs or foundations. In acting by duty, we act without motive. Argumentation proves to be superfluous and even inappropriate.

How do we explain the stunning influence of these ideas in British analytical philosophy? MacIntyre advances a mischievous hypothesis. The "ought" that Prichard analyzes is a "taboo," the taboo being a reason for acting or abstaining from action whose origins are no longer understood.[32]

In the journal of his third voyage, from 1778 to 1779, Captain James Cook records his discovery of the word "taboo." The English seamen are surprised to discover that the Polynesian women, with lax sexual habits, could not dine with the men. When questioned about the reasons for this prohibition, the Polynesians answered that this practice was taboo. No other response could be obtained. "Taboo" did not only mean "prohibited" but manifestly constituted a reason for prohibition, although a reason could not be specified. Ethnologists suspected that the Polynesians themselves no longer understood the motivations for prohibition. Undoubtedly in the past the prohibition had some serious raison d'être. But the disappearance of a social setting and cosmological background gradually deprived it of all foundation and rendered it unintelligible, thus conferring the word "taboo" with the odor of arbitrariness that remains to this day. The injunction or prohibition remains in force, but the roots are dead, and the trunk's base is beginning to rot. By "taboo," we therefore designate those rules that subsist but whose meaning is lost. Their purpose is obscured without yet bearing any harm to their prestige.

"Ought" suggests a *reason* for acting or abstaining from action, but without that reason being specified. When questioned on the motives of moral action, a student of Prichard must answer that it is "because it is my duty," without being able to add anything else. Captain Cook remarks that the word has a "mysterious significance." Similarly, MacIntyre notes that the "ought" in question makes one think of "a kind of nervous cough with which we accompany what we hope will be the more impressive of our injunctions."[33] The force of conviction of the analysis offered in the article "Does Moral Philosophy Rest on a Mistake?" holds not so much for its argumentative value as for the accuracy of the sociological and psychological intuition behind it. It reveals a rare impoverishment of existence, the disappearance of the tradition of enquiry, within whose framework duty could be the object of true justification. "But is this view of man true? Or is it a view—true to some extent at least of liberal, individualist men—made true indeed by their believing it to be true?"[34] Prichard's discovery does not bear on the atemporal meaning of the concept of obligation but on its *use* in Edwardian England. It is philosophically doubtful but empirically correct. By depriving duty of any basis *in law*, his analysis attests to the disappearance of any basis in fact.[35]

In 1819, Kamehameha II abolished the taboos in Hawaii, without encountering any resistance. "Why should we not think of Nietzsche as the Kamehameha II of the European tradition?" MacIntyre asks, echoing the voyages of Cook.[36] Nietzsche denounces the toxic character of the "dragon of Thou Shalt." MacIntyre ratifies the Nietzschean description: (German) nihilism, (British) emotivism, and (French) existentialism and neo-Nietzschean postmodernism analyze what liberal society has *become*. The catastrophic narrative that opens *After Virtue* is itself a commentary on the book's title: in the West, we live *After Virtue*, surrounded by "last men," as Nietzsche would say. We have become individuals withdrawn into ourselves, entirely preoccupied with our personal interests, acting according to our private fantasies, disposing of our little pleasures for the day and our little pleasures for the night.

Here I open a brief parenthesis about the novel. Unlike nineteenth-century European literature, which depicts the rise of the bourgeoisie and the decline of the aristocracy, twentieth-century literature by contrast seems to bear on the most asocial individuals and the most extreme cases.

Human relations take a back seat, if they do not purely and simply disappear. The social animal of nineteenth-century literature is replaced by an ontologically solitary being, a monad without windows. Man is henceforth described as a detached subject, isolated from every tradition, incapable of relating to another, and who only incidentally communicates. Marcel Proust, Louis-Ferdinand Céline, the *nouveau roman*, and the Theatre of the Absurd expose the imposture of human relationships, the inanity of love, and the falsity of language. Among the Marxists, this evolution incited two types of reaction. György Lukács denounced this literature for what appeared to him as its degenerate formalism, psychopathologizing aestheticism, patent anarchism, and perverted Rousseauism. He felt nostalgic for Honoré de Balzac, whose analyses are more easily akin to those of Marx. Others discover in this literature less the delirium of decadent avant-gardes than the reflection of a real malaise. Art does not reproduce social reality in an immediate, direct, and mechanical way. As Theodor Adorno writes, "The absurdity of reality forces us to a form that shatters the realistic façade."[37] MacIntyre's position is closer to Adorno than to Lukács.[38] Not content to criticize Lukács, he often refers to this literature as the best testimony of contemporary reality.[39] Liberal empiricism seems to him to have destroyed any dramatic setting, any belief that one could be the character of a vast history with its clashes and twists, its peaks and troughs.[40] "The modern world," he writes, "was a culture of theories rather than stories."[41] The loosening of the human bond and the sense of unfitness for action, described in modernist literature, are some of his favorite foils.

In the early 1960s, MacIntyre entitled his course at the University of Oxford "What *Was* Morality?" After a long period of gestation, the twentieth century saw the triumph of emotivism, existentialism, and postmodernism. These constitute the almost natural completion of a theory of freedom reduced to individualism or the absence of coercion. When the forms of excellence embodied in traditions are disregarded, reason is impoverished and reduced to emotion. Thus MacIntyre reckons that we live "after virtue."[42] He insists on the fact that emotivism has been *realized*, so to speak. MacIntyre gradually shifts the terrain from philosophical grammar to sociology. Philosophers reproach him for being too much of a sociologist, and sociologists reproach him for being too much of a philosopher.

For the concept of an "internal good" oscillates between a conceptual determination and a social and historical determination.[43]

Like some reactionaries before him, and like the theorists of postmodernism, MacIntyre merely takes atomism's modern supporters at their word. They are the very ones who emphasize radical novelty by emphatically distinguishing themselves from the "ancients" and by replacing virtue with commerce and liberty. In taking up the Marxist critique of Hegel for himself, MacIntyre rediscovers an atomistic description of the human world that bears a curious resemblance to that of some liberal philosophers, except that he does not approve of individualism, but deplores it. "The only theory that is necessary to [this] communitarian critique of liberalism is liberalism itself."[44] To demonstrate liberalism's intrinsic perversity, MacIntyre reckons that it is sufficient to show liberalism at work, inspecting it in the reality of contemporary history: in short, to take it at its word. On this stage, liberalism finally speaks its true language, whether it is individualistic, utilitarian, or emotivist. Liberalism's confirmation bears its own condemnation.

Here we find again the theme that I explored in this book's second chapter. Positivism in principle separates the right from the good. But it in fact presupposes a particular moral philosophy, an individualist, noncognitivist moral philosophy. Conflicting with any conception of authority in morality, it is emotivism, existentialism, and nihilism. As positivism imposes itself, this morality, which MacIntyre denounces as the negation of all morality, imposes itself with it. By disregarding the perspective of the good embedded in stories and traditions, the *individual* loses the very foundation of practical rationality. For MacIntyre, practical reason depends on a substantial context. If we consider ourselves as autonomous individuals, independent from every tradition of enquiry, we lose the foundation of practical rationality. The power of moral life is fatally weakened.

Charles Taylor, whom I have often likened to MacIntyre, is nevertheless markedly more individualist than him. Whereas MacIntyre remains very distrustful toward the moral resources of the individual and is concerned to insist on *the resources of traditions*, Taylor explores the many resources of subjectivity and happily expands on *the sources of the self*. Following the intellectual lineage that goes from Montaigne to Constant and that triumphs in the German idea of *Bildung* and then in John Stuart

Mill, Taylor elaborates an ethic of authenticity, which puts to good use the autonomy that the modern individual enjoys.[45] The latitude that each disposes of in the liberal regime renders a type of sincerity or self-knowledge possible, which for their part antiliberal regimes do not encourage. As social pressure diminishes, man can show himself as he is and deepen his particularity or his vocation, discovering what in himself is unique and incomparable. By working on himself, the individual can bring to bear dispositions which are his own and which have never existed in this form. Taylor identifies in particular with the moral tradition that, starting with Francis Hutcheson, criticizes the reduction of morality to calculation and insists on the "moral sense," the "inner voice" with which people are allegedly endowed. Taylor develops this element, which he calls "expressivist" and which he strives to reconcile with the holistic dimension of the cultures to which we belong.

While Taylor shows that individualism brings its own forms of excellence and that authenticity relates freedom to truth, MacIntyre considers that we live in a regime that is ruinous to all moral life, a regime that has neglected "virtue." He casts an unfriendly glance toward Hutcheson's intuitionism. MacIntyre's and Taylor's disagreement bears on an essential question: Is the ethic of authenticity a life raft or an "emotivist" irrationalism? Is it an invitation to wallow in relativism and mediocrity, as MacIntyre insists, or an invitation to know oneself, as Taylor insists? Communitarians, such as Taylor, start less from an analysis of the community, to come to the individual, than they start from personal identity, to conclude that there is a need for community. Taylor begins by analyzing the richness of the soul, the "resources of the self," to affirm that we cannot isolate them in a narrow and inconvenient box, the private sphere. The individual needs to be recognized in his particularity; he needs to give a social texture to the use he makes of his freedom. MacIntyre's approach is the opposite. He starts not from the richness of the soul, the "resources of the self," but from their impoverishment in the absence of a community that could give them life. MacIntyre's own movement consists in starting from the misery of a self separated from every tradition.

While Taylor aligns himself with an ethic of authenticity that grants a large place to subjectivity, MacIntyre insists on the objective dimension of moral life and defends an ethic of virtue. While Taylor grants a trust in personal conscience that could border on Protestantism, MacIntyre follows in the footsteps of St. Benedict and Thomas Aquinas. We can summarize the heart of their disagreement by one question: *Is moral conscience an expression of subjectivity or of tradition?* MacIntyre insists on the collective character of the exercise of practical reason and, correlatively, on the central role of *authority* in morality. Taylor brings himself to qualify MacIntyre's remarks and to reconcile his own holism with moral individualism. This is why, contrary to MacIntyre, he does not use the term "natural law" (which is akin to the law of a *tradition*). We do not find in Taylor the concern to anchor reflection on positive freedom in metaphysical reflection or natural theology.[46] Taylor is in this respect more phenomenological, more Wittgensteinian, and more "antifoundationalist" than MacIntyre.

Inspired by Wittgenstein, Taylor insists on the social character of language, conceived as an internal good. As for MacIntyre, he analyzes the social nature of man less in relation to *language* than in relation to *traditions*. Knowledge and truth, he insists, are the fruit of cooperation within the framework of a tradition of enquiry. Freedom is nourished by the natural desire to live in society. Against liberalism, which seeks to maintain or obtain freedom through artifices and social or political constructs, MacIntyre contrasts a social life ordered to individual freedom, not only as a mere means but also as an end in itself. While Taylor aligns himself with multi*culturalism*, MacIntyre refuses to be associated with this movement and tends to only see "traditions" where Taylor sees "cultures" (which presuppose the separation of the state and civil society). Authenticity is an extension of "culture"; virtue is an extension of "tradition." "Culture" has the thickness of language and what language carries with it, whether poetry or literature. The disagreement between MacIntyre and Taylor here bears on the nature and status of language. While Taylor considers language to pertain to *poiēsis* or creation, MacIntyre considers language to pertain to *praxis*, action, and therefore to practical truth. For MacIntyre, language and culture do not have the "autonomy" that Taylor, following German Romanticism, ascribes to them. MacIntyre does not deny the existence of cultures, he does not see language as a mere tool, and he is concerned to show what is the essential relationship between language and thought. But language and therefore "culture" must be ordered to theology and philosophy. In privileging "cultures," Taylor incorporates a certain individualism that MacIntyre rejects. For these "cultures" are not mediated by authority: neither that of reason nor that of faith. Taylor identifies with the modern ideal of the "artist." MacIntyre contrasts this with the medieval ideal of the craftsman, which relegates individuality, the singularity of the artist, to the background.

To criticize utilitarianism, MacIntyre develops on the one hand a theory of the internal good and on the other hand a theory of the incommensurability of traditions of enquiry. These two theories join together. Both theories deny the existence of a measurement that enables comparison by reduction to a calculation of pleasures and pains. We cannot easily compare two internal goods in different practices, because they are precisely "internal." And by definition we cannot compare what is "incommensurable." These two criticisms of utilitarianism include a social dimension: internal goods are inseparable from "practices," and incommensurability refers to "forms of life." In Taylor, this social dimension is present, but he adds a more individualistic dimension to his critique of utilitarianism. If he develops an ethic of authenticity, it is to emphasize that each soul is unique, incomparable. In this respect, his critique is more existentialist than Aristotelian.

Taylor's work sometimes pertains to philosophy properly speaking, and sometimes to the history of ideas. As a philosopher, he is inspired by phenomenology, hermeneutics, and Wittgenstein to criticize scientism or positivism. As a historian, he highlights the existence of an "expressivist" tradition within modernity, of intellectual and moral resources that are not sufficiently used. Taylor distinguishes two traditions within the Enlightenment. One is reductionist, mechanistic, materialist, atomist, and positivist. The other, which goes back to Montesquieu, is respectful of the diversity of life forms, concerned with the purpose of human beings, and disposed to combine scientific progress with a certain sense of community. By imputing modernity's failures to the first of these two traditions, Taylor tends to exonerate the second. Taylor strives to distinguish between two types of liberalism. One yields to the myth of interiority—we can think of Bentham, or Rawls in *A Theory of Justice*. The other, a more sociological or anthropological sensibility, accommodates holistic demands—we can think of Montesquieu. Correlatively, Taylor distinguishes two tendencies within communitarianism itself. One, with which he identifies, denounces the abstract character of liberalism and opposes atomism to an ontology of the social compatible with the spirit of liberalism. This is linked to Montesquieu's tradition. MacIntyre illustrates the other, markedly more anti-modern. It counters individualism with a politics of rootedness, with "community" serving as the principle of both intelligibility and practical intention.[47] MacIntyre refuses to distinguish two heterogeneous traditions within the Enlightenment: he tends to blur liberalism, the Enlightenment, and "modernity."[48]

Taylor and MacIntyre both belong to the Catholic Church. But we should place their two standards of faith opposite each other: St. Benedict and Matteo Ricci, the Jesuit who evangelized China and whom Taylor made his hero in a conference on the relationship between Christianity and modernity.[49] While MacIntyre tends to want to reject liberal society, whose economic organization seems to him to be ruinous to the soul, Taylor carries out reinterpretive work. In his view, it is a question of finding *homo religiosus* not outside the century, but within the century itself. Ricci here symbolizes a gradual infusion of Christian theology within a pagan culture. While the Benedictine monastic community presupposes a rupture toward the city and putting in place essentially distinct forms of sociability, the evangelization of China illustrates the attempt par excellence for an inculturation of the Christian faith. While Taylor proposes to build bridges between Catholicism, Protestantism, and modernity, MacIntyre tempers the subjectivist trend of modern voluntarism with a call for the objectivity of the good and of tradition. While for the former, "modernity" develops certain Christian intuitions, for the latter, "modernity" ruptures the balance between individual will and the objective order: moral conscience is not so much the expression of subjectivity as it is the expression of a tradition, a judgment informed by knowledge. The former's ecclesiology is more liberal than the latter's. In *Sources of the Self,* Taylor starts from the Augustinian metaphysics of interiority; individualism begins with Christianity. In *Whose Justice? Which Rationality?* MacIntyre places the principal rupture in the late seventeenth century. Taylor makes Augustine his starting point, whereas MacIntyre places Augustine in the midst of a tradition that leads from Plato to Thomas Aquinas. In MacIntyre's view, it was not until the seventeenth century that voluntarism and subjectivism became radicalized to the point of losing any sense of the objective world. For Taylor, by contrast, the fundamental rupture is between Augustine and those who preceded him; since Augustine, there have been multiple course corrections, but no radical change in direction.

MacIntyre maintains that true morality presupposes education and discernment, which is to say, an authority and a community in which that authority can be exercised. In longing for a "new St. Benedict," MacIntyre no doubt thinks of the monastery as the place par excellence where passions are governed—the three vows of poverty, chastity, and obedience are intended to examine, select, and transform desires. MacIntyre's call for a renewal of monasticism owes perhaps as much to St. Benedict himself as to the contempt that Hobbes, Montesquieu, and Hume, the three progenitors of the morality of self-interest rightly understood, reserved for monkish virtues.[50]

Taylor is a communitarian. Within his liberal interpretation, he considers the separation of the private from the public to be against nature. Like Rousseau, he considers it to divide the soul and to be fundamentally hypocritical, since what is shown in private is hidden in public. He therefore advocates a "politics of recognition," which abolishes this tension by publicly recognizing individual particularities. He calls for an ethic of sincerity. MacIntyre is also sensitive to the artificial character of the separation of private and public, but he is not a communitarian. In his eyes, it is naïve to believe that a politics of recognition will be enough to put an end to hypocrisy. The separation of private and public must not be overcome by giving primacy to personal identity, but by giving primacy to the collective element, to shared traditions.

Whereas for Taylor, individual freedom should enable the emergence of new truths, MacIntyre considers that the individual as such cannot discover anything: truth only appears within the framework of the development of existing intellectual traditions. It follows that we cannot reconcile anthropological holism and moral individualism, for individualism is but an invitation to wallow in utilitarianism or emotionalism. Moral conscience is not so much an expression of subjectivity as that of a judgment informed by the knowledge of a tradition. While MacIntyre appeals to the logic of a commandment, Taylor appeals to the conscience of each individual in his particularity. While MacIntyre prefers to express himself in terms of practical rationality rather than freedom, as if freedom were ultimately only a means of placing the good at the disposal of the soul, Taylor prefers to express himself in terms of freedom rather than rationality. In his eyes, those who within the framework of liberal democracy are drawn to literature, art, and religion attain a kind of sincerity, an unprecedented purity, because they are no longer bound to a political regime, to any form of domination. MacIntyre is doubtful of this purity and sincerity, as he is unconvinced that we can so easily come to know ourselves. Their disagreement bears on the value of "autonomy." It is about the existence of what we commonly call (in the Anglo-American world) a perfectionist liberalism and what I call here a *liberal spirituality.*

Liberal democracy is often analyzed as a mere modus vivendi. For it succeeds in making citizens with divergent and apparently incompatible views and ends live within the same political framework. The liberal technique par excellence consists in circumventing disagreements. If citizens are divided, if they dispute about this or that subject or question, we come to consider the object of the dispute as "private"; it becomes a personal matter, a matter of individual choice. Thus religion is not a matter of state, but a matter for each individual, because this is the only way to avoid "the wars of religion." From this perspective, liberalism is not so much guided by an *ideal* of freedom, as it is guided by a theory of tolerance as the lesser evil. Many philosophers consider this analysis to be insufficient. They insist that individual autonomy is not a mere modus vivendi, but an ideal that enables citizens to reach the maturity to which they are called, to fulfill their humanity. These philosophers claim a "liberal spirituality." Taylor belongs to the individualist school that strives to describe and propose this spirituality; MacIntyre belongs to the anti-individualist school that denies its existence. Thus we find here the guiding thread of this intellectual biography: liberalism flees from evil; it does not propose to look for the good. Unlike Taylor, MacIntyre does not consider that this flight from evil in politics necessarily facilitates the *sincere* search for good in morality; above all, he does not give sincerity any specific place in the catalogue of virtues.

The insufficiency of secular spiritualities implies that we turn to a spirituality with less dubious credentials. There is no liberal spirituality, because we do not seek God as an individual but as a member of a community, and to the extent that one participates in the "tradition" that is based around that community. Moral conscience is less an expression of subjectivity than of tradition. The traditions with which MacIntyre aligns himself are not essentially theological. They are first and foremost philosophical traditions that relate a certain conception of justice to a certain moral philosophy. But this philosophy of tradition is inseparable from two types of considerations. First, supporters of a secularist approach to politics tend to base their separation of politics and religion on a separation of justice and morality; if the right is not entirely separable from the good, it is not certain that a reflection on justice can pass natural theology by. Second, to be philosophically acceptable, theology must grant an important place to the concept of tradition.

III. The Theology of the Tradition

In as much as she is "one, catholic, and apostolic," the Christian church is universal. All are called to belong to her, without distinction. The Enlightenment proposes to go further than Christianity, to outbid it. From the point of view of the Enlightenment's abstract universalism, the concrete universalism of the Church is too particular. Is not the Church attached to a revelation made in a specific place and time and, in her Roman version, to a specific tradition? Moreover, is she not rooted in the singularity of the Jewish people? Against the particularism of tradition and revelation, the Enlightenment counters with the universalism of reason. Every man as a man—which is to say, as endowed with reason—can be enlightened, without having to belong to a given community of believers that excludes other communities. Accustomed to struggling against particularisms and placed in an awkward position by this unexpected "competition," the Church has become divided. While some have held (and hold) to the classical or medieval interpretation of Christian universalism, others have proposed (and propose) to adapt the Church to the age of Enlightenment. These liberal Christians, who are often Protestant but also sometimes Catholic, relativize the criteria of belonging. They open the Church to the world and silence the rights of truth.

Liberal democracy proposes to make the most varied forms of life harmoniously coexist. From a religious point of view, however, this liberalism can give rise to grave suspicions. Islam, Judaism, and Christianity each respectively present themselves as the true religion, and not as one "culture" among others. By reinterpreting the Christian message, by softening its sharper aspects, liberalism could come to soften faith and deprive it of its substance. Tolerance, erected as the foundation of the political order, sometimes tends to relativize doctrines; but is not the *sacred* precisely that which resists all relativization? God is, by nature, the Absolute. In the 1950s, MacIntyre was inspired by Karl Barth, who defended this Absolute to denounce theological liberalism. The theorists of liberalism strive to put faith on the same level as "culture." Barth systematically reacted against these tendencies and reconstituted the walls of separation that had been gradually destroyed since the seventeenth century. He partitions, retraces the boundaries, and insulates reason from revelation in order to regain revelation's radicality. He presents reason and revelation as incommensurable, alien to each other, and he separates philosophy from theology to avoid subordinating the latter to the former and submitting divine intelligence to human intelligence. Theological concepts do not lend themselves to a philosophical explanation, since the Church is based on the Word of God alone, revealed in Jesus Christ. He insulates revelation in order to render it all its purity and preserve the radicality of the Gospels. Against the philosophical "cleansing" of dogmas that liberalism proposes, he counters with a theology that is completely separate from philosophy.

Before becoming interested in political philosophy, MacIntyre looked at the philosophy of religion. Since he was a disciple of the theologian Karl Barth, his first critique of liberalism's abstract universalism was a critique of theological liberalism. His first theory of the incommensurability of conceptual schemes is a theory of the incommensurability of reason and faith,[51] of a secular language and a religious language.[52] Following Friedrich Schleiermacher, liberal theologians such as Rudolf Bultmann, Dietrich Bonhoeffer, and Paul Tillich attempted to reconcile their faith with the presuppositions of modern political thought and to extract the universal dimension of faith from the ore of particularism. Following Karl Barth, MacIntyre compares them to Ludwig Feuerbach and goes so far as to accuse them of atheism:[53] "If I were God, I do not think that I would want to be studied by most contemporary theologians. This is not only because the general intellectual level of theological argument is perhaps lower than at any time since the tenth century. It is also because the peculiarly deep secularization of our pluralist culture offers traps to the theologians into which they continually fall. . . . If Pope Pius IX had genuinely understood what modern liberalism really is, he would have been quite right to condemn it."[54]

By wishing to adapt religion too much and by showing systematically that nothing serves man so much as serving God, we reduce the concern for the divine to the concern for the human, to the point of depriving the ultimate truth of all reality. Here, MacIntyre rediscovers the Wittgensteinian critique of reductionism. By wishing to replace a language bearing on God with a language oriented toward the needs of each person, we end up adopting categories of thought that, in no longer presupposing the existence of God, gradually make him a useless entity. In 1963, MacIntyre caused a scandal by denouncing the atheism of John Robinson, Anglican bishop of Woolwich. Robinson was a disciple of Bultmann and Tillich and author of the then-famous book *Honest to God.*[55] In order to make the faith more accessible, Robinson intended to make the language of theology explicit in a more ordinary language. But this concern for clarification, which leads him to *transpose* theological intuitions into philosophical intuitions, to *decode* the language of faith, and shortly thereafter to *reduce* revelation to reason, confers an air of redundancy upon the Word of God. According to MacIntyre, Robinson is so careless about these implications that, in the end, we no longer know whether or not he believes in God. The reinterpretation of Christian discourse makes it sometimes trivial and sometimes false. Subtle "demythologizations" of dogma culminate in platitudes that in spite of themselves adopt the values of their time. "The creed of the English is that there is no God and that it is wise to pray to him from time to time."[56]

In the first half of the 1950s, MacIntyre identified with Karl Barth's theology, and in particular with Barth's denunciation of natural theology and philosophy. He wrote that behind faith there is not an argument but the believer's determination. Barth separates theology and philosophy in order to preserve the former from the latter. The young MacIntyre's attitude was deeply Barthian. But from 1955 onwards, he relied on the philosophical restraint shown by analytical philosophers to sketch a rapprochement between reason and revelation.[57] He advocated a moderate use of philosophy and denied that we can entirely separate ordinary language from religious language.[58] Quite quickly, he dismissed in succession the orthodox Protestant Barthian view, which sometimes goes so far as to suggest that certain assertions in the Bible are unintelligible without special grace, and the liberal Protestant view, according to which religious language must be decoded to be made accessible to believers. His position came close to that of the Swiss theologian Emil Brunner, who had helped to introduce Barthism in Great Britain.[59] In a 1959 pamphlet, *Difficulties in Christian Belief*, MacIntyre emphasized philosophy's interest in faith, while nevertheless refuting the proofs for the existence of God. The language of revelation is not so peculiar that it refuses all philosophical analysis, but it does not follow that we should immoderately give ourselves over to natural theology.

Around 1960, MacIntyre lost his faith and turned away from theology, but without abandoning the problems that occupied him. In "Is Understanding Religion Compatible with Believing?" (1964), he pondered the meaning that words such as "God" or "grace" could assume, as they are found on the lips of skeptics or believers.[60] Compared to the 1950s, his way of dealing with the problem had changed direction, to reflect on the relationship between different cultures. The skeptic and the believer give different meanings to identical words. Their ways of seeing the world, their mores and their hopes, are not the same—as if they belong to different cultures. But if this is so, why not have recourse to what ethnology teaches about the relationship between cultures, in order to analyze what binds and separates the believer and the unbeliever? MacIntyre drew inspiration from the late Wittgenstein to criticize the superficial universalism of an ethnology that judges very different societies in light of one and the same rationality, that of the Enlightenment. This was the period of his debate with Winch.

Starting in the mid-1970s, while continuing to ponder the same questions, he changed his way of asking them by examining Thomas Kuhn's works. In the 1980s, he treated the problem from the angle of incommensurability and translatability. Beginning in the late 1980s, MacIntyre envisaged these questions anew, from a different angle. This time he examined the problem of the nature of truth. He strove to integrate a theory of truth as coherence with a theory of truth as adequation, in such a way as to take into account the irreducibility of conceptual sets, without renouncing one universal truth. The theory of truth as coherence harmonizes with the thesis of incommensurability, coherence being understood by reference to a given conceptual scheme. The theory of truth as adequation harmonizes with the thesis of universal commensurability, adequation being understood with reference to a unique, universally recognizable reality. In the eyes of the author of *Whose Justice? What Rationality?* Thomas Aquinas succeeds in balancing commensurability and incommensurability on the basis of a conception of truth as adequation.[61]

To speak about God, we use the words "good," "true," "beautiful," and "just"; but these words were conceived in a more human context. Can we use the same words to express ourselves about God and about the most ordinary realities? Can these concepts have the same meaning when applied to an infinite and perfect being and to finite and imperfect human beings? The doctrine of analogy, found in Thomas Aquinas, is one answer to this problem that MacIntyre began to pose in the analytical climate of the 1950s.[62] As the author of a synthesis between Augustine and Aristotle, Aquinas seems to prove by this his ability to relate two apparently incompatible traditions of enquiry. His thinking seems to give a place to both incommensurability and commensurability, for it integrates these traditions, but not without respecting their integrity. The Thomistic synthesis is not only a synthesis between traditions of enquiry; it is also, if not above all, a synthesis of philosophy and theology, which, in principle, respects the demands proper to each.

Karl Barth insulates theology from philosophy in order to preserve the integrity of revelation, to avoid lowering God to more flatly immanent realities. By insulating itself, by insisting on its specificity, and even on its absurd (Kierkegaard) or paradoxical (Barth) character, theology protects itself. But, according to MacIntyre, this invulnerability has a cost: senselessness.[63]

Defending religion as irrefutable is more fatal to it than any attack, insists the author of *After Virtue*. What does God's goodness mean, if this goodness in no way relates to what we otherwise understand as goodness? What meaning can we attribute to theological propositions if they pertain to a register so particular that their meaning has no link with the meaning we attribute to nontheological propositions? "Which God ought we to obey and why?" MacIntyre asks himself in an article bearing that title, an article where he takes to task the supporters of radical voluntarism. "They will not however be able to deny without inconsistency that it is on their view possible for their god to command what we—or some of us at least—now call unjust."[64]

MacIntyre is caught in a dilemma. Either practical reason is autonomous and human beings have little use for theology—this is Weber's best explanation of the story[65]—or moral life is a function of God's commandments and human beings have little use for practical reason—this is Karl Barth's basic thesis.[66] In the first case, there is no more *religious* morality, and in the second case, there is no more religious *morality*.[67] Faith seems either superfluous or unintelligible. As Pascal wrote: "If we submit everything to reason, our religion will have nothing of the mysterious and supernatural. If we upset the principles of reason, our religion will be absurd and ridiculous."[68]

MacIntyre did not cease to fight with this unpleasant alternative. In order to give God's transcendence its due, he first felt compelled to renounce all practical rationality, all reference to human needs. He could therefore only grant God his due by limiting human capacity, by renouncing practical reason, in order to root faith in natural desire. But, according to MacIntyre, Barth does not escape the dilemma that Plato articulated in the *Euthyphro*. By making it so that faith is not superfluous (as Robinson did), Barth makes it unintelligible. It is only with Thomas Aquinas that MacIntyre will escape these difficulties, through finding a theory of practical reason that recognizes its dependence on faith. Practical reason and grace must work together.

The young MacIntyre joins antiliberalisms together: Barthism in theology, Marxism in politics. In both cases, it is a question of denouncing the liberal interpretation of the relationship between practical reason and community. But how do we reconcile Marxism with the Barthian interpretation of Christianity? Above all, how do we reconcile the Barthian rejection of all philosophy with the conviction that the intelligibility of Christian revelation depends on a certain conception of reason—this conviction being presupposed by MacIntyre's thesis of secularization? While Barth insists on the irreducibility of the transcendent to the immanent, of revelation to reason, and of the Church to the world, Marxist Christianity emphasizes the complementarity of Christianity and the Enlightenment. The combination of Jesus and Marx leads back to Hegel, whereas the great Protestant theologian leads back to the Kierkegaardian critique of Hegel. It is only twenty years later, on a Thomistic basis, that MacIntyre attains a synthesis. Following the author of the *Summa contra Gentiles*, he reckons himself capable of giving nature as well as grace their due, the incarnate dimension of faith as well as its transcendent dimension. Whereas in 1981, in *After Virtue*, MacIntyre again affirmed the primacy of tragedy and gave the Kierkegaardian and Barthian *Either-Or* central importance, a few years later he came to deny the existence of irreducible moral dilemmas.[69]

In 1983, he converted to Catholicism, following the example of other British philosophers: in particular, Peter Geach, Elizabeth Anscombe, and Michael Dummett. Thomism is the doctrine that, at the end of his journey, authorizes him to hold together the two hitherto contradictory elements: on the one hand, Barth's zeal (which opposes reason to faith), and on the other, the neo-Hegelian rationalism of Marxist Christianity (which confuses reason and faith). "The truths about those precepts declared to us by God . . . are no other than the truths to which we have already assented as rational persons, or rather to which we would have assented, if we had not been frustrated in so doing by our own cultural, intellectual, and moral errors and deformations."[70]

MacIntyre discusses the question of the commensurability of conceptual schemas in various forms, which fall within Wittgenstein's legacy. In the 1950s, he countered Barth with an analytical philosophy that owed much to the author of *Philosophical Investigations*. Following that, he opposed the relativistic interpretation of Wittgenstein that Winch, William Van Orman Quine, and Donald Davidson offered. Winch defended a theory of incommensurability that echoed Barth's, condemning traditions to incomprehension. MacIntyre is then inspired by Geach and Anscombe, who embodied the Catholic wing of the Wittgensteinian school and strove to link the thought of the author of *Philosophical Investigations* with that of Thomas Aquinas. Starting from a radical position, that of the incommensurability of reason and revelation, MacIntyre strove to find a middle ground between commensurability and incommensurability. This was the case when he came close to Brunner or when, reaching the end of his journey, he defends a Thomistic position that looks to escape both the universalism of the Enlightenment and "postmodern" relativism, a position that looks to render faith neither superfluous nor unintelligible.

In looking to open the Christian church to the world and to make the faith intelligible, liberal theologians perhaps ended up making it superfluous. By wishing to save the Word of God from redundancy, by insulating theology from philosophy, Barth tended to make it unintelligible. With St. Thomas, MacIntyre reckons that he finds a way of articulating reason and faith that enables him to understand why the Church must remain attached to herself, at the same time as she must remain faithful to her universalism and apostolic dimension.

MacIntyre asks, "Which God ought we to obey and why?" It is a question of pondering God's attributes. God the Creator is also God the Legislator. God's *unity* enables us to reconcile the realist aspect and the voluntarist aspect of the good: God as the one who commands (the *law*) and God as the one who creates the nature from which intelligence begins (*natural* law). "The precepts of the natural law are those precepts promulgated by God through reason."[71] Nature is good: the fall has not completely corrupted it.

Remember that MacIntyre looks to escape the incommensurability between traditions by showing that the most accomplished tradition of enquiry must be capable of offering the most satisfactory interpretation of the strength and limitations of other traditions. This interpretation presupposes a certain kind of self-knowledge and wisdom, since the most satisfactory understanding is related to the most satisfactory way of living. Thus MacIntyre rediscovers the Aristotelian figure of the *spoudaios*, who *is* the moral standard. But is the recourse to the figure of the *spoudaios* sufficient to justify the kind of universalism that MacIntyre calls for? No doubt out of a desire to remain faithful to the antimetaphysical dimension of Wittgenstein's thought, Taylor refrains from going any further. As for MacIntyre, he does not hesitate to take the step. Natural justice is that which makes dialogue between traditions possible. Certainly, one cannot "exit" a tradition, for goods remain "internal," but the very possibility of comparison refers to a set of presuppositions common to all traditions, which are articulated in their own way. From the point of view of the Catholic tradition, the justification for this point calls for further development and a detour through natural theology. There can only be natural law if there is natural order, if the world is not chaos. We can speak of absolute rights only by reference to a Providence that orders the world, to a God who legislates.[72] In order that the concept that unites nature and law may be conceivable and coherent, there must be an essential harmony between the world insofar as it is created and the world insofar as it is commanded. There must therefore be a Providence that *orders* the world.

In the last analysis, the existentialism of Kierkegaard or Barth presupposes something like Cartesian dualism. This dualism in effect refers to a radically voluntarist theology, which separates God from the world, with the world being nothing more than matter or extension.[73] The sense that man is not at home in the world, the conviction that there is no human "nature," that the human condition is "inauthentic," refers to this dualism, as does the thesis according to which only (nonrational) "resolution" ensures freedom. By contrast, the Wittgensteinian critique of Cartesian dualism leads MacIntyre back to the medieval tradition. While existentialism depicts man as abandoned to insecurity, facing a terrifying abyss, MacIntyre starts from the goodness of nature. He does not contrast "facts" (bad, ugly) with "values" (human). He does not invite men to flee or to surpass their nature, but looks to root freedom in nature. He does not merely contrast security in God to the insecurity of the world. He suggests that the experience of faith is not contrary to natural human inclinations and that grace does not destroy nature but perfects it.

Let us return again to the conceptual tangle from which MacIntyre strives to escape: either practical reason is autonomous and human beings have no use for theology; or moral life is a function of God's commandments and human beings have no use for practical reason. To keep faith pure, MacIntyre was tempted to rely on decisionism, but decisionism condemned him to deny the rootedness of faith in reason. MacIntyre circumvents this alternative through the concept of *tradition*.

According to MacIntyre, the morals of interest and duty grant very little place to either belonging to a community of believers or to authority, rendering unintelligible the authority that the Church invokes.[74] The theorists of the morality of duty tend to base their moral philosophy on a theory of autonomy, which hardly grants any place for ecclesiology.[75] The calculus of utilitarians can only integrate a spiritual dimension on a secondary level. For MacIntyre, virtue involves roles and a hierarchy of ends articulated in the traditions of a community, which can be sacred or secular, a social body or a mystical body.

From the late 1940s, when he envisaged becoming a Presbyterian minister, MacIntyre had had plenty of leisure to reflect on belonging to a community, but less from a political or philosophical angle than from an ecclesiological angle. Later, he writes: "For Odysseus the Cyclopes stand condemned because they lack agriculture, an *agora* and *themis*. For Aristotle the barbarians stand condemned because they lack the *polis* and are therefore incapable of politics. For New Testament Christians there is no salvation outside the apostolic church."[76] "No practical rationality outside the *polis* is the Aristotelian counterpart to *extra ecclesiam nulla salus*," he adds elsewhere.[77] But MacIntyre gets rid of certain individualistic elements in Aristotle's thought. We read these disconcerting lines for an Aristotelian to put onto paper: "To be a man is to fill a set of roles each of which has its own point and purpose: member of a family, citizen, soldier, philosopher, servant of God. It is only when man is thought of as an individual prior to and apart from all roles that 'man' ceases to be a functional concept."[78]

Should a "philosopher" be put on the same level as a "member of a family, citizen," and "soldier"? Is the philosopher not the one who, having left the cave, returns as an "individual," with his own views and with knowledge irreducible to the opinions of the city? By relating morality directly to social roles, MacIntyre only plays down the tension between the good man and the good citizen, as Aristotle articulates it in the central book (book 3) of his *Politics*. MacIntyre diminishes the individualistic elements in Plato and Aristotle. Socrates's death and his irony, which seal the antagonism between philosophy and the city, are almost absent from his works.[79] He proposes an interpretation of the *Republic* in which the allegory of the cave, and consequently the difference between philosophic and civic life, only play a minimal role. Far from insisting on the distinction between the city and man, MacIntyre reasons in terms of "tradition of enquiry" and ecclesiology, unifying these two dimensions.

In insisting on individual freedom, some liberals lose sight of revelation's objectivity, the Word of God's transcendent character. The question of the rights of truth is at the basis of theological antiliberalism, for some forms of liberalism seem condemned to consider (revealed) truth as mere opinion. By contrast, MacIntyre rebalances will and reason, subjectivity and objectivity, personal conscience and authority, religious freedom and the objectivity of revelation. In his eyes, the theorists of liberalism tend to forget that life is meaningful only if we are ready to sacrifice ourselves for the traditions by which we live. The city can only be maintained if it understands itself by reference to what surpasses it. How could the truth remain if no one is truly ready to bear witness to it? Rationality is inseparable from a sense of dependence on something greater than oneself.

MacIntyre reconciles two partially contradictory demands. On the one hand, he wants to show that we cannot reduce the divine to human needs. On the other hand, he wants to show that the divine is all the less alien to our desires, as it is happiness itself.[80] Practical reason, which tends toward happiness, deepens and corrects desires, and thus tends toward the knowledge of God. Philosophy and theology support each other, granting their place to natural desire at the same time as to the glory of an essentially mysterious God. MacIntyre thus proposes to rediscover what we could call the keystone of Thomistic morality: the *natural desire for God*.[81] Man feels a natural desire to know fully the essence of the first cause, even if he is unable to ascend to it on his own. The final end is not separated from human ends. It is a natural end that can be attained only by grace. There is an ordered continuity between the earthly beatitude and the heavenly beatitude. Grace completes nature in the sense that its inclinations are already begun. Nature, which has its own consistency, is not actually closed in on itself: it is open to a supernatural end. MacIntyre himself does not linger on this natural desire for God, to which I attach some importance here, but it is nevertheless toward this that he thoroughly tends. At the end of his journey, he rediscovers the teaching of Thomas Aquinas, who, in striving to define what is proper to man, had insisted on two desires: the desire to live in society and the desire to know God.

If we analyze the Hegelian critique of Kant (which MacIntyre takes up) from a theological point of view, we would say that Kantian self-legislation comes to interiorize God and to deepen the spirit of Lutheranism, to the point of getting rid of all mediation and, through this, the whole "visible" church. While the Reformation tends to reduce desire to concupiscence, the Catholic Church grants to Protestants that concupiscence is a sin, but considers that desire itself offers openings through which sin can be attacked. MacIntyre thus emphasizes the existence of naturally good desires. This attachment to the workings of mores and natural justice is more akin to the Catholic than to the Reformation interpretation of Christianity. From the Catholic point of view, the Barthian—which is to say the Protestant—position can go so far as to sacrifice practical life and incarnate existence to the greatness and omnipotence of God. For it fears that concern for practical life verges on idolatry; it rejects the idea of a tradition, against which it counters with Scripture alone. But the affirmation of divine transcendence must not lead to the loss of the agent's point of view. By giving a central place to action, to agency, MacIntyre rejects *sola fide*, the rejection of works. We must take care neither to sacrifice freedom for the glory of God nor the glory of God for freedom—neither to sacrifice nature for grace nor grace for nature. MacIntyre rejects Barth's unilateralism, which he counters with the Thomistic position. After his conversion to Catholicism, the theme of tradition became central to his work, for Thomas Aquinas seemed to offer the means of escaping the dilemma with which he had long lived. So it was as a Catholic that MacIntyre regained his faith in 1983.

The history of the Church is not only a "human" history, which would refer to the incarnation only "from the outside," as if it belonged to a bygone past. There must, therefore, be a tradition. This is a conversation indefinitely taken up and renewed, an active subject's transmission of what is revealed.[82] For a Catholic, tradition is the fruit of grace working within human life, acting through human practices. MacIntyre's central thesis, the thesis that individual reasoning is participation in collective reasoning, is a theory that presupposes or harmonizes itself with the Christian faith, as interpreted by the Catholic Church. Divine laws are known through the practices and living traditions of the Church. Thoughtful and inspired individuals use their reason to make explicit the content of the divine plan, but they do this within the framework of a tradition that they accept. In particular, these theses are based on God's promise to bring the Church to "the whole truth."[83] The wisdom and justice of the tradition depend on faith in God's promise to support and guide the community's reasoning. Individual reasoning is part of an order that God maintains. These theses contrast with the Protestant interpretation of Christianity. For Luther and his disciples, truth is identified in Scripture. An individual, whose reasoning is illuminated by charity, interprets Scripture. Scripture is not interpreted within the framework of a community or tradition. The community is corrupt, and no tradition is authoritative.

To summarize, in theology liberalism's critics insist on the objective character of revelation, on the absolute transcendence of God. They oppose subjectivism, as well as the reduction of faith to ethics. However, the more one insists on the transcendence of God, the more one runs the risk of separating faith from practical life, and the more one tends to make faith unreal, separated from any concrete community of believers, isolated from human needs and desires. Antiliberalism in theology seems contradictory. We are confronted with a dilemma: either we privilege God and lose practical reason and the sense of a faith rooted in our true desires, or we privilege practical reason and lose God. To escape this dilemma, MacIntyre has recourse to two concepts: the concept of natural law and the concept of tradition. Natural law reconciles the two aspects of God: God as legislator or as will, the author of the *law*, and God as creator and as reason, author of a *natural* law. In a manner parallel with natural law, tradition takes into account the multiple forms of practical reason, but not without ordering them to God. Tradition remains faithful to the inheritance it receives at the same time as it develops it. It lives from human aspirations and desires, which it transforms in order to bring them back to God. Having shown in philosophy that rationality and desire coincide in virtue and natural law, MacIntyre shows in theology that human rationality and desire coincide with divine law.

MacIntyre sings the praises of the encyclical *Veritatis Splendor*, in which he finds elaborated the theory of freedom that he has worked tirelessly to develop. The encyclical has as its object the relationship between freedom and truth. It denounces "an alleged conflict between freedom and law."[84] From a Christian point of view, it is through natural law, through divine law, and through belonging to the Church that we attain freedom. In this encyclical, Pope John Paul II reestablishes the balance that a libertarian interpretation of Vatican II could threaten. While the council, in defending religious freedom, had seemed to stress particularly the rights of conscience, the encyclical *Veritatis Splendor* shows that freedom has meaning only by reference to an objective concept of truth—whence its title. John Paul II puts the rights of conscience back into perspective. If liberalism tends to subordinate truth to freedom, the Church considers that it is not enough to search for the truth. It is still necessary to proclaim the truth revealed and known through tradition. Insofar as there is a freedom of conscience and a duty to follow one's conscience, even if it is erroneous, this freedom is ordered to the search for truth.

It is in accordance with their dignity as persons—that is, beings endowed with reason and free will and therefore privileged to bear personal responsibility—that all men should be at once impelled by nature and also bound by a moral obligation to seek the truth, especially religious truth. They are also bound to adhere to the truth, once it is known, and to order their whole lives in accord with the demands of truth. However, men cannot discharge these obligations in a manner in keeping with their own nature unless they enjoy immunity from external coercion as well as psychological freedom. Therefore the right to religious freedom has its foundation not in the subjective disposition of the person, but in his very nature.[85]

The Church foregrounds truth, but she also affirms that adherence to this truth must be free. It was notably to develop a grammar of assent that Augustine developed the concept of "will" that is at the origin of our own idea of individual freedom. St. Augustine in effect distinguishes two types of freedom: freedom to choose between good and evil (*liberum arbitrium* or negative liberty), and freedom for the good (*libertas* or positive liberty), which is the good use of *liberum arbitrium*.[86] The freedom to perfect oneself (freedom for the good) takes precedence over the freedom of indifference, the freedom to choose the greater good over the freedom to choose between good and evil. We can overcome the conflict between subjectivity and law, between particular inclinations and universal duty, for it is truth that gives meaning to freedom. Or, to put it differently, it is the duty to seek the truth that underlies negative freedom. "The Truth shall set you free."[87]

It is by rediscovering a worthwhile tradition that we will rediscover an equally worthwhile rationality. The leitmotif of MacIntyre's thought is the collapse of the rationality of the Enlightenment. For him, this collapse confers on faith a value and importance that is suddenly much more manifest, including for reason itself. Whereas in the nineteenth century the Catholic Church called triumphant Reason back to its finitude, countering the atheistic rationalism of positivism with faith, the Church at the end of the twentieth century paradoxically comes to exalt the powers of reason against postmodern irrationalism. We can think of John Paul II's encyclical *Fides et Ratio*. In a world that no longer believes in philosophy and that sometimes even begins to criticize the natural sciences, it is curiously the Church that claims the discipline of intelligence, whose strength and greatness she proclaims.

Do the Enlightenment, science, and technology contribute to the edification of a universal society that will guarantee comfort, security, and equality? The political failure of the USSR, which understood itself as the embodiment of the most advanced version of the modern project, seems to show the limits of the project itself. Can one still align oneself with this project if the fullest attempt to take seriously idealism and constructivism ruined the very freedom it was supposed to serve? The thinkers that occupy us here were born too late in the century to adopt sincerely its utopias. The "postmodern" school delights in this disarray, which condemns us to prove our intellectual probity and to consider reality in all its ugliness, the absence of God in all its ignominy. MacIntyre, making the best of a bad situation, challenges these conclusions. To be sure, the revolution was aborted and emancipation did not take place. But this disappointment teaches a lesson and indicates a direction. If happiness and freedom do not come from the attempt to escape every tradition and determination, then perhaps they come from a recognition of the finitude of the human condition. Let us recall: it is a question of pondering the most adequate response to Stalinism. Why did the Enlightenment not keep its promises? Because the West lost all sense of a kind of justice that responds both to the demands of the soul and to the demands of the city—all sense of natural justice. We cannot *decide* what is just and what is unjust.

MacIntyre emphasizes the limits of modern rationalism, whether emancipatory, agnostic, or atheistic. By losing the sense of dependence on a revealed tradition, human beings lose their reason! Since modernity was defined both against Christianity and against Greece, MacIntyre is a supporter of Greek philosophy and Christianity. The erasure of the Enlightenment project and the Nietzschean moment to which MacIntyre grants so much importance give religions back some of their significance. The most interesting questions are neglected by a now weary reason. If Catholicism in the eighteenth century was politically strong though intellectually weakened, today Catholicism is politically weak but intellectually strong. "For democracy, political sovereignty and dialectical impotence; for the Church, political submission and dialectical advantage. The relationship that set the movement of the Enlightenment in motion is today, in short, reversed."[88] Through a curious historical paradox, the Church has perhaps become the best ally of liberalism, to the same extent that it pronounces itself in favor of a certain rationalism.[89]

MacIntyre feels that by developing the faith, modern societies would be stronger and more just. By promoting religion in a country, the Church is an eminent contributor to its prosperity. Progress in faith is the basis for progress in understanding, for the knowledge of God is the goal of that same understanding. MacIntyre's Christianity gains from being understood as a response to the frailty or fraying of the reason of the Enlightenment. MacIntyre clarifies the limits of the process of secularization and the fact that, in spite of many predictions, philosophy has not replaced theology and Reason has not deposed the Church. In MacIntyre, the theological theme comes to complete his analysis of the crisis of practical reason: the return to faith is a reaction to the impoverishment of existence. He appeals from eighteenth-century rationalism to thirteenth-century rationalism.

Marcel Gauchet illustrates this point in his own analysis of contemporary communitarianism. He insists that with the privatization of religion having now reached its final stage, modern politics has lost its adversary par excellence and, so to speak, its very objective. To be a citizen is no longer to renounce one's particularity in the name of a universal ambition (to put an end to established religion) but to claim one's identity in the absence of any real project, of any universal ambition. The question of pluralism replaces that of tolerance, and civil society pulls in a new kind of politics.

> Nourished by the confrontation with the sacred, democracy drew from it a sort of sacredness of contamination that uncontestably raised it above profane things. Turned towards "the exit of man from the state of adolescence," a fundamental seriousness inhabited democracy. This made it a vocation, a ministry, an object of unconditional devotion. Tending towards the achievement of autonomy, democracy gained the dimensions of a global project, embracing the entire human condition and appearing to be sufficient for everything. During the ardor of the struggle for it, how

great was its cause! Yet how ungrateful and prosaic it is in the aftermath of its victory! How drab politics is now that we are metaphysically emancipated! It is this collapse of the Enlightenment militant in the midst of the Enlightenment triumphant that is reshaping the face of democracy. It is this collapse that is calling religions into the public sphere and, in so doing, changing them. It is this collapse that is fundamentally transforming the relationship of representation between civil society and politics: between a civil society redefined in its mode of composition by the principle of identity, and a politics redefined in its justification by the principle of coexistence.[90]

The trouble of religion induces the trouble of secularism. Aiming at the "principle of coexistence," contemporary liberalism hardly resembles classical liberalism, for it no longer looks so much to tame religion as to make already tamed confessions live together. With the Enlightenment project having succeeded, the West no longer lives by any worthwhile purpose. Significantly, Gauchet considers that it was around 1970 that the break occurred, which is to say, at the time when MacIntyre made the turnaround I have already described. In the West, the triumph of freedom owes much to the old quarrel that opposes the supporters of the Church and the supporters of the city. As an Augustinian and as a Thomist, MacIntyre proposes to rediscover this dialectic, albeit in a peaceful way, in order to revive a more vibrant and substantial freedom.

It remains the case that in the second half of his life MacIntyre did not publish much in theology. As a young man, he could be considered a philosopher of religion. Having attained maturity, he wrote little on these matters. By this silence, he emphasizes that his reflection bears less directly on revelation than on practical reason and natural justice. Against the indifference or hostility of nonbelievers, he counters neither with the particularity of his religious community nor with his faith, but with his *reasons* to strive for the good. He invites the faithful not to isolate themselves in their certainties, but to show, if they can, that they understand better, that they are the most intelligent.

Epilogue

In the twentieth century, liberalism was the target of two successive waves of critique: communism and fascism. In the 1930s, caught in the grip of these two threats, liberal democracies seemed in the short term to be doomed. In the Second World War, the alliance of liberals and communists triumphed over fascism. Then private property's adversaries lost the Cold War. Today, liberalism is the only one left in the arena. The conflicts of the twentieth century have demonstrated that the regime that was in its beginning denounced as the weakest proved to be the strongest. But the questions raised by fascists and communists remain. "What place does liberalism give to greatness, to beauty?" ask some. "What place is there for justice?" ask others. These questions still resonate. Beneath the apparent consensus, liberalism is undermined. In 1945 and in 1989, might liberalism have won only by default? The bodies are satisfied, because comfort and security reign supreme. The soul is troubled.

Today, in reaction to the Nazi and Soviet infamies, human rights are triumphant. We answer totalitarianism with a politics of individual rights. We counter modern tyrannies with a theory of freedom as the absence of coercion. Naturally, these solutions have their merits. But throughout these pages I have tried to explain that in the eyes of Alasdair MacIntyre, they cannot be enough. We must protect ourselves from evil and guard against tyranny, but we must also support the desire for the good and the true, nourish it, and make it bear fruit. Pascal concisely summarizes my conclusions: "It is dangerous to make man see too clearly how he equals the beasts without showing him his greatness."[1] The passion for taking away our innocence has its limits: the desire to open our eyes to the atrocities of which human beings are capable must not lead to denying that man desires the good and that he is capable of the good. By absolutizing individual rights, we run the risk of ruining the very meaning of freedom that we propose to cultivate, of favoring a deleterious moral relativism, and of losing any sense of worthwhile purpose. Liberalism needs the habits, customs, and mores that individualism tends to destroy. The arrangement of the laws and the balance of powers is not enough: representative democracy also demands a sense of what a fulfilled life can look like. For MacIntyre, the political response that the cruelty of the twentieth century requires does not merely involve techniques of government, a sort of constitutional engineering, and a systematic circumventing of a human nature deemed too unreliable and too dangerous. It also involves, no doubt on a deeper level, nature itself and man himself.

After having for a long time explored human nature with a particular intensity, the West has bracketed off human nature, to the point of separating it from freedom. We must return to this separation. We must anchor freedom in human nature and relate existence to the two sources of the West, to the two desires by which the scholastic philosophers had understood humanity, and around which they had articulated practical reason: the desire to live in society and the desire to know the truth about God. If we believe the tradition with which MacIntyre aligns himself, freedom is not only the power to choose what pleases us. It is also the ability to act to achieve what is obviously good, in the pursuit of perfection. Yet the good is not always obvious. Knowledge of the good generally presupposes a moral authority. Liberalism delegates the search for the good to the individual alone; it affirms that it is up to the individual to find for himself his own idea of happiness. But it is possible that the good can only be discovered, lived, and deepened by a collective effort. It is not enough to say that political reasoning starts from the fact that human beings are capable of the worst and that moral reasoning starts from the fact that human beings are capable of the best. For we cannot separate or even distinguish an essentially individual and private morality from an essentially amoral politics. Morality develops within a collective framework, which includes an important political dimension. Therefore, the individual could prove to be powerless to find the good. Often, moral authority is not so much the opposite of freedom as its necessary condition. According to MacIntyre, it is not true that the modern "individual," by freeing himself from moral authority, has won his independence and his title to reason. It is not true that it is only the being who is freed from the grip of tradition that is capable of rationality. That individual has in reality *lost his reason*. It was the moral authority embodied in a tradition that ensured a minimum of practical rationality.

The revolt against paternal authority or against the authority of the law, associated with the movements of 1968, is rooted in the climate of the 1950s. MacIntyre deliberately reacted against this. He belongs to the generation that, after those movements, saw the transformations happen, which largely condition our mores and mentalities today. Without defending the often restrictive habits these transformations replaced, he offered one of the sharpest critiques of the "liberations" that these transformations pretend to have evidently ensured.[2]

In effect, if it is true that moral reasoning is rooted in practices and traditions, then the "individual" who looks to disregard these practices and traditions gradually impoverishes his moral reasoning. To the extent that individualism presupposes an essentially private morality, it presupposes that everyone disregards the practices and the traditions within whose framework moral reasoning develops. The individual is left to rely on intuition or the good will, contesting even the very idea of moral authority and practical rationality. This ethic of authenticity is the only one compatible with the separation of the right and the good; it gains in favor as positivism progresses. The more we sterilize political and legal language, the more we strive to make it amoral to satisfy the demands of a so-called neutrality of the law, the more we limit the intelligence of the human world, the more we refrain from understanding the demands of justice. In separating justice and morality too much, we come to disregard the practices and traditions that nourish both. We leave the "individual" at the mercy of a poorly taught subjectivity. The separation of the right and the good that contemporary liberalism would like to invoke is not true neutrality. It in fact implies a particular moral philosophy that can be described under different names: "nihilism," "existentialism," "emotivism"—moral philosophies that can be characterized by their rejection of all practical rationality and, in the end, by their extreme poverty.

Most contemporary theorists of liberalism follow in the footsteps of John Rawls. They are in search of "formal," "procedural" freedom. They also look as carefully as possible to circumvent any idea of the "good," any conception of the "good life." Far from reacting to our problem, they intensify its gravity and are part of the problem itself. Instead of contributing to the defense and renewal of liberalism, they precipitate the decadence of the political system they believe themselves to be defending. They slip down the slope without questioning where this slope takes human beings, which they would have to climb back up to fix. They are awkward thinkers; they have not taken the measure of their time.

Liberalism, whose fate has long seemed indissociable from the Enlightenment, needs to renew its reflection to face the crisis of modern rationalism. No regime can satisfy all our needs and aspirations; the human problem is stronger than its solutions. This conviction constitutes one of the starting points of liberalism and therefore part of its strength. At the same time, it encompasses the liberal regime itself: the self-imposed silence on the nature of truth and goodness inevitably raises many difficulties. By too unilaterally insisting on individual autonomy, we deprive life of its content, of its substance. That is the reason why, in spite of (or, more likely, because of) the liberal triumph, antiliberal political movements are prospering and renewing themselves. MacIntyre shows why the dissolution of the Enlightenment project leaves us distraught today and why, whether we like it or not, the void our societies create around themselves pulls in powerful winds. The collapse of the Enlightenment signifies that at the very moment when liberalism seems to triumph politically, it could lose its philosophical foundations.

Why read MacIntyre? The sharpness of his critiques, which are sometimes too over the top and sometimes too politically reactive, leaves very many questions unanswered. But they echo with great eloquence the malaise that today's triumph of moral relativism incites. MacIntyre tends too much to conceive of the history of philosophy as the history of moral philosophy, to the detriment of political philosophy. He tends too much to diminish the importance of patriotism as a remedy for the malaise he describes. He tends too much to neglect civic virtue and to relate moral virtue only to subpolitical or transpolitical "communities"—religious communities in particular. This leads him to neglect the importance of liberalism itself, which proposes to articulate or reconcile the sometimes contradictory demands of theological and civic virtues. By relegating politics to the background, he perhaps forgets the existence of a theological-political problem. The demands of the life of the soul and of communal life are often only reconciled within the framework of a liberal regime. The fact remains that no one can intelligently or effectively combat contemporary antiliberalism without taking the measure of the sometimes legitimate grievances it puts forward. Let us take care that the eulogy for a fake freedom does not create a reaction that takes away real freedom. The beautiful and fragile liberal balance could perish from the contempt of those who distort it while believing that they are defending it. MacIntyre perhaps does not bring answers to a number of our political questions, but he assuredly offers a corrective to our ways of thinking about them and asking them.

In the last analysis, MacIntyre is perhaps less remarkable for the originality of his thought—a classicism that he himself claims by following the Aristotelian and Thomistic tradition—than for his intellectual biography, which is a marvelous translation of the embarrassments and contradictions of our time. This is why I have not so much wished to treat his thought here in a systematic way, as I have wished to retrace the evolution of a sincere philosopher. First carried away by the political passions of his century, MacIntyre gradually rediscovered a kind of wisdom. First enthused by Marxism, he was led to put back into the foreground a theory of natural justice that combines, against positivism, politics with morality. Thus, for those who shared in the demoralizing uncertainties and the nihilistic temptation, he cleared a somewhat bumpy road, but one that has the merit of going in a sensible direction.

We could thus characterize the present situation as follows: on the one hand, English, an evermore international language, is making progress; and on the other, regional languages are progressing at the expense of the properly national languages. By erasing differences in the name of universality, we are pushing toward erasing universality in the name of differences. Consider transnational deterritorialization and ethnic reterritorialization. Or the globalization of trade and renewal of identity passions. Or the logic of human rights against cultural relativism. Or the universality of human dignity against the respect for the diversity of cultures. The universal and the particular, which until recently were apparently reconciled in the nation-state, are being separated. Whereas the universal becomes more and more abstract, the particularities are arming themselves and sharpening their weapons. Against the "ever-larger" World Trade Organization, we counter with the "ever-smaller" of identity. In the name of Reason, some want to escape all local rootedness, all tradition; in the name of Tradition, others react brutally against uprootedness by an exaltation of blood and soil, by an attachment to tradition that turns against reason. Is the principal danger threatening our times the alarming return of an antiliberalism that puts forward rootedness at the expense of freedom? Or is it a liberalism that is too abstract, unaware of its moral and spiritual limits? In the first case, I will conclude with a classic warning: antiliberalism does not offer a coherent political program. In the second case, I will conclude that, though liberals teach us not to underestimate individual freedom, the most pertinent critiques of liberalism remind us that it must be ordered to a truth that we do not always discover alone. These two conclusions are undoubtedly not mutually exclusive. It is important to moderate the particularist appetite of antiliberals, just as it is important to moderate the abstract universalism of the most dogmatic liberals. For we do not find truth outside of the framework of a tradition that is, up to a certain point, authoritative. It is within the framework of such a tradition that human beings show themselves capable of the good they desire.

MacIntyre remains faithful to his antiliberal premises even though he has no constitutional or political alternative to counter liberal democracy. This tension between de facto political liberalism and philosophical, theological, or moral antiliberalism manifests a tension in the very substance of our lives. Liberalism presupposes a social order that it does not produce and that it even tends to destroy. By absolutizing individual consent, by reducing truth to mere opinion without granting importance to otherwise recognized authorities, liberalism nourishes a relativism that subverts the mores and habits it needs. The moral is that liberalism does not stand to win if its program is completely realized. Liberalism only lasts if we periodically counter it with our objections. Without this it collapses in on itself. The tension between liberalism and these criticisms, between freedom and truth, does not weaken the West. On the contrary, this tension constitutes one of the secrets of its vitality.

Notes

Foreword

1. See Aurel Kolnai, "Conservatism and the Natural Order of Things: A Review of Michael Oakeshott's Rationalism in Politics," in *Privilege and Liberty and Other Essays in Political Philosophy*, ed. Daniel Mahoney (Lanham, MD: Lexington Books, 1999).

2. See pages 120–21.

Introduction

1. Pascal, *Pensées*, ed. Lafuma, §118.

2. Alasdair MacIntyre, "Against Utilitarianism," in *Aims in Education*, ed. T. H. B. Hollins (Manchester: Manchester University Press, 1964), 1. [Translator's note: The second phrase in the quotation is omitted in the text, but without any indication of an intended ellipsis. I include it here to clarify the passage.]

3. Hobbes, *Leviathan*, chap. 11.

4. Hobbes, *Leviathan*, chap. 6.

5. This is what authors like Jacques Maritain (after the Second World War) and Bertrand de Jouvenel do; or today, what John Finnis, David Wiggins, and Vincent Descombes do.

6. Harvey Mansfield, "Liberal Democracy as a Mixed Regime," in *The Spirit of Liberalism* (Cambridge, MA: Harvard University Press, 1978), 1–15; Bernard Manin, *Principes du gouvernement représentatif* (Paris: Calmann-Lévy, 1995).

7. However, this book was first a doctoral thesis, defended in June 2000 at l'École des hautes études en sciences sociales, in Paris. I would like to thank the members of the jury for their suggestions: Philippe Raynaud, who was the president, Monique Canto-Sperber, Alain Boyer, Pierre Manent, and Charles Taylor. Thanks are equally due to John Rist, Raymond Geuss, Alasdair MacIntyre, Melissa Lane, Philippe de Lara, Marcel Gauchet, John Dunn, Charles Larmore, Ralph Lerner, Christophe Saint-Yves, Guillaume Lagane, and Louis Perreau-Saussine. I also thank three philosophers as of yet unknown, Daniel Doneson, Jonathan Hand, and Amanda Perreau-Saussine. With Pierre Manent, I found not only a thesis supervisor always generous with his time and with his knowledge but also an example of intellectual life and of nobility that very much helped make a reputedly grueling exercise a renewed source of joys.

8. Robin Blackburn, "MacIntyre, the Game Is Up," *Black Dwarf* 14, no. 27 (January 1970): 11. The allusion to the CIA refers to MacIntyre's collaboration with *Encounter*, which I shall come back to later.

9. Alasdair MacIntyre, "An Interview for *Cogito*," in *The MacIntyre Reader*, ed. Kelvin Knight (Cambridge: Polity Press, 1998), 269.

10. Alexis de Tocqueville, *Recollections: The French Revolution of 1848 and Its Aftermath*, ed. Olivier Zunz, trans. Arthur Goldhammer (Charlottesville: University of Virginia Press, 2016), 5. [*Souvenirs* (1893), in *Oeuvres complètes* (Paris: Gallimard, 1964), 12:32].

ONE.   Politics: Impoverished Lives

1. In a book that appeared in Great Britain in 1959, sociologist Ralf Dahrendorf described this process, showing how society changed since the end of the Second World War. See *Class and Class Conflict in Industrial Society* (Stanford, CA: Stanford University Press, 1959).

2. [Translator's note: Hugh Gaitskell was leader of the British Labour Party from 1955 to 1963; his economic views often aligned with the policies of the British Conservative Party. Guy Mollet was prime minister of France from 1956 to 1957 and leader of the Section française de l'Internationale ouvrière (SFIO); while nominally a socialist, his government implemented more conservative policies.]

3. [Translator's note: The name l'Union Sacrée refers to the political movement that, facing the German invasion of France in 1914, called for a truce between the factions of the left and the right to support the government in the name of patriotism. As the war progressed, socialist support for l'Union Sacrée eroded.]

4. Alasdair MacIntyre, "The End of Ideology and the End of the End of Ideology," in *Against the Self-Images of the Age* (Notre Dame, IN: University of Notre Dame Press, 1978 [1971]), 3. Cf. MacIntyre, "Breaking the Chains of Reason," in *Out of Apathy*, ed. E. P. Thompson (London: Stevens and Sons, 1960), 195–240; Charles Taylor, *The Pattern of Politics* (Toronto: McClelland, 1970), 1–14. Cf. Chaim I. Waxman, ed., *The End of Ideology Debate* (New York: Funk and Wagnalls, 1968).

5. Charles Taylor, "The Agony of Economic Man," in *Essays on the Left*, ed. Laurier Lapierre et al. (Toronto: McClelland and Stewart, 1971), 221–23. Cf. Georges Perec, *Things: A Story of the Sixties*, trans. David Bellows (Jaffrey, NH: David R. Godine, 1990; originally published as *Les choses: Une histoire des années 1960* [Paris: Julliard, 1965]).

6. Daniel Bell, *The End of Ideology* (New York: Collier Books, 1962), 404. See also Bell, "The Debate on Alienation," in *Revisionism*, ed. Leopold Labedz (London: George Allen & Unwin, 1962), 210, where Bell mentions MacIntyre.

7. James Burnham, *The Managerial Revolution* (New York: John Day Company, 1941). See also Michael Barrat Brown, "The Controllers," *Universities and Left Review*, no. 5 (1958–59): 53–61; no. 6 (1958–59): 38–41; no. 7 (1958–59): 43–39; and Brown, "Crosland's Enemy—a Reply," *New Left Review*, no. 19 (March–April 1963): 23–31.

8. Friedrich Engels, *Socialism: Utopian and Scientific*, trans. Edward Aveling (Moscow: Progress Publishers, 1970 [1892]).

9. Alasdair MacIntyre, "Labour Policy and Capitalist Planning," in *Alasdair MacIntyre's Engagement with Marxism: Essays and Articles, 1953–1974*, ed. Paul Blackledge and Neil Davidson (Leiden: Brill, 2008), 284 [*International Socialism*, no. 15 (Winter 1963–64): 5]. Cf. MacIntyre, "The 'New Left,'" *Labour Review* 4, no. 3 (1959): 99; MacIntyre, *Against the Self-Images of the Age*, 38–42.

10. Alasdair MacIntyre, "A Rejoinder to Left Reformism," in Blackledge and Davidson, *Alasdair MacIntyre's Engagement with Marxism*, 193 [*International Socialism*, no. 6 (Autumn 1961): 22]. Cf. MacIntyre, "From MacDonald to Gaitskell," *Socialist Labour League Pamphlet* (London: Plough Press, 1960).

11. Alasdair MacIntyre, *After Virtue*, 3rd ed. (Notre Dame, IN: University of Notre Dame Press, 2007), xvii.

12. Kenneth Allsop, *The Angry Decade* (London: Peter Owen, 1958); Robert Hewison, *In Anger: British Culture in the Cold War (1945–1960)* (Oxford: Oxford University Press, 1981), 127–59.

13. Raphael Samuel, "Born-Again Socialism," in *Out of Apathy: Voices of the New Left Thirty Years On*, ed. R. Archer et al. (London: Verso, 1989), 39–57;

Notes to Pages 16–18   163

Peter Worsley, "Non-alignment and the New Left," in Archer et al., *Out of Apathy*, 88. In devoting a long monograph to William Morris, E. P. Thompson, the editor in chief of *The New Reasoner*, had chosen him as an intellectual godfather. His *William Morris: Romantic to Revolutionary* (London: Lawrence & Wishart, 1955) neglected the reactionary dimension of romanticism and conferred on Morris the status of a socialist revolutionary of the first rank.

14. Raphael Samuel, "New Authoritarianism—New Left," *Universities and Left Review* 5 (Autumn 1958): 68.

15. Peter Sedgwick, "Liquidating the Thirties," review of *History of Socialist Thought*, by G. D. H. Cole, vol. 5, *New Left Review* 7 (January–February 1961): 67; Sedgwick, "G. D. H. Cole," *Universities and Left Review* 6 (Spring 1959): 72, Stuart Hall, "The 'First' New Left: Life and Times," in Archer et al., *Out of Apathy*, 15.

16. Bertrand de Jouvenel, *Problèmes de l'Angleterre socialiste* (Paris: La Table Ronde, 1947), 244. See also G. D. H. Cole, "Democracy Face to Face with Hugeness," in *Essays in Social Theory* (London: MacMillan, 1950), 90–96; Cole, *What Marx Really Meant* (New York: Knopf, 1934), 177–205. Cf. André Philip, *Guild socialisme et trade-unionisme: Quelques aspects nouveaux du movement ouvrier anglais* (Paris: Presses Universitaires de France, 1923), 49–63; W. H. Greenleaf, *The British Political Tradition*, vol. 2, *The Ideological Heritage* (London: Methuen, 1983), 349–539.

17. Alasdair MacIntyre, "Seven Traits for the Future—Designing Our Descendants," *Hastings Center Report* 9, no. 1 (1979): 7.

18. Alasdair MacIntyre, "Marxist Tracts," in Blackledge and Davidson, *Alasdair MacIntyre's Engagement with Marxism*, 27–28 [*Philosophical Quarterly* 6 (1956): 36]; MacIntyre, "Prediction and Politics," *International Socialism*, no. 13 (Summer 1963): 15–19.

19. Daniel Bell, *The Cultural Contradictions of Capitalism* (London: Heinemann, 1976).

20. Charles Taylor, *Hegel* (Cambridge: Cambridge University Press, 1975), 459.

21. Alasdair MacIntyre, *Dependent Rational Animals* (London: Gerald Duckworth and Co., 1999), 9.

22. Karl Marx and Friedrich Engels, *The Communist Manifesto*, 1888 English edition translated by Samuel Moore (London: Penguin Books, 2002), part 1, p. 222. Cf. Hegel, *Elements of the Philosophy of Right*, §189–208 and 257–58, and Marx's *Critique of Hegel's Philosophy of Right*; Jean Hippolyte, "La conception hégelienne de l'État et sa critique par Karl Marx," in *Études sur Marx et Hegel* (Paris: Marcel Rivière, 1955), 120–41.

23. Alasdair MacIntyre, "Breaking the Chains of Reason," in E. P. Thompson, *Out of Apathy*, 210–11, 235, 240; MacIntyre, "Patients as Agents," in *Philosophical*

Medical Ethics, ed. S. F. Spicker and H. T. Engelhardt (Dordrecht: Reidel, 1977), 197–212; MacIntyre, *After Virtue*, 26–27, 48.

24. Alasdair MacIntyre, *Whose Justice? Which Rationality?* (London: Gerald Duckworth & Co., 1988), 210–12. On Bradley, see MacIntyre, "My Station and Its Virtues," *Journal of Philosophical Research* 19 (1994): 1–8.

25. Jean-Paul Sartre, *L'être et le néant* (Paris: Gallimard, 1943), 98–100. Cf. MacIntyre, *Against the Self-Images of the Age*, 96–108.

26. MacIntyre, *After Virtue*, 23–35.

27. MacIntyre, "Utilitarianism and the Presuppositions of Cost-Benefit Analysis," in *Values in the Electric Power Industry*, ed. K. Sayre (Notre Dame, IN: University of Notre Dame Press, 1977), 217–37; MacIntyre, "Social Science Methodology as the Ideology of Bureaucratic Authority," in *Through the Looking Glass*, ed. M. J. Falco (Washington, DC: University Press of America, 1979), 42–58; MacIntyre, *After Virtue*, 27–29.

28. Jürgen Habermas, *Theory of Communicative Action*, vol. 1, *Reason and the Rationalization of Society*, trans. Thomas A. McCarthy (Boston: Beacon, 1984), 339–402. In a Weberian vein, Charles Taylor also shows how the progress of instrumental reasoning contributes to modernity's malaise. See *Le malaise de la modernité* (Paris: Cerf, 1994).

29. Alasdair MacIntyre, "Poetry as Political Philosophy," in *On Modern Poetry*, ed. V. Bell and L. Lerner (Nashville: Vanderbilt University Press, 1988), 149; MacIntyre, "The Theses on Feuerbach: A Road Not Taken," in Knight, *MacIntyre Reader*, 227.

30. Alasdair MacIntyre, "An Interview for *Cogito*," in Knight, *MacIntyre Reader*, 272; MacIntyre, "The Privatization of Good: An Inaugural Lecture," *Review of Politics* 52 (1990): 344–61; MacIntyre, "A Partial Response to My Critics," in *After MacIntyre*, ed. John Horton and Susan Mendus (Cambridge: Polity Press, 1994), 302–3; MacIntyre, *Dependent Rational Animals*, 131ff.

31. Alasdair MacIntyre, "An Interview with Giovanna Borradori," in Knight, *MacIntyre Reader*, 258–59; MacIntyre, "Manchester: The Modern Universities and the English Tradition," *The Twentieth Century* 159 (February 1956): 123–29.

32. George Orwell, *England Your England, and Other Essays* (London: Secker and Warburg, 1953), 210.

33. [Translator's note: The Prague coup d'état happened in February 1948, the expulsion of Yugoslavian leader Josip Broz Tito from Cominform in June 1948, and the show trial of the Hungarian communist politician László Rajk in September 1949, with his execution on October 15, 1949.]

34. J. Saville, "The XXth Congress and the British Communist Party," *The Socialist Register* 13 (1976): 1–23. *The New Reasoner* was a little like the British

equivalent of *Arguments*, the journal of Edgar Morin, Kostas Axelos, and Jean Duvignaud. We find the same relative spirit of openness, the same obsessive fear of dogmatism (whether it be Stalinist or not), and the same interest for the ethical dimension. Gil Delannoi, "*Arguments* (1956–62) ou la parenthèse de l'ouverture," *Revue française de science politique* 34, no. 1 (1984): 137–39.

35. David R. Holden, "The First New Left in Britain (1956–1962)" (PhD diss., University of Wisconsin–Madison, 1976), 286n11.

36. [Translator's note: The text says the PSU was created in 1959, but this is incorrect: it was officially created on April 3, 1960.]

37. MacIntyre, "Rejoinder to Left Reformism," 191 [*International Socialism*, no. 6 (Autumn 1961): 22].

38. Alasdair MacIntyre, "The Algebra of the Revolution," review of *Marxism and Freedom*, by Raya Dunayevskaya, in Blackledge and Davidson, *Alasdair MacIntyre's Engagement with Marxism*, 43 [*Universities and Left Review* 5 (Autumn 1958): 79–80].

39. Alasdair MacIntyre, "Communism and British Intellectuals," in Blackledge and Davidson, *Alasdair MacIntyre's Engagement with Marxism*, 121–22 [*The Listener*, 7 January 1960, 23].

40. MacIntyre, "Rejoinder to Left Reformism," 195 [*International Socialism*, no. 6 (Autumn 1961): 23]. Cf. MacIntyre, *Against the Self-Images of the Age*, 52–59; J. Callaghan, *British Trotskyism* (Oxford: Blackwell, 1984), 72, 222n17.

41. [Translator's Note: The Club was a Trotskyist group operating within the British Labour Party during the 1950s, led by Gerry Healy. In 1959 it was reconstituted as the Socialist Labour League.]

42. George Thayer, *The British Political Fringe: A Profile* (London: A. Blond, 1965), 142. MacIntyre's name does not disappear from the editorial board of *International Socialism* until 1968. In French, we only find a little information on these diverse movements, noting however Claude Journès, *L'extrême gauche en Grande-Bretagne* (Paris: LGDJ), 1977.

43. [Translator's note: To clarify Perreau-Saussine's partial quotation of MacIntyre, it is helpful to quote the "law" MacIntyre describes in the prior sentence: "In the normal conditions of capitalist society everyone's actions tend to be to the right of their principles."] Alasdair MacIntyre, "In Place of Harold Wilson?," in Blackledge and Davidson, *Alasdair MacIntyre's Engagement with Marxism*, 371 [*The Listener*, 10 October 1968, 476]; MacIntyre, "Mr Wilson's Pragmatism," *The Listener*, 29 July 1971, 150–51; MacIntyre, "The Strange Death of Social Democratic England," *The Listener*, 4 July 1968, 7–8 (the article, which alludes to the book of George Dangerfield, *The Strange Death of Liberal England* [1935], takes up a text read on the BBC's airwaves, which often gave academics a platform).

44. Alasdair MacIntyre, "Politics and the University," review of *Student Politics*, by S. M. Lipset, *New Society*, 16 May 1968, 724. I owe this anecdote to Geoffrey Hawthorn, who then taught at the University of Essex.

45. Blackburn, in an article to which I already referred ("MacIntyre, the Game Is Up"), denounced MacIntyre's "Carnaby Street Marxism," an allusion at once to King's Street, the British Colonel-Fabien [the headquarters of the Communist Party] and to Carnaby Street, the hotspot for 1960s "pop" culture. He is charged, pell-mell, with philistinism, empiricism, and Stalinism, and treated as a "miserable charlatan." In the *New Society*'s autumn 1968 issues, MacIntyre is ironic: "The Events of May," 10 October 1968, 532–33; "The Cannabis Taboo," 5 December 1968, 848; "Fallen among Fantasies," 12 December 1968, 886–87.

46. Alasdair MacIntyre, *Herbert Marcuse: An Exposition and Polemic* (London: Viking, 1970).

47. Alasdair MacIntyre, "Son of Ideology," *New York Review of Books*, 9 May 1968, 26.

48. Alasdair MacIntyre, *Marxism and Christianity* (New York: Schocken Books, 1968).

49. Peter Coleman, *The Liberal Conspiracy: The Congress for Cultural Freedom and the Struggle for the Mind of Post-War Europe* (New York: Free Press, 1989), 59–79. *Encounter* was therefore the British equivalent of the French journal *Preuves*.

50. Michael Kenny, "Neither Washington nor Moscow: Positive Neutralism and the Peace Movement," in *The First New Left* (London: Lawrence & Wishart, 1995), 168–96; Peter Shipley, "Neither Washington nor Moscow . . ." in *Revolutionaries in Modern Britain* (London: Bodley Head, 1976), 130–50. Inside the cover of *Marxism and Christianity* (London: Pelican, 1971), it was specified—tongue in cheek—that "among those by whom he [MacIntyre] has not been employed are the CIA and the Soviet Government."

51. Alasdair MacIntyre, "Sartre as Social Theorist," in Blackledge and Davidson, *Alasdair MacIntyre's Engagement with Marxism*, 204 [*The Listener*, 22 March 1962, 512]. [Translator's note: MacIntyre is paraphrasing Lukács on Sartre.]

52. MacIntyre, *Against the Self-Images of the Age*, 72; MacIntyre, "Freedom and Revolution," *Labour Review* 5, no. 1 (February–March 1960): 19–24. Cf. Raymond Aron, "Marxisme et existentialisme" [1948], in *Marxismes imaginaires* (Paris: Gallimard, 1970), 45–50.

53. MacIntyre, "Sartre as Social Theorist," 207.

54. MacIntyre, *After Virtue*, 34–35.

55. [Translator's note: On February 25, 1956, in a speech called "On the Cult of Personality and Its Consequences," Soviet leader Nikita Khrushchev gave

a report on the abuses of Joseph Stalin to the Twentieth Congress of the Communist Party of the Soviet Union.]

56. R. Crossman, A. Koestler, I. Silone, A. Gide, R. Wright, L. Fisher, and S. Spender, *The God That Failed: Six Studies in Communism* (London: Hamish Hamilton, 1950). Cf. François Furet, *Le passé d'une illusion: Essai sur l'idée communiste au XXe siècle* (Paris: Éditions Robert Laffront, 1995), 503–46.

57. Cf. Peter Sedgwick, "The Ethical Dance: A Review of Alasdair MacIntyre's *After Virtue*," *The Socialist Register* 19 (1982): 265. In 1953 MacIntyre married Ann Perry, whom he divorced in 1963. (Cf. Alasdair MacIntyre, "Case History," *New Statesman*, 8 October 1960, 532.) That same year, he married Susan Margery Willis. He divorced her in 1977, when he married Lynn Sumida Joy. He has two daughters from his first marriage and a son and daughter from his second marriage.

58. Alasdair MacIntyre, "Toleration and the Goods of Conflict," in *The Politics of Toleration*, ed. S. Mendus (Edinburgh: Edinburgh University Press, 1999), 142–44. Cf. MacIntyre, "How to Be a North American" (Washington, DC: Federation of State Humanities Councils, 1987), 4; MacIntyre, "Interview with Giovanna Borradori," 266; MacIntyre, *Three Rival Versions of Moral Enquiry* (Notre Dame, IN: University of Notre Dame Press, 1990), 216–36; Alan Ryan, "Liberal Anti-liberalism," review of *Three Rival Versions Moral Enquiry*, by MacIntyre, *New Statesman and Society*, no. 3 (17 August 1990): 37–38.

59. Philippe de Lara, "Communauté et communautarisme," in *Dictionnaire de philosophie politique*, ed. Philippe Raynaud and Stéphane Rials (Paris: Presses Universitaires de France, 1996), 96–101; Pierre Hassner, "Vers un universalisme pluriel?," *Esprit*, December 1992, reprinted in *La violence et la paix* (Paris: Seuil, 2000), 270–82.

60. Charles Taylor, *Reconciling the Solitudes: Essays on Canadian Federalism and Nationalism* (Montreal: McGill-Queen's University Press, 1993). Cf. Taylor, *Pattern of Politics*, 160.

61. Maurice Isserman, *If I Had a Hammer: The Death of the Old Left and the Birth of the New Left* (New York: Basic Books, 1987), 77–123.

62. Thomas D. Pearson, "Interview with Alasdair MacIntyre," *Kinesis: Graduate Journal in Philosophy* 20, no. 2 (1994): 44.

63. Alasdair MacIntyre, *Marxism: An Interpretation* (London: SCM, 1953), 121–22.

64. MacIntyre, *After Virtue*, 263. [Translator's note: The 3rd edition (2007) is cited here as elsewhere.]

65. James McDyer, *Fr. McDyer of Glencolumbkille: An Autobiography* (Dingle, Co. Kerry, Ireland: Brandon, 1982), 62–63. I owe this information to MacIntyre.

66. Alasdair MacIntyre, "Politics, Philosophy, and the Common Good," in Knight, *MacIntyre Reader*, 246–50.

67. Alasdair MacIntyre, review of *On Democratic Theory: Essays in Retrieval*, by C. B. MacPherson, *Canadian Journal of Philosophy* 6, no. 2 (1976): 180–81; MacIntyre, *After Virtue*, 261.

68. MacIntyre, *Against the Self-Images of the Age*, 11.

69. MacIntyre, "Privatization of the Good"; MacIntyre, "A Partial Response to my Critics," in Horton and Mendus, *After MacIntyre*, 302–3; MacIntyre, *Dependent Rational Animals*, 131–32.

70. [Translator's note: Charles Taylor held the Chichele Chair in Social and Political Theory at Oxford from 1976 to 81, after which he returned to Montreal.]

71. Charles Taylor, *Multiculturalism and the Politics of Recognition* (Princeton: Princeton University Press, 1992).

72. MacIntyre, *Whose Justice? Which Rationality?*, 257–58.

73. Ibid., 217–19, 281–99. It should be noted that the hero of Charles Taylor is not Fletcher but Johann Gottfried von Herder.

74. [Translator's note: It is unclear whether Perreau-Saussine is here referring to a private conversation he had with MacIntyre on this subject, or repeating what he has heard secondhand.]

75. MacIntyre, "Poetry as Political Philosophy," 149.

76. Alasdair MacIntyre, "I'm not a communitarian, but . . . ," *The Responsive Community* 1, no. 3 (1991), 91–92; MacIntyre, "A Partial Response to My Critics," in Horton and Mendus, *After MacIntyre*, 302; MacIntyre, "Politics, Philosophy, and the Common Good," in Knight, *MacIntyre Reader*, 243–46.

77. Alasdair MacIntyre, "Some Skeptical Doubts," in *Affirmative Action in the University*, ed. Steven M. Cahn (Philadelphia: Temple University Press, 1993), 264–68.

78. MacIntyre, *Dependent Rational Animals*, 142.

79. [Translator's note: French communitarians, *communautaristes*, support greater independence within France for certain cultural groups. More extreme proponents criticize French republicanism, argue that certain groups should be exempt from the customs and laws of the French Republic, and support separatism.]

80. Marcel Gauchet, *La religion dans la démocratie: Parcours de la laïcité* (Paris: Gallimard, 1998).

81. D. Widgery, *The Left in Britain (1956–1968)* (Harmondsworth: Penguin, 1976), 57–60, 493–94, 509–10.

82. Ken Coates, [article in] *The Listener*, 6 October 1960, 563–64. It should also be noted that in an article partially dedicated to the moral critique Stalinism, Walzer follows Taylor's lead. His position is more supportive of Taylor's

individualism than MacIntyre's position is supportive of Kolakowski's individualism. Michael Walzer, "Political Action: The Problem of Dirty Hands," *Philosophy and Public Affairs* 2 (1973): 160–80. [Translator's note: For Perreau-Saussine's discussion on MacIntyre and Kolakowski, see below, 70.]

83. Charles Taylor, "Marxism and Socialist Humanism," in Archer et al., *Out of Apathy*, 59–70.

84. MacIntyre, *After Virtue*, 187–96. Cf. Karl Polanyi, *Trade and Market in the Early Empires* (New York: Free Press, 1957), 64–94.

85. [Translator's note: See St. John of the Cross, *The Ascent of Mount Carmel*.]

86. MacIntyre, *After Virtue*, 262. Utopia is henceforth not linked to politics but to local life—for example, that of the university. Cf. MacIntyre, *Three Rival Versions of Moral Enquiry*, 234–35.

87. Stuart Hall, "A Conversation with C.L.R. James," in *Rethinking C.L.R. James*, ed. Grant Farred (Oxford: Blackwell, 1996), 15–44. James's reflections on cricket influenced the notion of a "practice" that MacIntyre develops (I owe this information to MacIntyre). Cf. MacIntyre, *After Virtue*, 190–91. MacIntyre, whom I questioned on this subject, affirmed that his three "heroes" were C. L. R. James, P. James McDyer, and Karl Polanyi.

88. MacIntyre, "Interview with Giovanna Borradori," 256. See, for example, George Thomson, *Marxism and Poetry* (London: Lawrence and Wishart, 1945).

89. François Furet, *In the Workshop of History*, trans. Jonathan Mandelbaum (Chicago: University of Chicago Press, 1984), 30.

90. MacIntyre, "Interview with Giovanna Borradori," 256. The MacIntyres left the Isle de Sky in the early fourteenth century and settled in Glenorchy, in the western Highlands, on lands that the Campbells had gradually conquered. They lived there for five centuries, then decided to replace traditional payment in kind with cash payment—a cash payment that they quickly could not afford. They therefore had to leave. The most famous figure of the clan was Duncan Ban MacIntyre (1724–1812), a hunter and poet born in Argyllshire.

91. Alasdair MacIntyre and Dmitri Nikulin, "Interview: Wahre Selbsterkenntnis durch Verstehen unserer selbst aus der Perspektive anderer," *Deutsche Zeitschrift für Philosophie* 44, no. 4 (1996): 671.

92. Alasdair MacIntyre, "Going into Europe," *Encounter* 113 (February 1963): 65.

93. Tom Nairn, *The Break-Up of Britain* (London: New Left Books, 1977).

94. Charles Taylor, "Alienation and Community," *Universities and Left Review* 3 (1958): 11–18; Raymond Williams, *Culture and Society (1780–1950)* (New York: Columbia University Press, 1983); Williams, "Knowable Communi-

ties," in *The Country and the City* (London: Chatto and Windus, 1973), 165–81. Cf. Peter Laslett, *The World We Have Lost* (London: Methuen, 1965); Asa Briggs, *Michael Young: Social Entrepreneur* (Basingstoke: Palgrave, 2001).

95. Richard Hoggart, *The Uses of Literacy: Aspects of Working Class Life* (London: Chatto and Windus, 1957); Hoggart, *A Local Habitation, 1918–40* (London: Chatto and Windus, 1988).

96. E.g., Charles Taylor, "From Marxism to the Dialogue Society," in *From Culture to Revolution*, ed. Terry Eagleton and B. Wicker (London: Sheed and Ward, 1968), 158–62.

97. In 1887, Queen Victoria inaugurated the People's Palace. Intended for working-class families, the building drew together picture galleries, concert halls, and lecture halls. *The Times* described it as a "happy experiment . . . in practical Socialism" (*The Times*, 14 May 1887, 13). Shortly thereafter, the People's Palace was transformed into East London College, before becoming Queen Mary College in 1934. After the war it was there, in the poorest borough of the British capital and not at Oxford or Cambridge, that MacIntyre studied Latin and Greek. MacIntyre related to me that Ruskin's disciples were behind the origin of the People's Palace. He also confirmed to me that he was strongly influenced by Ruskin (cf., for example, *Unto This Last* [1860]). Nevertheless, George Godwin (*Queen Mary College: An Adventure in Education* [London: Acorn Press, 1939) does not mention Ruskin. Quentin Bell, author of *Ruskin* (London: Hogarth Press, 1963), was MacIntyre's colleague and friend.

98. [Translator's note: In the French edition, Perreau-Saussine has a parenthetical remark about how to best translate *enracinement* in English. He adjusts his first translation, "rooted," to "embedded," *enchâssé*. I translate *enracinement* and its cognates as "rooted," and *enchâssé* as "embedded."]

99. Jean-Pierre Rioux, "Apothéose de Clio?," in *Encyclopaedia Universalis*, ed. Encyclopaedia Universalis France (Paris: Universalia, 1982), 99–106; Marcel Gauchet, "Changement de paradigme en sciences sociales?" *Le débat* 50 (1988): 165–70.

100. MacIntyre, *After Virtue*, 69. Cf. Alasdair MacIntyre, *A Short History of Ethics* (London: Routledge and Kegan Paul, 1966), 154–56; MacIntyre, "The Right to Die Garrulously," in *Death and Decision*, ed. E. McMullin (Boulder, CO: Westview Press, 1978), 75–77; MacIntyre, *After Virtue*, 244–55; Alasdair MacIntyre, *Are There Any Natural Rights?* (Brunswick, ME: President and Trustees of Bowdoin College, 1983). Generally we do not pay sufficient attention to MacIntyre's oft-quoted and -repeated phrase. The unicorn is a symbol of purity, and in some societies, witches play a vital social role. To compare subjective right to witches and unicorns is not to maintain, as Bentham does, that the concept is

"nonsense on stilts." Rather it is to maintain that the concept has no meaning except by reference to its social and political context. MacIntyre's phrase is therefore paradoxical. He writes that subjective rights (by nature abstract, independent of any specific practice, attached to an individual) are in fact concrete, dependent on social practices, and attached to forms of life.

101. MacIntyre, *Whose Justice? Which Rationality?*, 321.

102. MacIntyre, *After Virtue*, 195.

103. Hannah Arendt, *The Origins of Totalitarianism* (London: Harcourt, 1968), 267–90.

104. Simone Weil, *The Need for Roots* (London: Routledge and Kegan Paul, 2002), 62–119.

105. [Translator's note: "Exodus" translates *l'exode*. This refers to the flight of millions of French people in the face of the German invasion of France during May and June 1940.]

106. Weil, *Need for Roots*, 35.

107. Alasdair MacIntyre, "*Sophrosune*: How a Virtue Can Become Socially Disruptive," in *Midwest Studies in Philosophy* 13 (1988): 1–11; MacIntyre, "Natural Law as Subversive: The Case of Aquinas," *Journal of Medieval and Early Modern Studies* 26, no. 1 (1996): 61–83; MacIntyre, *After Virtue*, 261–63.

108. Alasdair MacIntyre, "Of Aristotle and the Way We Live Now," interview by Andrew Brown, *The Independent*, 23 March 1989, 27; MacIntyre, "Politics, Philosophy, and the Common Good," in Knight, *MacIntyre Reader*, 237; MacIntyre, "An Interview for *Cogito*," in Knight, *MacIntyre Reader*, 272.

109. During the 2004 US presidential election, MacIntyre calls for not voting, for both political parties seem to answer the wrong questions. The Republican Party's pro-life politics, which MacIntyre supports, only have meaning when supported by the Democratic Party's social politics, which support the poorest in raising their children. See Alasdair MacIntyre, "The Only Vote Worth Casting in November," available at chamberscreek.net, accessed 15 January 2020, https://chamberscreek.net/library/macintyre/macintyre2004vote.html.

110. See MacIntyre, "Why the Enlightenment Project Had to Fail," in *After Virtue*, 51–61; MacIntyre, "Some Enlightenment Projects Reconsidered," in *Questioning Ethics*, ed. R. Kearney and M. Dooley (London: Routledge, 1999), 245–57. In the same vein, MacIntyre not only emphasizes the kinship between America and the modern project, but he also emphasizes (if not above all else) that America is an "idea." MacIntyre, "The Idea of America," *London Review of Books*, 6 November 1980, 14–15; MacIntyre, "The American Idea," in *America and Ireland (1776–1976)*, ed. D. N. Doyle and O. D. Edwards (Westport, CT: Greenwood Press, 1980), 57–68.

111. On the subject of René Descartes's *Discourse on Method*, Péguy writes: "It is an agenda, alas, and it is almost the agenda of a political campaign." Charles Péguy, *Note sur M. Bergson et la philosophie bergsonienne* [1914], *Oeuvres en prose completes* (Paris: Gallimard, 1992), 3:1257.

112. On this conservatism, see J. Bouveresse, "Wittgenstein et le monde modern," in *Remarques sur le "Rameau d'or" de Frazer*, by Ludwig Wittgenstein (Lausanne: L'Age d'Homme, 1982), 62–81; H. Putnam, "Convention: A Theme in Philosophy," in *Realism and Reason: Philosophical Papers* (Cambridge: Cambridge University Press, 1983), 3:170–83.

113. Cf. the condemnations of Stephen Holmes in *The Anatomy of Antiliberalism* (Cambridge, MA: Harvard University Press, 1993), 88–121. In his reply MacIntyre denounces Holmes's condemnations as "agitprop." MacIntyre, "The Spectre of Communitarianism," *Radical Philosophy* 70 (1995): 34–35. One conservative magazine praises MacIntyre as "the most subversive conservative thinker since T. S. Eliot." Thomas Fleming, "Phronesis, Prudentia, Justice," *National Review* 40, no. 9 (13 May 1988): 50.

114. MacIntyre, *After Virtue*, 221–22.

115. Ibid., 181–85, 239–43. The rapprochement between Jane Austen and Aristotle is habitually British. For example, Gilbert Ryle, "Jane Austen and the Moralists," *Oxford Review* 1 (February 1966): 5–18.

116. Isaiah Berlin, "Two Concepts of Liberty," in *Liberty*, ed. Henry Hardy (Oxford: Oxford University Press, 2002), 169; Charles Taylor, "What's Wrong with Negative Liberty," in *Philosophy and the Human Sciences: Philosophical Papers* (Cambridge: Cambridge University Press, 1985), 2:211–29.

117. I shall illustrate this through the intellectual journey of E. P. Thompson. In 1955, Thompson dedicated an important study to William Morris, for Morris defended a conception of moral realism. This study gave a central place to conscience, and it distanced Morris from the mechanistic materialism of Engels at the same time as it drew him closer to the young Marx. Morris thus offered an intellectual articulation of Thompson's doubts about the USSR. Thompson's study helped him to clarify his reasons for resigning from the British Communist Party. In 1963, Thompson published *The Making of the English Working Class*, where he insisted on the role the working class played in its own formation. The first lines commented on the title. "*Making*, because it is a study in an active process, which owes as much to agency as to conditioning. The working class did not rise like the sun at an appointed time. It was present at its own making" (New York: Vintage Books, 1966), 9. Finally, in 1978, he launched a systematic attack against the Althusserism of the second New Left. He challenged the cult of the structure to the detriment of the acting subject, thus replying to the Althusserist critique of Marxist

humanism (cf., for the Althusserist side, Perry Anderson, *Arguments within English Marxism* [London: Verso Editions, 1980], 16–58). These three moments illustrate the continuity in the historian's thought and his concern for fidelity to Marxism, at the same time as it illustrates his critical spirit toward the Party. Above all, it professes the preoccupations of MacIntyre's intellectual milieu. In drafting *The New Reasoner*'s agenda, Thompson took Marxist orthodoxy to task and insisted on individual creativity to revolt against a determinist, impersonal, and mechanical conception of history. This reflection on the lot of the agent was a response to the horrors of Stalinism. In the name of the absolute primacy of politics, communist parties had sacrificed consciences, truth, and often lives for the cause's progress. E. P. Thompson, "Socialist Humanism: An Epistle to the Philistines," *New Reasoner* 1 (Summer 1957): 119–29. See also Thompson, "Agency and Choice," *New Reasoner* 5 (Summer 1958): 89–110. Cf. C. Wright Mills, "Letter to the New Left," *New Left Review* 5 (1960): 18–23.

TWO. Philosophy: Collective Reasoning

1. [Translator's note: As noted earlier, Perreau-Saussine published a version of this section under the title "The Moral Critique of Stalinism," in *Virtue and Politics: Alasdair MacIntyre's Revolutionary Aristotelianism*. This edited version omitted and edited some parts. When discrepancies arise in this section between the published English article and the original French text, I follow the original French text.]

2. Edgar Morin, *Autocritique* (Paris: Julliard, 1959), 54–55.

3. Ibid., 153.

4. Ibid., 152–53.

5. Jean-Paul Sartre, "Pour tout vous dire . . ." *Les temps modernes* 82 (August 1952): 383.

6. Ibid., 366.

7. Albert Camus, "Lettre au directeur des Temps modernes," *Les temps modernes* 82 (August 1952): 331.

8. Isaiah Berlin, "Does Political Theory Still Exist?," in *Philosophy, Politics and Society: Second Series*, ed. Peter Laslett and W. G. Runciman (Oxford: Blackwell, 1962), 1–33.

9. Rawls developed his critique of utilitarianism in the 1950s. See John Rawls, *Collected Papers* (Cambridge, MA: Harvard University Press, 1999).

10. G. W. F. Hegel, *Philosophy of Right*, §135, §207; MacIntyre, *A Short History of Ethics*, 208; MacIntyre, *After Virtue*, 52; MacIntyre, "How Moral Agents Became Ghosts, or Why the History of Ethics Diverged from That of the Philoso-

phy of Mind," *Synthese* 53, no. 2 (1982): 295–312; Taylor, *Hegel*, 403–16, 458–61, 570–71. Cf. Charles Larmore, *Patterns of Moral Complexity* (Cambridge: Cambridge University Press, 1987), 77–130; Onora O'Neill, "Kant after Virtue," *Inquiry* 26, no. 4 (1983): 387–405.

11. For example, Bernard Bosanquet, *The Philosophical Theory of the State* (London: MacMillan, 1899), 124–54. When MacIntyre discusses the "Enlightenment," it is in the sense of German historiography. Ernst Tugendhat notes that "from a methodological point of view, MacIntyre is closer to the German tradition than Anglo-Saxon ethics." See "L'éthique conservatrice: Hegel et l'école de Ritter; *After Virtue* d'Alasdair MacIntyre," in *Conférences sur l'éthique* [1993], trans. from the German by M. N. Ryan (Paris: Presses Universitaires de France, 1998), 214.

12. Alasdair MacIntyre, "Hegel on Faces and Skulls," in *Hegel: A Collection of Critical Essays*, ed. Alasdair MacIntyre (New York: Doubleday, 1972), 219–36.

13. Alasdair MacIntyre, *Is Patriotism a Virtue?* (Lawrence: Department of Philosophy, University of Kansas, 1984), 11, available at https://mirror.explodie .org/Is%20Patriotism%20a%20Virtue-1984.pdf.

14. Leon Trotsky, *In Defence of Marxism* (New York: Pathfinder, 1973), 11.

15. Philippe Raynaud, "Société bureaucratique et totalitarisme: Remarques sur l'évolution du groupe Socialisme ou Barbarie," *Revue européenne des sciences sociales, Cahiers Vilfredo Pareto* 86 (1989): 255–68.

16. Jean-François Lyotard, *The Postmodern Condition: A Report on Knowledge*, trans. Geoffrey Bennington and Brian Massumi (Manchester: Manchester University Press, 1984). Note the importance of the critique of Stalinism in Lyotard's approach: "Note sur le marxisme," in *Tableau de la philosophie contemporaine*, ed. A. Weber and D. Huisman (Paris: Fischbacher, 1957), 59.

17. Jean-François Lyotard, *La guerre des Algériens: Écrits, 1956–1963* (Paris: Galilée, 1989), 37–38. Jacques Derrida, who was never a member of Lefort's group, expresses a similar view: "Many young people today (of the type 'readers-consumers of Fukuyama' or of the type 'Fukuyama' himself) probably no longer sufficiently realise it: the eschatological themes of the 'end of history,' of the 'end of Marxism,' of the 'end of philosophy,' of the 'ends of man,' of the 'last man' and so forth were, in the '50s, that is, forty years ago, our daily bread. We had this bread of apocalypse in our mouths naturally, already, just as naturally as that which I nicknamed after the fact, in 1980, the 'apocalyptic tone in philosophy.' What was its consistency? What did it taste like? It was, *on the one hand*, the reading or analysis of those whom we could nickname *the classics of the end*. They formed the canon of modern apocalypse (end of History, end of Man, end of Philosophy, Hegel, Marx, Nietzsche, Heidegger, with their Kojèvian codicil and the codicils of Kojève himself). It was, *on the other hand and indissociably*, what we had known

or what some of us for quite some time no longer hid from concerning totalitarian terror in all the Eastern countries, all the socio-economic disasters of Soviet bureaucracy, the Stalinism of the past and the neo-Stalinism in process (roughly speaking, from the Moscow trials to the repression in Hungary, to take only these minimal indices). Such was no doubt the element in which what is called deconstruction developed—and one can understand nothing of this period of deconstruction, notably in France, unless one takes this historical entanglement into account." Jacques Derrida, *Spectres of Marx: The State of the Debt, the Work of Mourning, and the New International*, trans. Peggy Kamuf (London: Routledge, 1994), 14–15.

18. Jean-François Lyotard, *The Differend: Phrases in Dispute*, trans. Georges Van Den Abbeele (Minneapolis: University of Minnesota Press, 1988), 146.

19. MacIntyre, *After Virtue*, 262.

20. Cornelius Castoriadis, *La montée de l'insignificance* (Paris: Seuil, 1996), 88.

21. Alasdair MacIntyre, "Notes from the Moral Wilderness I," in Knight, *MacIntyre Reader*, 34 [*The New Reasoner*, 1958–59].

22. MacIntyre, *After Virtue*, 215–23; Charles Taylor, *Sources of the Self* (Cambridge: Cambridge University Press, 1989), 25–52; cf. Leszek Kolakowski, "Why Do We Need Kant?," in *Modernity on Endless Trial* (Chicago: University of Chicago Press, 1990), 44–54.

23. Daniel Bell, *The Coming of Post-Industrial Society: A Venture in Social Forecasting* (London: Heinemann, 1974), 165–265.

24. John Rawls, *Political Liberalism* (New York: Columbia University Press, 1993), 215–57; Charles Taylor, "Justice after Virtue," in Horton and Mendus, *After MacIntyre*, 16–43.

25. Cf. MacIntyre, *Three Rival Versions of Moral Enquiry*; MacIntyre, "John Finnis' *Moral Absolutes, Tradition, Revision, and Truth*," *Ethics* 103, no. 4 (1993): 811–12; MacIntyre, "How Can We Learn What *Veritatis Splendor* Has to Teach?" *The Thomist* 58, no. 2 (1994): 176–88; MacIntyre, "Anthony J. Lisska: *Aquinas' Theory of Natural Law*," *International Philosophical Quarterly* 37, no. 1 (1997): 95–99.

26. Elizabeth [or G. E. M.] Anscombe, *An Introduction to Wittgenstein's Tractatus* (London: Hutchinson, 1959), 13; cf. MacIntyre, *After Virtue*, 53, 260; cf. Elizabeth Anscombe and Peter Geach, *Three Philosophers* (Oxford: Blackwell, 1961); Roger Pouivet, *Après Wittgenstein, saint Thomas* (Paris: Presses Universitaires de France, 1997).

27. Inspired by a certain respect for Hume, emotivism's progenitors also adopted the conclusions of the Vienna Circle (which in the 1920s, reunited theorists of logical positivism) by explaining that metaphysical and theological propo-

sitions are not so much false as they are meaningless. A. J. Ayer, *Language, Truth, and Logic* (London: Victor Gollancz, 1936). MacIntyre criticized this theory in 1950–51, when writing his master's thesis: "The Significance of Moral Judgments" (MA thesis, University of Manchester, 1951). This developed some of the themes that he took up again in *After Virtue*.

28. C. L. Stevenson, *Ethics and Language* (New Haven: Yale University Press, 1944), 169.

29. P. M. S. Hacker, *Wittgenstein's Place in Twentieth Century Analytic Philosophy* (Oxford: Blackwell, 1996), 137–82. We can add one useful witness: Mary Warnock, *A Memoir: People and Places* (London: Duckworth, 2000).

30. Alasdair MacIntyre, "On Not Misrepresenting Philosophy," *Universities and Left Review* 4 (Spring 1958): 72–73; Ernest Gellner, "Reply to Mr MacIntyre," *Universities and Left Review* 4 (Spring 1958): 73–74; Gellner, *Words and Things: A Critical Account of Linguistic Philosophy and a Study in Ideology* (London: Victor Gollancz, 1959), 21, 182, 211, 234.

31. J. Bouveresse, *Le mythe de l'intériorité: Expérience, signification et langage privé chez Wittgenstein* (Paris: Minuit, 1976).

32. Wittgenstein applies the distinction between "causes" and "reasons" to philosophy of action in his remarks on Freud. MacIntyre draws from this for his book dedicated to the analysis of the unconscious. See also Hans-Johann Glock, "Causation," in *A Wittgenstein Dictionary* (Oxford: Wiley-Blackwell, 1996), 72–76; Vincent Descombes, "Causes de l'action, causes, raisons et circonstances de l'action," in *Dictionnaire d'éthique et de philosophie morale*, ed. Monique Canto-Sperber (Paris: Presses Universitaires de France, 1996), 227–32.

33. I refer to a very enlightening book: Philippe de Lara, *Le rite et la raison: Wittgenstein anthropologue* (Paris: Ellipses, 2005).

34. Cf. Vincent Descombes, "L'inconscient adverbial," review of *The Unconscious: A Conceptual Analysis*, by Alasdair MacIntyre, *Critique* 40 (1984): 775–96; J. Bouveresse, *Philosophie, mythologie et pseudo-science: Wittgenstein lecteur de Freud* (Paris: L'Éclat, 1991).

35. G. E. M. Anscombe, "Mechanism and Ideology," review of *The Explanation of Behaviour*, by Charles Taylor, *New Statesman*, 5 February 1965, 206.

36. Alasdair MacIntyre, "Describing and Explaining," in *The Unconscious: A Conceptual Analysis* (New York: Routledge, 2004), 81–104; MacIntyre, *Against the Self-Images of the Age*, 200, 216–20; MacIntyre, "A Mistake about Causality in Social Sciences," in Laslett and Runciman, *Philosophy, Politics and Society*, 48, 58–59; MacIntyre, "Is Understanding Religion Compatible with Believing?," in *Faith and the Philosophers*, ed. John Hick (New York: St. Martin's Press, 1964), 124–26; MacIntyre, "The Intelligibility of Action," in *Rationality, Relativism and the Human*

Sciences, ed. J. Margolis, M. Krausz, and R. M. Burian (Dordrecht: Martinus Nijhoff, 1986), 71; MacIntyre, "Post-Skinner and Post-Freud," in *Scientific Controversies*, ed. H. T. Engelhardt and A. L. Caplan (Cambridge: Cambridge University Press, 1987), 306–7.

37. G. E. M. Anscombe, *Intention*, 2nd ed. (Cambridge, MA: Harvard University Press, 1963), §25 (p. 45).

38. On virtue ethics, see G. E. M. Anscombe, "Modern Moral Philosophy" [1958], in *Ethics, Religion, and Politics* (Oxford: Blackwell, 1981), 26–42. Cf. Alasdair MacIntyre, "The Return to Virtue Ethics," in *The Twenty-Fifth Anniversary of Vatican II*, ed. R. E. Smith (Braintree, MD: Pope John Centre, 1990), 239–49; MacIntyre, "Virtue Ethics," in *Encyclopedia of Ethics*, vol. 2, ed. L. C. Becker and C. B. Becker (New York: Garland, 1992), 1276–82; G. H. von Wright, *The Varieties of Goodness* (London: Routledge and Kegan Paul, 1964); Peter Geach, *The Virtues* (Cambridge: Cambridge University Press, 1977); Philippa Foot, *Virtues and Vices* (Berkeley: University of California Press, 1978). MacIntyre opposes the argument that utilitarianism and Kantianism constitute the alternative par excellence: "Egoism and Altruism," in *The Encyclopedia of Philosophy*, ed. Paul Edwards (New York: MacMillan, 1967), 2:462–66; MacIntyre, "Truthfulness, Lies, and Moral Philosophers: What Can We Learn from Mill and Kant?," in *Tanner Lectures on Human Values 16*, ed. G. B. Peterson (Salt Lake City: University of Utah Press, 1995); MacIntyre, *Against the Self-Images of the Age*, 136–56. MacIntyre remains sensitive to the importance of this alternative in the modern context. Cf. Henry Sidgwick, *Outlines of the History of Ethics for English Readers* (London: MacMillan, 1886), 197–98, and the flattering remarks MacIntyre dedicates to Sidgwick: preface to *A Short History of Ethics*, 2nd ed. (Notre Dame, IN: University of Notre Dame Press, 1998), xi–xii, 243–44; MacIntyre, *Three Rival Versions of Moral Enquiry*, 186–89.

39. MacIntyre, *After Virtue*, 211; MacIntyre, *Whose Justice? Which Rationality?*, 385–86.

40. Tzvetan Todorov, *Poétique de la prose* (Paris: Seuil, 1971), 129–50.

41. MacIntyre, *After Virtue*, 175–77, 202. Cf. MacIntyre, "Contexts of Interpretation: Reflections on H. G. Gadamer's *Truth and Method*," *Boston University Journal* 26 (1980): 175–77.

42. MacIntyre, *After Virtue*, 204–25; cf. David Carr, *Time, Narrative and History* (Bloomington: Indiana University Press, 1986), 73–99; Paul Ricoeur, *Soi-même comme un autre* (Paris: Seuil, 1990), 186–90.

43. Vincent Descombes, preface to G. E. M. Anscombe, *L'intention*, translated into French by Mathieu Maurice and Cyrille Michon (Paris: Gallimard, 2002), 15.

44. Anscombe, *Intention*, §15 (p. 24).

45. On "forms of life" see Ludwig Wittgenstein, *Philosophical Investigations*, §§19, 23, 174, 241, 226.

46. Ludwig Wittgenstein, *Philosophical Investigations*, §337. Cf. MacIntyre, "Mistake about Causality in Social Sciences," 61–62.

47. MacIntyre, *After Virtue*, 185, 193–94. Wittgenstein came to prefer the utterance "grammatical relation" to "internal relation," which was probably in his eyes too charged with metaphysical connotations.

48. The distinction between internal goods and external goods takes up what medieval philosophers designated by the analogical character of the good—analogical, which is to say neither univocal nor equivocal.

49. Cf. Peter Geach, "Good and Evil," *Analysis* 17 (1956): 33–42; Vincent Descombes, "Considérations transcendantales," in *La faculté de juger*, ed. J.-F. Lyotard (Paris: Minuit, 1985), 55–85.

50. MacIntyre, *After Virtue*, 181–225; cf. MacIntyre, *Three Rival Versions of Moral Enquiry*, 196–97.

51. Ved Mehta, *Fly and the Fly-Bottle: Encounters with British Intellectuals* [1961] (New York: Columbia University Press, 1983), 50.

52. G. E. M. Anscombe, "Mr Truman's Degree," in *The Collected Papers of G.E.M. Anscombe*, vol. 3, *Ethics, Religion, and Politics* (Oxford: Blackwell, 1981), 62–71; Vincent Descombes, "Action," in *Notions de philosophie*, ed. Denis Kambouchner (Paris: Gallimard, 1995), 2:162–71.

53. We stand to gain by contrasting Anscombe's book with Jeremy Bentham's remarks in *An Introduction to the Principles of Morals and Legislation*, VIII, 13. When I asked Anscombe which philosophers had brought her to reflect on intentionality, even if only by reaction, she replied: "Bentham."

54. MacIntyre, *After Virtue*, 191.

55. Ibid., 194.

56. Ibid., 198.

57. Alexis de Tocqueville, *Democracy in America*, trans. and ed. Harvey C. Mansfield and Delba Winthrop (Chicago: University of Chicago Press, 2000), 403 (vol. 2, pt. 1, chap. 1).

58. MacIntyre, *Whose Justice? Which Rationality?*, 133.

59. MacIntyre, *Is Patriotism a Virtue?*, 12.

60. Michael Sandel, *Liberalism and the Limits of Justice*, 2nd ed. (Cambridge: Cambridge University Press, 1998), 183.

61. MacIntyre, *Short History of Ethics*, 124–25; MacIntyre, *Against the Self-Images of the Age*, 161–62. Cf. Henry Maine, *Ancient Law: Its Connection with the Early History of Society and Its Relation to Modern Ideas* [1861] (London: John Murray, 1906), 172–74.

62. MacIntyre, *After Virtue*, 57–61; MacIntyre, *Whose Justice? Which Rationality?*, 152–56, 286–90. Cf. Dorothy Emmet, *Rules, Roles, and Relations* (London: MacMillan, 1966), 138–66, which bears on the favorable review that MacIntyre dedicates to her ("Laying an Ethical Ghost," *New Society*, 1 September 1966, 344), as well as what Dorothy Emmet dedicates to him: *Philosophers and Friends: Reminiscence of Seventy Years in Philosophy* (London: Macmillan, 1996).

63. MacIntyre, *Is Patriotism a Virtue?*, 12.

64. MacIntyre, *After Virtue*, 57–58.

65. Ibid., 190.

66. MacIntyre, *Against the Self-Images of the Age*, x.

67. Alasdair MacIntyre, "Moral Rationality, Tradition, and Aristotle: A Reply to Onora O'Neill, Raimond Gaita, and Stephen R. L. Clark," *Inquiry* 26 (1983): 447.

68. Cf. Alasdair MacIntyre, "Colors, Culture, and Practices," *Midwest Studies in Philosophy* 17 (1992): 1–23. This article constitutes an example of MacIntyre's debt toward Wittgenstein. Following Wittgenstein, MacIntyre shows that human description is not reducible to the scientific description of colors (Charles Taylor and M. Kullman, "The Pre-Objective World," *Review of Metaphysics* 12, no. 1 [September 1958]: 108–32). On the critique of positivism around 1960, we find a useful summary in G. H. von Wright, *Explanation and Understanding* (London: Routledge and Kegan Paul, 1971), 1–33.

69. James Frazer, *The Golden Bough* (London: MacMillan, 1890); B. Malinowski, *Argonauts of the Western Pacific* (London: Routledge, 1922); E. E. Evans-Pritchard, *Witchcraft, Oracles, and Magic among the Azande* (Oxford: Clarendon, 1937); Peter Winch, *The Idea of a Social Science and Its Relation to Philosophy* (London: Routledge and Kegan Paul, 1958). Cf. Robert C. Ulin, *Understanding Cultures: Perspectives in Anthropology and Social Theory* (Austin: University of Texas Press, 1984).

70. MacIntyre, *Against the Self-Images of the Age*, 253. See also 211–29.

71. MacIntyre, "Is Understanding Religion Compatible with Believing?," 122. Cf. L. Dumont, "La communauté anthropologique et l'idéologie," in *Essais sur l'individualisme* (Paris: Seuil, 1983), 187–221.

72. Ernest Gellner, "The Entry of the Philosophers," *Times Literary Supplement*, 4 April 1968, 347.

73. We can find the principal elements of the debate in Bryan R. Wilson, ed., *Rationality* (Oxford: Blackwell, 1970). We can add Peter Winch, "Human Nature," in *Ethics and Action* (London: Routledge and Kegan Paul, 1972), 73–89.

74. MacIntyre, *Against the Self-Images of the Age*, 251–53.

75. Charles Taylor, "Understanding and Ethnocentricity," in *Philosophy and the Human Sciences: Philosophical Papers* (Cambridge: Cambridge University Press, 1985), 2:118. Cf. inter alia, Taylor, *Sources of the Self*, 60–62. In what concerns the philosophy of social sciences, an exchange between Taylor and MacIntyre enables us to judge their proximity. See MacIntyre, "Predictability and Explanation in the Social Sciences," *Philosophy Exchange* 1 (1972): 5–13; Taylor, "A Response to MacIntyre," *Philosophy Exchange* 1 (1972): 15–20.

76. MacIntyre, *Short History of Ethics*, 1. Cf. Quentin Skinner, *The Foundations of Modern Political Thought* (Cambridge: Cambridge University Press, 1978), 1:x, n. 2.

77. Cf. Alasdair MacIntyre, "Persons and Human Beings," *Arion*, 3rd series, 1, no. 3 (1991): 188–94.

78. Alasdair MacIntyre, "Epistemological Crises, Dramatic Narrative, and the Philosophy of Science," *The Monist* 60 (1977): 453–72; MacIntyre, "Objectivity in Morality and Objectivity in Science," in *Morals, Science and Sociality*, ed. H. T. Engelhardt and D. Callahan (Hastings-on-Hudson, NY: Hastings Center, 1978), 21–39.

79. MacIntyre, *After Virtue*, 83–84; MacIntyre, *Whose Justice? Which Rationality?*, 370–71; MacIntyre, "Incommensurability, Truth, and the Conversation between Confucians and Aristotelians about the Virtues," in *Culture and Modernity*, ed. E. Deutsch (Honolulu: University of Hawaii Press, 1991), 113–15. Cf. Ruth Chang, ed., *Incommensurability, Incomparability, and Practical Reason* (Cambridge, MA: Harvard University Press, 1997).

80. MacIntyre, "Moral Relativism, Truth, and Justification," in *Moral Thought and Moral Tradition: Essays in Honour of Peter Geach and Elizabeth Anscombe*, ed. L. Gormally (Dublin: Four Courts Press, 1994), 6–24; MacIntyre, "The Form of the Good, Tradition, and Enquiry," in *Value and Understanding: Essays for Peter Winch*, ed. R. Gaita (London: Routledge, 1990), 242–62. In his review "Ayer, Anscombe, and Empiricism," *London Review of Books*, 17 April 1980), 10, MacIntyre expresses his high esteem for Anscombe's interpretation of Wittgenstein.

81. Against Winch's Aristotelian relativism, MacIntyre counters with Aristotle's fidelity to Plato: he keeps the realism of the Ideas. Aristotle's anthropological holism accommodates itself to the objective character of the Platonic Ideas. MacIntyre, "Form of the Good, Tradition, and Enquiry," 242–43. Cf. Peter Winch, "Reconstructing a 'Good for Man,'" review of *After Virtue*, by Alasdair MacIntyre, *Times Higher Education Supplement*, 18 September 1981, 14–15. See also Winch's review of *Whose Justice? Which Rationality?*, *Philosophical Investigations* 15, no. 3 (1992): 285–90. The relativist interpretation of Wittgenstein was

developed above all by Saul Kripke, *Wittgenstein on Rules and Private Language* (Oxford: Blackwell, 1982).

82. MacIntyre, *Against the Self-Images of the Age*, 3–11, 92; MacIntyre, "Justice: A New Theory and Some Old Questions," review of *A Theory of Justice*, by John Rawls, *Boston University Law Review* 52 (1972): 332.

83. MacIntyre, *Three Rival Versions of Moral Enquiry*, 117. Cf. MacIntyre, *Dependent Rational Animals*, 77.

84. MacIntyre, "Partial Response to my Critics," 283.

85. Charles Taylor, "Interpretation and the Sciences of Man," in *Philosophy and the Human Sciences*, 2:53–54.

86. Taylor, "Interpretation and the Sciences of Man," 57. Cf. Taylor, *Sources of the Self*, 66, 76–77; Sandel, *Liberalism and the Limits of Justice*, 179–80. Even though Sandel is generally considered to be one of the figures of communitarianism, I have hardly discussed Sandel up to now. There are two reasons for that. On the one hand, he belongs to a different generation than Taylor, Walzer, and MacIntyre, being younger than they. On the other, his work tends to limit itself to a critique of Rawls. We can note with interest that at the start of his book, Sandel thanks Charles Taylor, because he "broadened Anglo-American horizons and taught the relevance of Aristotle and Hegel." Michael Sandel, *Liberalism and the Limits of Justice*, 1st ed. (Cambridge: Cambridge University Press, 1982), ix. [Translator's note: Not only was Sandel (as a graduate student) Taylor's student at Oxford, but he was also (as an undergraduate) MacIntyre's student at Brandeis. The translator is grateful to Ronald Beiner for providing this anecdote—Beiner himself told MacIntyre this in 1997. Prior to that MacIntyre did not recall teaching Sandel.]

87. Aristotle, *Nicomachean Ethics*, 1113a32, 1143a35–47, 1176a16–17, 1176b26, 1179b27–1180a5.

88. Philippe de Lara, introduction to Charles Taylor, *La liberté des modernes*, ed. and trans. Philippe de Lara (Paris: Presses Universitaires de France, 1999), 7–12. Michael Walzer distinguishes a "reiterative" universalism from a "covering-law" universalism. See "Nation and Universe," in *Thinking Politically: Essays in Political Theory*, ed. David Miller (New Haven: Yale University Press, 2007), 183–218.

89. MacIntyre, "How Can We Learn," 187.

90. MacIntyre, *Whose Justice? Which Rationality?*, 30–102.

91. Ibid., 326–48. Cf. Jean Porter, "Tradition in the Recent Work of Alasdair MacIntyre," in *Alasdair MacIntyre*, ed. Mark C. Murphy (Cambridge: Cambridge University Press, 2003), 38–69.

92. MacIntyre, *Against the Self-Images of the Age*, 283.

93. MacIntyre, *After Virtue*, 23–55.

94. MacIntyre, *Dependent Rational Animals*, 8. Cf. Philippe de Lara, "Si un lion pouvait parler . . . l'humanité de l'homme selon Wittgenstein," *Revue européenne des sciences sociales* 37 (1999): 199–217. MacIntyre, however, hardly expresses himself on reproduction or more generally on sexual desire. Are there properly masculine or feminine virtues? His "virtue" is asexual.

95. MacIntyre, *Is Patriotism a Virtue?*, 12.

96. MacIntyre, *After Virtue*, 156. Through the intermediary of Bloomsbury, MacIntyre joins Forster's position to emotivism.

97. MacIntyre, *After Virtue*, 263.

THREE. Theology: The Community of Believers

1. The history of Greece, as seen by MacIntyre, owes much to Eric A. Havelock, *The Liberal Temper in Greek Politics* (New Haven: Yale University Press, 1957) (see *Whose Justice? Which Rationality?*, 392), and to Arthur W. H. Adkins, *Merit and Responsibility: A Study in Greek Values* (Chicago: University of Chicago Press, 1960). Leo Strauss, who insists on the existence of the theologico-political problem, completely refutes this tradition. Cf. Strauss, "The Liberalism of Classical Political Philosophy," review of *The Liberal Temper in Greek Politics*, by Eric A. Havelock, in *Liberalism Ancient and Modern* (Chicago: University of Chicago Press, 1995), 26–64.

2. MacIntyre, *Marxism: An Interpretation*, 9–10.

3. The concept of "secularization" does not explain much; it is often confusing. But it refers to the debates in which MacIntyre participated, where secularization loosely means "the privatization and weakening of religious beliefs."

4. Pierre Manent, "L'Europe et le problème théologico-politique," in *Histoire intellectuelle du libéralisme* (Paris: Calmann-Lévy, 1987), 17–30.

5. For example, "Against Utilitarianism" (1964), 2; "Patients as Agents," in *Philosophical Medical Ethics*, ed. S. F. Spicker and H. T. Engelhardt (Dordrecht: Reidel, 1977), 197–98; "How to Identify Ethical Principles?," in *The Belmont Report: Ethical Principles and Guidelines for the Protection of Human Subjects of Research I*, DHEW pub. no. (OS) 78-0013 (Washington, DC: United States Department of Health, Education, and Welfare, 1978), 8–14; "Moral Philosophy, What Next?" in *Revisions: Changing Perspectives in Moral Philosophy*, ed. Alasdair MacIntyre and Stanley Hauerwas (Notre Dame, IN: University of Notre Dame Press, 1983), 1; "Does Applied Ethics Rest on a Mistake?," *Monist* 67 (1984): 499–501; "How to Be a North American?" (Washington, DC: Federation of State Humanities Councils, 1987), 1.

6. "But the true consciousness of the loss of community is Christian: the community desired or pined for by Rousseau, Schlegel, Hegel, then Bakouine, Marx, Wagner, or Mallarmé is understood as communion, and communion takes place, in its principle as in its ends, at the heart of the mystical body of Christ. . . . The thought of community or the desire for it might well be nothing other than a belated invention that tried to respond to the harsh reality of modern experience: namely, that divinity was withdrawing infinitely from immanence, that the god-brother was at bottom *himself* the *deus absconditus* (that was Hölderlin's insight) and that the divine essence of community—or community as the existence of a divine essence—was the impossible itself. One name for this has been the death of God." Jean-Luc Nancy, *The Inoperative Community*, trans. Peter Connor (Minneapolis: University of Minnesota Press, 1991). We can distinguish between Wittgensteinian communitarians and Heideggerian communitarians, such as Nancy. Cf. Charles Taylor, "*Lichtung* or *Lebensform*: Parallels between Heidegger and Wittgenstein," in *Philosophical Arguments* (Cambridge, MA: Harvard University Press, 1995), 61–78.

7. Augustine, *The City of God* 1.35, 11.1, 20.9.

8. Alain Besançon, *Les origines intellectuelles du léninisme* (Paris: Calmann-Lévy, 1977).

9. André Laudouze, *Dominicains français et Action française (1899–1940): Maurras au couvent* (Paris: Les Éditions Ouvrières, 1989); François Leprieur, *Quand Rome condamne: Dominicains et prêtres-ouvriers* (Paris: Plon-Cerf, 1989).

10. Cf. Gaston Fessard, *De l'actualité historique: Progressisme chrétien et apostolat ouvrier*, s.l. (Paris: Desclée de Brouwer, 1960), 33–48.

11. MacIntyre, *After Virtue*, 178–80; MacIntyre, *Whose Justice? Which Rationality?*, ix–xi; MacIntyre, foreword to Herbert McCabe [1926–2001], *God Still Matters* (London: Continuum, 2002), vii–ix.

12. Emmanuel Mounier, *L'affrontement chrétien: Les cahiers du Rhône* 58 (April 1945): 14. Pius XI: "The greatest scandal of the Church in the nineteenth century was that it lost the working class."

13. Louis Althusser, "Une question de faits," *Jeunesse de l'Église*, Cahier 10 (1949): 13–24.

14. In the mid-1960s, after MacIntyre lost his faith (and before he found it again), one commentator remarked that even as an atheist he continued to give the impression of being a Christian. G. Lienhardt, "British Christian Atheism," review of *Secularization and Moral Change*, by Alasdair MacIntyre, *The Listener* 77 (29 June 1967): 860. Steven Lukes and Thomas Nagel equally insist on MacIntyre's Christianity. Steven Lukes, "Return to a World We Have Lost," *New Statesman and Society* 1 (19 August 1988): 35–36; Thomas Nagel, "MacIntyre

versus the enlightenment" [1988], in *Other Minds: Critical Essays (1969–1994)* (Oxford: Oxford University Press, 1995), 206, 209.

15. Dominique Gonnet, *La liberté religieuse à Vatican II: La contribution de John Courtney Murray* (Paris: Cerf, 1994), 40–42.

16. Cf. Gérard Cholvy, "1975: Tournant spirituel et intellectuel," *Revue des Deux Mondes*, May 1996, 96–106. More generally, we can refer to the ample literature on the "desecularization" of the contemporary world—e.g., Daniel Bell, "Return of the Sacred? The Argument on the Future of Religion," *British Journal of Sociology* 28, no. 4 (1977): 419–49; José Casanova, *Public Religions in the Modern World* (Chicago: University of Chicago Press, 1994).

17. Is Christian Marxism the latest heir to the radicalism of the Pilgrim Fathers? Michael Walzer dedicated a monograph to this subject: *The Revolution of the Saints: A Study in the Origins of Radical Politics* (Cambridge, MA: Harvard University Press, 1982).

18. Alasdair MacIntyre, "The Privatization of the Good," *Review of Politics* 52 (1990): 344–61; MacIntyre, "Politics, Philosophy, and the Common Good," in Knight, *MacIntyre Reader*, 237. Cf. Andrew Lytle, *A Wake for the Living: A Family Chronicle* (New York: Crown, 1975); Paul Merchant, ed., *Wendell Berry* (Lewiston, ID: Confluence Press, 1991). More generally, we can refer to Thomas Bender, *Community and Social Change in America* (New Brunswick, NJ: Rutgers University Press, 1978), 45–120.

19. Cf. Pierre Manent, *Tocqueville et la nature de la démocratie* (Paris: Fayard, 1993), 117–49.

20. Michel Foucault, *Les mots et les choses* (Paris: Gallimard, 1966), 339.

21. MacIntyre, *Marxism: An Interpretation*, 120.

22. Cf. MacIntyre, *Against the Self-Images of the Age*, vii–viii; MacIntyre, "Public Virtue," *London Review of Books*, February–March 1982, 14; Aristotle, *Nicomachean Ethics* 1094b11–1095a4, 1104b11–12. Cf. Richard Bodéüs, *Le philosophe et la cité: Recherches sur les rapports entre morale et politique dans la pensée d'Aristote* (Paris: Les Belles Lettres, 1982), 181–219.

23. MacIntyre, *After Virtue*, 159. Cf. MacIntyre, *Whose Justice? Which Rationality?*, 104; MacIntyre, "Politics, Philosophy, and the Common Good," 250. Cf. Aristotle, *Politics* 1277b33–1278b5.

24. Alasdair MacIntyre, "Despúes de tras la virtud," interview by Ricardo Yepes Stork, *Atlántida* 1, no. 4 (1990): 92.

25. MacIntyre, *Short History of Ethics*, 60, 66, 68, 79; MacIntyre, *After Virtue*, 158–60; MacIntyre, *Dependent Rational Animals*, 7, 127; Aristotle, *Nicomachean Ethics* 1123a34–1125a17; R.-A. Gauthier, *Magnanimité: L'idéal de la grandeur dans la philosophie païenne et dans la théologie chrétienne* (Paris: Vrin,

1951). I note the following in passing. In thinking about the opposition between Christian humility and pagan virtues, a great liberal such as Isaiah Berlin comes to consider that human beings pursue different or contradictory ends. Mark Lilla, Ronald Dworkin, and Robert B. Silvers, eds., *The Legacy of Isaiah Berlin* (New York: New York Review of Books, 2001), 106–7.

26. MacIntyre, *After Virtue*, 183, 185, 197–99.

27. Alasdair MacIntyre, *Secularisation and Moral Change* (Oxford: Oxford University Press, 1967), 54.

28. Alasdair MacIntyre, "The Debate about God: Victorian Relevance and Contemporary Irrelevance," in *The Religious Significance of Atheism*, ed. Alasdair MacIntyre and Paul Ricoeur, (New York: Columbia University Press, 1969), 31–32.

29. Max Weber, citing John Wesley, in *The Protestant Ethic and the Spirit of Capitalism* [1904–5], trans. Talcott Parsons (London: Routledge Classics, 2001), 118–19. Cf. MacIntyre, "The Debate about God," 39–40.

30. Weber, *Protestant Ethic and the Spirit of Capitalism*, 34.

31. H. A. Prichard [1871–1947], "Does Moral Philosophy Rest on a Mistake?," *Mind* 21, no. 81 (1912): 21–37. Cf. Philippa Foot, "La vertu et le bonheur," in *La philosophie morale britannique*, by Monique Canto-Sperber et al. (Paris: Presses Universitaires de France, 1994), 133–35.

32. MacIntyre, *Short History of Ethics*, 1; MacIntyre, "Some More about 'ought,'" in *Against the Self-Images of the Age*, 166–67; MacIntyre, *After Virtue*, 111–13; MacIntyre, *Three Rival Versions of Moral Enquiry*, 178–85. "It may be surmised that the taboo of Polynesian savages is after all not so remote from us as we were at first inclined to believe; the moral and customary prohibitions which we ourselves obey may have some essential relation to this primitive taboo the explanation of which may in the end throw light upon the dark origin of our own 'categorical imperative.'" Sigmund Freud, *Totem and Taboo*, trans. A. A. Brill (New York: Moffat, Yard and Company 1918), 38. MacIntyre does not cite this passage, which nevertheless well illustrates his purpose.

33. MacIntyre, "Notes from the Moral Wilderness," in Knight, *MacIntyre Reader*, 42.

34. MacIntyre, *Against the Self-Images of the Age*, 92. This genre of analysis is typical with Marxists (or former Marxists). E.g., Lucien Goldmann, *La communauté humaine et l'univers chez Kant* (Paris: Presses Universitaires de France, 1948), 194.

35. MacIntyre is influenced here by Anscombe, "Modern Moral Philosophy" [1958], in *Ethics, Religion, and Politics* (Oxford: Blackwell, 1981), 26–42. More generally see W. D. Hudson, ed., *The Is-Ought Question* (London: Macmillan, 1969).

36. MacIntyre, *After Virtue*, 113.

37. Theodor W. Adorno, "An Open Letter to Rolf Hochhuth," in *Notes to Literature*, ed. Rolf Tiedemann, trans. Shierry Weber Nicholsen (New York: Columbia University Press, 2019), 494.

38. MacIntyre, *Against the Self-Images of the Age*, 60–69; cf. György Lukács, *The Meaning of Contemporary Realism* (London: Merlin Press, 1962); Adorno, "Open Letter to Rolf Hochhuth," 491–96.

39. MacIntyre, *After Virtue*, 24–25, 156, 212–14, 263.

40. MacIntyre, "A Society without a Metaphysics," *The Listener*, 13 September 1956, 375–76.

41. MacIntyre, "Interview with Giovanna Borradori," 255; MacIntyre, "Interpretation of the Bible," *Yale Review* 65, no. 2 (1976): 251–55; MacIntyre, *How to Be a North American?*, 8–10. Cf. Walter Benjamin, *Selected Writings, 1935–38*, ed. Howard Eiland (Cambridge, MA: Belknap Press, 2006), 3:143–66.

42. In the writings of Alain Renaut, we read: "It is evidently the loss of such a concept of social roles that MacIntyre's antimodernism and antiliberalism deplores: an analysis to be sure that allows us to switch the signs [and affirm what he deplores] (which, for my part, I evidently do without hesitating); but it is an analysis that descriptively seems correct to me." Would Renaut be inclined to philosophize "with a hammer"? No! Renaut cannot simply "switch the signs," because MacIntyre himself has already switched them [to deplore what modernity affirms]. Renaut therefore merely puts modern philosophy back up. Alain Renaut, *La rationalité des valeurs*, ed. Sylvie Mesure (Paris: Presses Universitaires de France, 1998), 204. On the subject of liberal England, Montesquieu writes, "The men in this nation would be confederates more than fellow citizens." *The Spirit of the Laws*, trans. and ed. Anne M. Cohler, Basia Carolyn Miller, and Harold Samuel Stone (Cambridge: Cambridge University Press, 1989), bk. 19, §27 (pp. 325–33). One objection against MacIntyre is that the theme of "virtue" had not completely disappeared with the philosophy of the Enlightenment. Certainly! But MacIntyre is not so much proposing the history of a word as the history of a concept.

43. Cora Diamond, "Losing Your Concepts," *Ethics* 98 (1988): 255–77; Anthony Kenny, "Transauthentic," review of *Religious Significance of Atheism*, ed. MacIntyre and Ricoeur, *The Listener*, 5 February 1970, 187; Gellner, "Entry of the Philosophers," 347–49.

44. Michael Walzer, "The Communitarian Critique of Liberalism," *Political Theory* 18, no. 1 (February 1990): 8.

45. Taylor, *Sources of the Self*. Taylor summarizes and popularizes his conclusions in a book significantly entitled *The Ethics of Authenticity* (Cambridge, MA: Harvard University Press, 1992).

46. Alasdair MacIntyre, "Critical Remarks on *The Sources of the Self* by Charles Taylor," *Philosophy and Phenomenological Research* 54, no. 1 (March 1994): 187–90, and Taylor's reply, 203–7. Cf. MacIntyre, "Charles Taylor: Philosophical Arguments," *Philosophical Quarterly* 47, no. 186 (1997): 94–96.

47. Charles Taylor, "Cross-Purposes: The Liberal-Communitarian Debate," in *Philosophical Arguments*, 181–203.

48. Significant in this respect is the discomfort some experience when they see that MacIntyre characterizes them as "liberals." Jeffrey Stout, "Homeward Bound: MacIntyre on Liberal Society and the History of Ethics," *Journal of Religion* 69, no. 2 (1989): 229–30.

49. Charles Taylor, *A Catholic Modernity?* (Oxford: Oxford University Press, 1999), 15–16, 36–37, 106–7 (at 22–23, Taylor seems to go so far as to take up the Reformation's critique of monasticism).

50. Montesquieu, *Spirit of the Laws*, bk. 5, §2. Cf. Edward Gibbon, *Decline and Fall of the Roman Empire*, chap. 37. Cf. MacIntyre, *After Virtue*, 231; MacIntyre, *Whose Justice? Which Rationality?*, 318.

51. Alasdair MacIntyre, "The Logical Status of Religious Beliefs," in *Metaphysical Beliefs*, ed. Alasdair MacIntyre, S. Toulmin, and R. W. Hepburn (London: SCM Press, 1957), 157–211. Barth's influence began to be felt in the United Kingdom from the 1930s onward. Cf. Anne-Kathrin Finke, *Karl Barth in Grossbritannien: Rezeption und Wirkungsgeschichte* (Neukirchen-Vluyn: Neukirchener, 1995).

52. J. Macquarrie, *Twentieth-Century Religious Thought: The Frontiers of Philosophy and Theology (1900–1960)* (London: SCM Press, 1963), 305–17.

53. MacIntyre, "Debate about God," 27–28; MacIntyre, *Marxism and Christianity*, 142–43. If we follow Bultmann, says MacIntyre ironically, "What Jesus really meant turns out to have been an anticipation of Martin Heidegger." MacIntyre, *Against the Self-Images of the Age*, 16.

54. Alasdair MacIntyre, "Theology, Ethics, and the Ethics of Medicine and Health Care," *Journal of Medicine and Philosophy* 4 (1979): 435.

55. Alasdair MacIntyre, "God and the Theologians," review of *Honest to God*, by John Robinson, in *Against the Self-Images of the Age*, 12–26. Cf. MacIntyre, preface to the 2nd edition of MacIntyre, Toulmin, and Hepburn, *Metaphysical Beliefs* (1970), x–xi; John Robinson, "Comment," in *The Honest to God Debate*, ed. John Robinson and David L. Edwards (London: SCM Press, 1963), 229–30. In general, MacIntyre's denunciation of Robinson was poorly received, even among the bishop's opponents. Ian T. Ramsey, *Christian Discourse* (London: Oxford University Press, 1965); E. L. Mascall, *The Secularisation of Christianity* (London: Libra, 1965). Cf. Rowan Williams, "John Robinson (1919–1983)," in *Anglican Identities* (London: Darton, Longman and Todd, 2004), 103–20.

56. MacIntyre, *Against the Self-Images of the Age*, 26.

57. Alasdair MacIntyre, *New Essays in Philosophical Theology* (London: SCM Press, 1955).

58. MacIntyre, "Logical Status of Religious Beliefs," 175–79. Cf. also the preface of the 2nd edition of *Metaphysical Beliefs*, vii–xii.

59. Alasdair MacIntyre, "Brunner, Emil," in Edwards, *Encyclopedia of Philosophy*, 1:403–5.

60. Alasdair MacIntyre, "Is Understanding Religion Compatible with Believing?," in *Faith and the Philosophers*, ed. John Hick (London: Macmillan, 1964), 115–33. Cf. MacIntyre, *Marxism: An Interpretation*, 13.

61. MacIntyre, *Whose Justice? Which Rationality?*, 164–82; MacIntyre, *Three Rival Versions*, 105–48; MacIntyre, *First Principles, Final Ends and Contemporary Philosophical Issues* [1990], in Knight, *MacIntyre Reader*, 171–201. More specifically see MacIntyre, *Whose Justice? Which Rationality?*, 170–71; MacIntyre, *Three Rival Versions*, 105–7, 112–13.

62. MacIntyre, "Analogy in Metaphysics," *Downside Review* 69, no. 215 (1950–51): 45–61. Cf. Thomas Aquinas, *Summa contra Gentiles* I.33; Thomas Aquinas, *Summa Theologiae* I.13.5 ad. resp.

63. MacIntyre, "Is Understanding Religion Compatible with Believing?," 130.

64. MacIntyre, "Which God Ought We to Obey and Why?," *Faith and Philosophy* 3, no. 4 (1986): 360. "If in ascribing goodness to God I do not mean what I mean by goodness; if I do not mean the goodness of which I have some knowledge, but an incomprehensible attribute of an incomprehensible substance . . . what do I mean by calling it goodness? and what reason have I for venerating it? . . . To say that God's goodness may be different in kind from man's goodness, what is it but saying, with a slight change of phraseology, that God may possibly not be good?" J. S. Mill, *An Examination of Sir William Hamilton's Philosophy* [1865], in *Collected Works of J. S. Mill*, ed. Marion Filipuik et al. (Toronto: University of Toronto Press, 1979), 9:102.

65. MacIntyre, "Which God Ought We to Obey and Why?," 366. On utilitarianism: MacIntyre, "Secularisation," *The Listener*, 15 February 1968, 193–95; MacIntyre, *Against the Self-Images of the Age*, 121. On Kantianism: MacIntyre, *Difficulties in Christian Belief* (London: SCM Press, 1961), 102; MacIntyre, *Short History of Ethics*, 194–95; MacIntyre, *Against the Self-Images of the Age*, 148–50.

66. MacIntyre, "Which God Ought We to Obey and Why?," 365. Barth understands ethics by reference to the will of God rather than to reason. See, for example, four chapter titles in the work he devotes to the subject: "The Reality of the Divine Command," "The Command of God the Creator," "The Command

of God the Reconciler," and "The Command of God the Redeemer." Karl Barth, *Ethics*, ed. Dietrich Braun, trans. Geoffrey W. Bromiley (Eugene, OR: Wipf and Stock, 2013).

67. Plato, *Euthyphro* 10a. Cf. Norman Kretzmann, "Abraham, Isaac, and Euthyphro: God and the Basis of Morality," in *Hamartia: The Concept of Error in the Western Tradition*, ed. Donald V. Stump et al. (New York: Edwin Mellen Press, 1983), 27–50.

68. Pascal, *Pensées*, ed. Lafuma, §173.

69. MacIntyre, *After Virtue*, 179–80; cf. MacIntyre, "Moral Dilemmas," *Philosophy and Phenomenological Research* 50 (1990): supplement, 367–82. Cf. John Davenport and Anthony Rudd, *Kierkegaard after MacIntyre* (Chicago: Open Court, 2001).

70. Alasdair MacIntyre, "How Can We Learn What *Veritatis Splendor* Has to Teach?," *The Thomist* 58, no. 2 (1994): 174–75. Cf. John Davenport and Anthony Rudd, "Once More on Kierkegaard," in *Kierkegaard after MacIntyre*, 350–53.

71. MacIntyre, *Dependent Rational Animals*, 111.

72. Anscombe, "Modern Moral Philosophy."

73. Jean-Luc Marion, *Sur la théologie blanche de Descartes* (Paris: Presses Universitaires de France, 1981).

74. Alasdair MacIntyre, *Secularisation and Moral Change* (Oxford: Oxford University Press, 1967), 54; MacIntyre, "Patients as Agents," 200–201.

75. J.-L. Bruch remarks: "Caught between the individualistic conception of the kingdom of ends and the communitarian conception of the ethical city, Kant tends to privilege the former, since he does not rework his initial concept of the autonomy of the will." *La philosophie religieuse de Kant* (Paris: Aubier-Montaigne, 1968), 171.

76. MacIntyre, *After Virtue*, 186.

77. MacIntyre, *Whose Justice? Which Rationality?*, 141.

78. MacIntyre, *After Virtue*, 59.

79. MacIntyre, *Short History of Ethics*, 18–25; MacIntyre, *Whose Justice? Which Rationality?*, 69–76. Concerning irony, MacIntyre has singularly harsh words. See *Dependent Rational Animals*, 151–54.

80. [Translator's note: Reading the sentence as "qu'il est pour ainsi [dire] le bonheur même."]

81. Thomas Aquinas, *Summa Theologiae* I.12.1; I-II.3, 8; Thomas Aquinas, *Summa contra Gentiles* III.37. On a very different but nevertheless parallel register, Wittgenstein defines man as a "ceremonial animal," thus refusing to contrast the empirical and the mystical.

82. Yves Congar, *La tradition et les traditions: Essai théologique* (Paris: Fayard, 1963). Cf. Alasdair MacIntyre, "Hume, Testimony to Miracles, the Order of Nature and Jansenism," in *Faith, Scepticism and Personal Identity: A Festschrift for Terence Penelhum*, ed. J. J. MacIntosh and H. Meynell (Calgary: University of Calgary Press, 1994), 83–99. In this article, MacIntyre proceeds to defend the centrality and legitimacy of witness in human experience against Hume's criticisms of miracles. MacIntyre thus lays the groundwork for an epistemology of the Tradition.

83. John 16:13.

84. MacIntyre, "How Can We Learn What *Veritatis Splendor* Has to Teach?," 185.

85. Vatican II, *Dignitatis Humanae: Declaration on Religious Freedom*, 2.2.

86. Étienne Gilson, *Introduction à l'étude de saint Augustin* (Paris: Vrin, 1942), 185–216; Jacques Maritain, "L'idée thomiste de la liberté," *Revue thomiste* 45 (July–September 1939): 440–59.

87. John 8:32.

88. Pierre Manent, "Christianisme et démocratie: Quelques remarques sur l'histoire politique de la religion ou sur l'histoire religieuse de la politique moderne," in *L'individu, le citoyen, le croyant*, ed. Pierre Colin (Brussels: Publications des Facultés Universitaires de Saint-Louis, 1993), 73.

89. Alasdair MacIntyre, "Catholic Universities: Dangers, Hopes, Choices," in *Higher Learning and Catholic Education*, ed. Robert E. Sullivan (Notre Dame, IN: University of Notre Dame Press, 2001), 1–21.

90. Marcel Gauchet, *La religion dans la démocratie: Parcours de la laïcité* (Paris: Gallimard, 1998), 103–4.

Epilogue

1. Pascal, *Pensées*, ed. Lafuma, §121.

2. Recall that in 1970 MacIntyre wrote a polemical essay against the theorist of the student movements: *Herbert Marcuse: An Exposition and Polemic*. Published in the Modern Masters collection, MacIntyre's essay turned that epithet into a lie.

Index of Names

Adkins, Arthur, 114
Adorno, Theodor, 21, 130
Althusser, Louis, 119, 173n117
Anscombe, Elizabeth, xii, 75, 78–80,
  81–83, 87, 94, 98, 122, 144,
  179n53, 181n80
Aquinas, Thomas, St., 10–11, 51, 73,
  107, 118–19, 121–22, 124, 126,
  133, 135, 142–44, 145, 148–49
Arendt, Hannah, 49, 62, 122–23
Aristotle, xii–xiv, xvi–xvii, 4–6, 8–11,
  36, 49–50, 53, 69–75, 81,
  85–87, 92, 97, 100–102, 104,
  107–9, 114, 118–19, 122,
  124–26, 134, 142, 145, 147,
  159, 173n115, 182n86
Arnold, Matthew, 46
Aron, Raymond, 62, 123
Attlee, Clement, 17, 22, 42
Augustine, St., 117, 135–36, 142,
  151, 154
Austen, Jane, 53–54, 173n115
Axelos, Kostas, 165n34

Bakouine, Michel (Bakunin, Mikhail),
  184n6
Balzac, Honoré de, 130
Barker, Sir Ernest, 114
Barth, Karl, 10, 12, 98, 114, 139–46,
  148–49, 188n51, 189n66
Baudrillard, Jean, 123
Beiner, Ronald, 182n86
Bell, Daniel, 163n6
Bell, Quentin, 171n97
Benedict, St., xiii, 31, 51, 69, 113,
  121–22, 124, 127, 133, 135–36
Bentham, Jeremy, 48, 74, 134,
  171n100, 179n53
Berlin, Isaiah, 61, 64, 123, 186n25
Bernard, St., 127
Bernstein, Eduard, 69
Berry, Wendell, 121
Blackburn, Robin, 167n45
Blake, William, 47
Bonhoeffer, Dietrich, 139
Boru, Brian, 46
Boyer, Alain, 162n7

Bradley, F. H., 20
Bruch, J. L., 190n75
Brunner, Emil, 141, 144
Bultmann, Rudolph, 139–40,
    188n53
Burke, Edmund, 37, 47–49, 52–53
Burnham, James, 16

Camus, Albert, xii, 60, 64, 70–71, 85
Canto-Sperber, Monique, 162n7
Castoriadis, Cornelius, 66, 69–70
Céline, Louis-Ferdinand, 130
Cliff, Tony, 24
Cole, G. D. H., 18, 31
Columban, St, 46
Constant, Benjamin, 120, 131
Cook, James, 128–29
Cornford, Francis MacDonald, 114
Cyran, St., 121

Dahrendorf, Ralf, 162n1
Daniel, Yvan, 119
Davidson, Donald, 144
de Flore, Joachim, 121
de Lara, Philippe, 162n7
Deleuze, Gilles, 69, 123
Derrida, Jacques, 69, 123, 175n17
Descartes, René, 87, 173n111
Descombes, Vincent, 161n5
Doneson, Daniel, 162n7
Dummett, Michael, 144
Dunn, John, 162n7
Duvignaud, Jean, 165n34

Eliot, T. S., 173n113
Emmet, Dorothy, 180n62
Engels, Friedrich, 17, 173n117
Evans-Pritchard, Sir Edward Evans,
    93, 96

Feuerbach, Ludwig, 139
Finnis, John, 161n5
Fletcher, Andrew, xiii, 36–37,
    169n73
Forster, E. M., 108, 183n96
Foucault, Michel, 69, 123
Franklin, Benjamin, 127
Frazer, James George, 92–96, 101
Freud, Sigmund, 27, 77–78, 177n32
Fukuyama, Francis, 175n17
Furet, François, 45

Gadamer, Hans-Georg, 75
Gaitskell, Hugh, 16, 26, 162n2
Gauchet, Marcel, 153–54, 162n7
Geach, Peter, 144
Geuss, Raymond, 162n7
Godin, Henri, 119
Gramsci, Antonio, 19
Guevara, Ernesto "Che", 25

Habermas, Jürgen, 62, 64–65, 71–72
Hall, Stuart, 44
Hand, Jonathan, 162n7
Hare, Richard, 82–83
Havelock, Eric, 114
Hayek, F. A., 62
Healy, Gerry, 24, 166n41
Hegel, Georg, 19–21, 26–28, 50, 53,
    64–65, 75, 84, 97, 113, 131,
    143–44, 148, 182n86, 184n6
Heidegger, Martin, 75, 175n17,
    184n6, 188n53
Herder, Johann Godfried, 169
Hitler, Adolf, 4, 64
Hobbes, Thomas, 8–9, 18, 73, 85,
    102–3, 105–6, 111, 113, 136
Hoggart, Richard, 47
Holmes, Stephen, 173n113

Homer, 6
Horkheimer, Max, 21
Howe, Irving, 31
Hume, David, 37, 136, 176n27,
    191n82
Husserl, Edmund, xiv, 75

James, C. L. R., 44–45, 170n87
Jefferson, Thomas, 35
John Paul II, St., 150, 152
Joy, Lynn Sumida, 168n57

Kamehameha II, 129
Kant, xii, 62–65, 67, 69–72, 75, 105,
    107, 148, 178n38, 189n65,
    190n75
Keynes, John Maynard, 18
Khrushchev, Nikita, 29, 58–59,
    167n55
Kierkegaard, Søren, 27, 142–44, 146
Kojève, Alexandre, 28, 175n17
Kolakowski, Leszek, 70, 85, 169n82
Kolnai, Aurel, xiv
Kripke, Saul, 181n81
Kuhn, Thomas, 141

Lagane, Guillaume, 162n7
Lane, Melissa, 162n7
Larmore, Charles, 162n7
Laslett, Peter, 61
Lefort, Claude, 66, 175n17
Lerner, Ralph, 162n7
Locke, John, 18, 29, 32, 44, 72
Louis-Philippe d'Orléans, 13
Lukács, György, 21, 130, 167n51
Lukes, Steven, 184n14
Luther, Martin, 148
Lyotard, Jean-François, 66–67, 101
Lytle, Andrew, 121

Machiavelli, Niccolò, 50, 61, 73, 102
MacIntyre, Duncan Ban, 170n90
Macmillan, Harold, 15–16
Madison, James, 35
Malinowski, Bronislaw, 93
Mallarmé, Stéphane, 184n6
Manent, Pierre, 162n7
Marcuse, Herbert, 25, 27–28
Maritain, Jacques, xvi, 118, 161n5
Marx, Karl, xvi, 9–11, 15, 18–21,
    23–27, 29, 32–35, 37–38,
    40–45, 47–52, 55–56, 57–60,
    62–73, 86, 91, 108, 113–15,
    117–19, 123–26, 130–31,
    143–44, 159, 167n45, 173n117,
    175n17, 184n6, 185n17, 186n34
McCabe, Herbert, 118
McDyer, James, 31, 170n87
Metternich, Klemens von, 17
Mill, John Stuart, 132
Mollet, Guy, 16, 162n2
Montaigne, Michel Eyquem de, 131
Montesquieu, Baron de (Charles-
    Louis de Secondat), 72, 134,
    136, 187n42
Montuclard, Maurice, 118–19
Morin, Edgar, 165n34
Morris, William, 16, 163n13,
    173n117
Mounier, Emmanuel, 119

Nairn, Tom, 44, 46
Nancy, Jean-Luc, 184n6
Napoleon I, 17
Nietzsche, Friedrich, 54, 67–70, 72,
    121, 129, 152, 175n17

Oakeshott, Michael, xiv, 62
Orwell, George, 22

Pascal, Blaise, 2, 143, 155
Péguy, Charles, xi, 173n111
Perreau-Saussine, Amanda, 162n7
Perreau-Saussine, Louis, 162n7
Perry, Ann, 168n57
Pius IX, 140
Pius XI, 184n12
Plato, 103, 114, 117, 135, 143, 147, 181n81
Polanyi, Karl, 170n87
Popper, Karl, 123
Prichard, H. A., 128–29
Proust, Marcel, 130

Quine, Willard Van Orman, 144

Rajk, László, 22, 165n33
Rawls, John, 62–65, 67, 70, 72, 119, 134, 158, 174n9, 182n86
Raynaud, Philippe, 162n7
Renan, Ernest, 46
Renaut, Alain, 187n42
Rhees, Rush, 93
Ricci, Matteo, 135
Richelieu, Cardinal-duc de (Armand Jean du Plessis), 50
Rist, John, 162n7
Robinson, John, 140, 143, 188n55
Rousseau, Jean-Jacques, 11–12, 18–19, 32, 72, 130, 136, 184n6
Ruskin, John, 47, 171n97

Sade, Marquis de (Donatien Alphonse François), 6
Saint-Yves, Christophe, 162n7
Sandel, Michael, 119, 182n86
Sartre, Jean-Paul, xii, 27, 60, 64, 70, 71, 167n51

Schlegel, Karl Wilhelm Friedrich von, 184n6
Schleiermacher, Friedrich, 139
Schmitt, Carl, 64
Smith, Adam, 89
Solzhenitsyn, Aleksandr, 32
Stalin, Joseph, xii, 4, 12, 22–24, 26, 29, 32, 55–56, 57–62, 65–73, 75, 83–84, 101, 103, 109, 123, 152, 165n34, 167n45, 167n55, 169n82, 173n117, 175nn16–17
Strauss, Leo, 62, 122, 183n1

Taylor, Charles, 19, 30, 32, 34–35, 39, 42–45, 47, 77–78, 97, 100, 119, 121, 123, 131–37, 145, 162n7, 165n28, 169n70, 181n75, 182n86, 187n45, 188n49
Thompson, E. P., 23, 47, 163n13, 173n117
Thomson, George, 44–45
Tillich, Paul, 139–40
Tito, Josep Broz, 22, 165n33
Tocqueville, Alexis de, 13, 35, 86
Todorov, Tzvetan, 80
Trotsky, Leon, 10–11, 22, 24, 26, 28–29, 31, 45, 64–66, 69, 71, 124, 166n41
Truman, Harry S., 83
Tugendhat, Ernst, 175n11

Victoria, 22, 94–95, 97, 104, 171n97
Voegelin, Eric, 122

Wagner, Richard, 184n6
Walzer, Michael, 30–31, 34, 39, 119, 123, 169n82, 182n86, 185n17

ÉMILE PERREAU-SAUSSINE (1972–2010)

was a lecturer in the Department of Politics and International Studies at the University of Cambridge and the author of *Alasdair MacIntyre: une biographie intellectuelle* and *Catholicisme et démocratie.*

NATHAN J. PINKOSKI

is a research fellow and director of academic programs at the Zephyr Institute.

PIERRE MANENT

is professor emeritus of political philosophy at the École des Hautes Études en Sciences Sociales. He is the author of numerous books, including *Montaigne: Life without Law* (University of Notre Dame Press, 2020).

CPSIA information can be obtained
at www.ICGtesting.com
Printed in the USA
LVHW080055260822
726871LV00003B/151